D0225787

FLORIDA STATE
UNIVERSITY LIBRARIES

MAY 18 1994

TALLAHASSEE, FLORIDA

Blake's Prophetic Workshop

Blake's Prophetic Workshop

A Study of *The Four Zoas*

George Anthony Rosso, Jr.

Lewisburg
Bucknell University Press
London and Toronto: Associated University Presses

© 1993 by Associated University Presses, Inc.

All rights reserved. Authorization to photocopy items for internal or personal use, or the internal or personal use of specific clients, is granted by the copyright owner, provided that a base fee of $10.00, plus eight cents per page, per copy is paid directly to the Copyright Clearance Center, 27 Congress Street, Salem, Massachusetts 01970. [0-8387-5240-3/93 $10.00 + 8¢ pp, pc.]

PR
4144
F683
R67
1993

Associated University Presses
440 Forsgate Drive
Cranbury, NJ 08512

Associated University Presses
25 Sicilian Avenue
London WC1A 2QH, England

Associated University Presses
P.O. Box 338, Port Credit
Mississauga, Ontario,
Canada L5G 4L8

The paper used in this publication meets the requirements of the American National Standard for Permanence of Paper for Printed Library Materials Z39.48-1984.

Library of Congress Cataloging-in-Publication Data

Rosso, G. A., 1954–
    Blake's prophetic workshop : a study of The four Zoas / George Anthony Rosso, Jr.
        p. cm.
    Includes bibliographical references and index.
    ISBN 0-8387-5240-3 (alk. paper)
    1. Blake, William, 1757–1827. Four Zoas. 2. Prophecies in literature. I. Title.
PR4144.F683R67   1993
821'.7—dc20   92-54660
                                                                 CIP

PRINTED IN THE UNITED STATES OF AMERICA

This book is dedicated to
the Rosso Clan
Vivian and George
Sandi, Susie, Tom, and Greg

The Four Zoas is more than fragments of a great poem. It is the workshop of an extraordinary poet.

—G. E. Bentley, Jr.

Contents

Preface

THE *Four Zoas* presents an extraordinary challenge. Its unfinished manuscript status, along with its narrative gaps, bold juxtapositions, multiple perspectives, and myriad allusions, all place exacting demands on the reader. *Blake's Prophetic Workshop* attempts to meet these demands by approaching the poem from a variety of critical viewpoints. It assumes some familiarity with Blake's prophecies, and the criticism built up around them, but is cast between the "consensual" and "incommensurable" positions of the two previous books on the poem (by Wilkie and Johnson, and by Ault). While building on a "consensus of Blakeans," this study treats *The Four Zoas* as a radically open-ended but ultimately partisan text, one requiring an engaged response if the reader is to participate in its meanings.

Given the daunting nature of Blake's text, I concentrate on patterns of coherence and attempt to synthesize rather than problematize my own argument. Although my predominant interpretive strategy is close reading, the narrative's transactive nature implies an extratextual dimension that, I believe, is best complemented by historical methods. Thus in chapters one, two, and four I sketch contexts and traditions relevant to the poem, while in chapters three, five, and six I provide close textual analyses within these contexts.

Chapter one presents a history of the poem's reception. It situates the various critical approaches to Blake within the respective historical moments in which they appear. Chapter two, moving in the opposite direction, sets *The Four Zoas* in an unusual and neglected context: the tradition of the eighteenth-century "long poem," a specifically Anglican tradition against which Blake pits his Nonconformist epic-prophecy. I argue that Blake critiques "actual" Newtonian poems, such as Pope's *An Essay on Man* and Young's *Night Thoughts,* to recover a Miltonic heritage eclipsed by Newtonian natural religion, which drops the Fall from its universe and subordinates inspired prophecy to empirical science.[1] Chapter three tests these assertions by surveying the poem's creation-fall narratives, which draw deeply on the rationalist and visionary cosmogonies that animate much of the century's apologetic literature.

Chapter four sifts the intellectual background that informs Blake's use of biblical typology, or of what Paul Korshin calls "abstracted typology" to indicate its modification by secular practice and criticism. In this context, chapters five and six scrutinize British and Continental philosophies of history and how they encroach on *The Four Zoas*, as well as situate the poem in the apocalyptic context of the 1790s. While Blake's apocalypse is interpreted usually as a purely internal event, these chapters argue for a dual individual and collective focus. Blake mediates apocalypse through the individual poet: Los undergoes a spiritual conversion in Night VII that empowers him to narrate the "Last Judgment" of Night IX. But Los's experience does not arrest the wars that continue into Night VIII: these wars cease only with the integration of *all* the zoas and emanations into the figurative community of the giant Albion in the final Night of the poem.

In both *The Four Zoas* and its criticism, history is a difficult and multivalent concept. I can suggest something of its problematic character by contrasting the historical-materialist and poststructural positions on the issue of the Fall, the central "event" in the poem. For Fred Whitehead and Jackie DiSalvo, Blake's "Fall" contains mythic allusions to ancient history that, reconstructed through anthropological research, yield a "definite sequence of historical events" in the poem. Since ancient myths encode information about traumatic social changes in the archaic period of European history, these critics describe the Fall in terms of a breakdown in primeval tribal equality "during the rise of urban society in the ancient Near East about 4000 B.C."[2] From this perspective, Blake's *in medias res* technique refers to a dual chronology, one leading up to the narrative and the other the temporal sequence of events actually narrated by the poet (Whitehead 1982, 232).

This notion of a *res* to history is precisely what the poststructural perspective denies. Donald Ault, for example, says that Blake's "Fall" has no structure or content "other than serving as a pretext for setting incommensurable perspectives in order" (Ault 1987, 11). For Ault, as for Paul Mann, *The Four Zoas* is "incorrigibly autotelic" and, therefore, cannot by definition refer to anything outside itself (Mann 1985, 3). Ault equates *res* with reification (not, of course, in a Marxian sense). Drawing on Stanley Fish's argument in *Surprised By Sin*, Ault contends that Blake strategically creates "the impression that he is plunging the reader into the narrative *in medias res* when there are in fact no *res*—things—in Blake's narrative world . . ." (Ault 1987, 26). While this approach retains a healthy skepticism toward Blake's prophetic intentions, it idealizes the literary text. And while historical-materialism may be a more realistic way to study the relation of literature and history, its insights into *The Four Zoas* derive as much from source material as from Blake's text.[3]

My position is a hybrid of various approaches. I realize that history is not in any simple way extrinsic to the text, but "is generated by the latter at the very moment in which it begins to work on and to alter it" (Jameson 1982, 343). The text, that is, brings into play a "history" to which the literary work is simultaneously a response. Thus I also regard "history" as the contingent force that disrupts the narrative, that links content and form, by pulling readers toward the world in which the work is created and received. I call this force the *kerygmatic* character of the narrative: it manifests itself precisely at moments of greatest fissuring, when demands for a committed, active response by readers are most acute. Secularizing the *kerygma*, I interpret *The Four Zoas* as a dynamic interplay between force and form, as an autonomous rhetorical construct governed by internal rules and a mediation between readers and their lives. *Kerygma* extends a text beyond its own formed boundaries into the human context, where narrative can function as dialogue.

But, of course, *The Four Zoas* only approximates such an experience. It remains, in Erdman's words, a "work in progress." I call *The Four Zoas* a "workshop" partly to echo this sentiment. Blake never shapes his poem into final form: in Bentley's curious phrase, it remains a workshop "with chips and broken tools left about among pieces of the partly completed manuscript" (Bentley 1963, xvii). Although no laborer worth his salt leaves broken tools about, Bentley directs us to the artisanal meaning of the metaphor. As historians have shown, early industrial capitalism shattered the ancient bonds and skills of the artisans, the workers of Blake's own social class, by fostering ever more specialized divisions of labor. Blake's trade of engraving suffered directly from these changes. On a deep level, *The Four Zoas* registers the dislocation of Blake's class and, thus, functions as the first anticapitalist epic, the epic of those literate craftsmen and women, small masters and artisans, whom Blake represents as an organic worker-intellectual (Crehan 1984, 11).

The Four Zoas is also where Blake works out his mature epic vision, expanding his scope from the Lambeth to the epic prophecies. It is where he becomes the most original and daring of Romantic poets, experimenting with the nature and limits of narrative form, reaching some dead ends, but exploring regions untrod in literature. It is the imaginative space from which Blake seeks to induce what he calls prophetic or expanded vision, challenging readers to engage in *intellectual* battle, thereby helping to transform a divided world into a community.

Let me define my use of the term *prophetic*. First, it refers to the affiliations and shared cultural materials of a group of poets that deeply influenced Blake, notably Milton, Spenser, Dante, and the biblical prophets, Isaiah, Ezekiel, Daniel, and John of Patmos, among others. As shaped by these writers over vast and disparate periods of history, prophecy develops a set of generic signals and expectations, including a visionary idiom, intertextual or allusive contexts, narrative disjunctions, multiple perspectives, a typological code, and a liberatory social ethic. Further, the composite medium of prophecy—its generic mixture—doubles as its message, which is designed to personally accost readers and render their cultural outlook and self-understanding problematic. The *prophetic*, finally, designates a living drama of contending voices whose generic cast retains its workshop status with each performance.

The prophetic of course is now under erasure. For some, it remains an embarrassing residue of either the poet's late eighteenth-century Christianity or the critic's late twentieth-century nostalgia for extrinsic reference. While Blake yields some interesting deconstructionist insights, I am persuaded that he wrote as a Christian visionary, albeit an exceptionally unorthodox one. But that does not mean that I ignore the following challenge:

> The question I am raising concerns the extent to which even a mode as self-confident as the prophetic may be beset with uncertainty and the extent to which that uncertainty may be implicit in the "contending perspectives" the prophetic voice struggles to establish as "complementary." (Rajan 1985, 140)

This is a fair statement, one to keep in mind when striving to make sense of Blake's nearly schizophrenic narrative strategies. Yet I would up the ante and argue that Blake hammers together the different segments and perspectives of the manuscript, not to allow the poem to create itself out of its own erasure, but to record—"on the ground," as Raymond Williams puts it—the individual and social fragmentation of late eighteenth-century England. The contending strands of narrative, in this view, embody the divisions not just of William Blake, but of British and European culture and society, adrift in a world without economic or transcendental guarantees.

Ultimately we must come to terms with the vexing issue of whether *The Four Zoas* remained a work in progress, became an abandoned fragment, or is a failed poem. As Wilkie and Johnson put it in an enduring question: "Did Blake finish the poem in the sense that he brought it to a stage where he was satisfied with it?" (Wilkie and Johnson 1978, xiii–xiv).

Where John Middleton Murry, Northrop Frye, and G. E. Bentley regard the poem as both a tragic, if tantalizing, failure and an abandoned but brilliant fragment, recent scholars make a virtue of the poem's unfinished condition.[4] Some deem *The Four Zoas* a self-deconstructing artifact; others develop their own theories to account for its strangeness. For deconstructionists, the uncertain status of the manuscript renders it an ideal text, one whose drive for unity is not only undercut by its own aporias but whose unfinished form suits the interminable world it explores. Others argue that because of deepening poverty and commercial failures, Blake abandoned the manuscript, or at least his intention of publishing it. Steering between the Scylla of old critical unity and the Charybdis of poststructural entropy, these critics sight land in a return to the physical manuscript—the manuscript *as* manuscript. In this view, critical commentary violates the pristine or "irreducible inaccessibility" of the material text and is able only to "re-produce" it as an ideal for interpretation.[5]

This notion of Blake's "singularity" stretches as far back as Blake's contemporary Allan Cunningham and continues through Alexander Gilchrist and T. S. Eliot to Donald Ault. While acknowledging the poem's heterogeneity and Blake's uniqueness, criticism need not embrace the indeterminate as the only way to keep interpretation open. To insist on Blake's singularity seems not only wrongheaded but counterproductive. It seals Blake from the public he longed to reach and distorts him for those who find him. Since any notion of *The Four Zoas*'s poetic status is unavoidably bound to each critic's own ideas about art and narrative, the time has come to move from the cloistered act of reading *in* Blake to the collective act of opening *up* Blake to wider audiences. I offer this book as a study in critical solidarity.

Note on the Manuscript

THE *Four Zoas* manuscript poses formidable obstacles to reading and comprehension. As its editorial and interpretive histories are sewn together, I provide a brief note on the manuscript to explain my choice of the 1982 Erdman edition as the textual basis for this study.

I would first acknowledge that no amount of editorial labor can give us a clear, unblemished text—leaving aside, for the moment, the text's intricate relation to the drawings, proofs, and sketches (see appendix). For Blake not only left the poem unfinished, but revised it almost to the point of illegibility. Sometime late in his life, Blake apparently turned the manuscript over to John Linnell, whose sons loaned it to John Ellis and William Butler Yeats in 1889, "un-paged and unsorted." Ellis and Yeats arranged, numbered, transcribed, and published the text in 1893. Blake never bound the manuscript; the British Museum bound it in 1960.

Many reliable descriptions of the manuscript exist (see D. J. Sloss and J. P. R. Wallis 1926; H. M. Margoliouth 1956; G. E. Bentley 1963; Anne K. Mellor 1974; David V. Eerdman 1982; David V. Erdman and Cettina T. Magno 1987; and Martin Butlin 1981). These descriptions, many of them excellent, have been contested because Blake did not leave a full set of instructions for editing the many additions, deletions, transpositions, scribblings, and glosses that riddle the *Four Zoas* manuscript. Culling the work of Bentley, Erdman, and Butlin, I offer the following general description.

The manuscript proper consists of seventy large sheets written on both sides (133 pages), with seven full-size drawings without text. From page 43 on, Blake uses the discarded proofs of designs intended for his *Night Thoughts* project, except for pages 87–90, which he made by cutting in half a print of his early "Edward & Eleanor" engraving. Drawings meant perhaps as illustrations or illuminations were done on eighty-four pages, including on the back of *Night Thoughts* proofs. According to Butlin, Blake seems

15

to have stitched together the first section of pages (1–18, 23–42) and, separately, most of the *Night Thoughts* pages (43–84, 111–12). However, while the manuscript seems to have begun as a fair copy in formal engraver's script, Blake revised it over a ten-year period, at first in a fairly neat hand but eventually in his normal hand, adding stanzas in between lines, filling margins, and writing extra pages. Because it underwent such massive reworking in ink, pencil, chalk, and watercolor, the manuscript's ultimate status remains in question.

The most comprehensive study remains Bentley's facsimile edition of 1963, which is the only full-size reproduction and helps clarify many textual problems in the manuscript. However, David Erdman's 1982 ("newly revised") transcription supercedes previous ones. This edition, while imperfect, offers the most reliable transcription of the manuscript text (as his and Cettina Magno's 1987 facsimile provides the most minute reproduction of the manuscript's visual designs). While he equips us with a text that certainly cannot, by the nature of Blake's writing, be Blake's actual text—and we should bear this point in mind—Erdman warns against drawing unfounded conclusions. "The complexities of the ms," he writes, "continue to defy analysis and all assertions about meaningful physical groupings or chronologically definable layers of composition or inscription must be understood to rest on partial and ambiguous evidence" (Erdman 1982, 818). Erdman's prudent caution, his attention to textual and visual detail, his unwillingness to normalize spelling and syntax (in most cases), and his patience with incompletion make him Blake's most astute and faithful editor.

But since all deities reside in the human breast, we should consider a critique of Erdman's text. For those critics known collectively as the Santa Cruz Blake Study Group (SCBSG), Erdman's 1982 edition concedes too much to print technology at the expense of the actual work, or of what they call the "minute graphological particulars" of the manuscript (SCBSG, 1986, 324). While they target the entire edition, their section iv examines *The Four Zoas,* the two Nights VII in particular.

The critique, titled "What Type of Blake," laments the passing of Blake as "the prophet of *ecriture*" because Erdman violates Blake's inimitable form of writing in the name of "contextual expectations" (SCBSG 1986, 302). Erdman's decisions to change commas into periods and rearrange passages filters Blake's text through the altering "I" of the editor, doing violence to the "visual semiotics of Blake's printed text" (SCBSC 1986, 306). As they point out, readers should remain alert to the "graphic potential" of Blake's work, which too often is subordinated to the bland format and normative code of letterpress and offset printing. Erdman's compliance with this code obscures the fact that Blake's books draw attention to themselves "as graphological production" (SCBSC 1986, 323). This insistence is well founded and the Group finds Erdman especially guilty of imposing his perspective on the two Nights VII, whose new arrangement marks his most radical departure from the earlier (1965) edition.

The problems regarding the two Nights VII, both in relation to each other and to Nights VI and VIII, are extremely complex. As students of the poem know, Blake left two Nights titled "Night the Seventh" without fully reliable instructions for arrangement. Readers should consult *Blake/An Illustrated Quarterly* 46 (Summer 1978), especially the essays by John Kilgore, Andrew Lincoln, Mark Lefebvre, and Erdman, both for a fuller sense of the issues involved and for the textual analysis that underpins Erdman's editorial decision. In a note to the 1982 edition, Erdman summarizes the analyses:

> Andrew Lincoln, arguing from an impressive hypothetical reconstruction of the evolution of the ms, would insert VIIa between the two portions of VIIb (as Blake rearranged them). Mark Lefebvre and John Kilgore, arguing mainly from fit, propose inserting all of VIIb between the two portions of VIIa (taking the first portion of VIIa as concluding with 85:22, originally followed by "End of the Seventh Night"). Kilgore would return the transposed parts of VIIb to their original order; Lefebvre would keep them in the order of Blake's transposing. In the present edition I have decided to follow the latter course. (Erdman 1982, 836)

The decision about how best to arrange the two versions of Night VII rests ultimately with the scholar-editor. As Wilkie and Johnson suggest, serious readers of *The Four Zoas* might well try five possible sequences (VI & VIIa & VIII; VI & VIIb & VIII; VI & VIIa & VIIb & VIII; VI & VIIa1 & VIIb & VIIa2 & VIII; *VI & VIIb1 & VIIa & VIIb2 & VIII*) and ponder the thematic and narrative patterns that result (Wilkie and Johnson 1978, 273). My own choice of arrangement, which I have italicized, follows Lincoln's.

I choose to place VIIa between two portions of VIIb for two reasons: first, it seems reasonably loyal to Blake's intentions, insofar as these can be gauged; second, it accords with my own interpretive position on the poem. As argued in chapter five, I believe that in Night VIIa the individual integration of the imaginative zoas—Los, Urthona's Spectre, and Enitharmon—is crucial but limited because, in narrative-historical terms, Los's integration does not stem the tide of blood inaugurated in Night VIIb and followed in Night VIII. Also, the poem moves toward the larger or more collective integrations of the zoas and emanations in Night IX. While I am aware that in *The Four Zoas* "unity" derives from interpretive and editorial decisions, I choose the Erdman-Lincoln arrangement because it enables me to resurrect the poem/manuscript to a provisional unity that, in turn, calls for response by other interested readers.

All quotations of Blake's work are from *The Complete Poetry and Prose of William Blake,* edited by David V. Erdman (Berkeley: University of California Press, 1982). Because of complexities in citing the *Four Zoas* manuscript in Nights VIIa, VIIb, and VIII, I include the page and line numbers from Blake's text with the Erdman page number in these Nights: thus (95:1; E 360) means page 95, line 1 of the *Four Zoas* manuscript found on page 360 of the Erdman text.

Acknowledgments

I first want to thank my family for unfailing belief in a project that lies outside their sphere of expertise. I also acknowledge the nurturing influence of Libby Baxter, who helped engender and cultivate this book. I thank my friends and mentors Steve Mowrey, Naomi Ayala, Tom Christensen, Dolora Cunningham, Leslie Tannenbaum, and the late (and sorely missed) Richard Bjornson. Leo Damrosch and Neil Fraistat made incisive and useful comments on an early draft and backed me when I needed it. To my colleagues at Southern Connecticut State—especially Mike Shea, Eleanor Lang, Vara Neverow-Turk, Mark Heidmann, and Peter Baker—I am indebted for timely utterance and support. Steve Badrich, Jackie DiSalvo, and Danny Watkins read parts of the manuscript and steered it in the right directions: each, in their distinct ways, has taught me what engaged scholarship is all about. My deepest gratitude is to Laura Wagner for her realistic intelligence and loving comradeship: without her I am in my spectre's power. And to Joe Wittreich goes my most enthusiastic acknowledgement for his creative intellect, boundless generosity, and unerring wisdom.

My sincere appreciation to Southern Connecticut State University for a research grant that got me to the British Library to study the *Four Zoas* manuscript in its naked glory. Thanks also to David Erdman for his kindness in loaning me several photographs from the *Four Zoas* manuscript. And thanks to Bucknell University Press and Associated University Presses for their professional support and cooperation.

Finally I thank the British Library for permission to reproduce illustrations from the *Four Zoas* manuscript and the University of California Press for permission to quote from *The Complete Prose and Poetry of William Blake*, edited by David V. Erdman.

19

Blake's Prophetic Workshop

1

A Reception History of *The Four Zoas*

His poems are variously estimated. They tested rather severely
the imaginative capacity of their hearers.
—Samuel Palmer

There has always been a tendency among critics of Blake to
interpret him in terms of the critic's own time.
—Northrop Frye

SAMUEL Palmer is only partly right. Blake's poems tested the rational as well as the imaginative capacity of their hearers, as is
amply demonstrated by the critical heritage of *The Four Zoas*. But
since the *Four Zoas* manuscript did not appear publicly until the
1893 Ellis-Yeats edition of Blake, we must reconstruct two previous stages of Blake's reception to situate the Ellis-Yeats moment:
namely the late eighteenth and early nineteenth centuries, when
Blake wrote the poem, and the Pre-Raphaelite phase of the mid-
nineteenth century, when Alexander Gilchrist, the Rossetti brothers, and A. C. Swinburne rescued Blake from near oblivion. Critics in both periods find fault with the obscurity of Blake's longer
poems, a charge that haunts Blake's twentieth-century reception.
This charge, however, stems as much from the critical tendency
to interpret Blake according to one's presuppositions about artistic form and content as from Blake's arcane literary style.

I

While the public did not see *The Four Zoas* in Blake's lifetime,
and while any profile of the poem's initial audience remains hypo-

23

thetical, underscoring Blake's artisanal background and republican politics at the outset will indicate how critics view Blake in terms of their own times.

In the 1790s, Blake's audience included the Dissenting radicals of London, comprised of both an "urban subclass" and the intellectual coterie surrounding the publisher Joseph Johnson.[1] Blake's affiliation with Johnson's circle, which included liberals such as Thomas Paine and Mary Wollstonecraft as well as Blake's friend Henry Fuseli, has been well documented.[2] Less understood is his connection to the Dissenting artisans of the lower middle class, those "second and third rate tradesmen" who were "linked by the capitalist market to teachers, journalists, and dissenting ministers" (Scrivener 1990, 115). Blake shares with the radical artisans and literate craftsmen an "autodidactic" education that belies the social gap between sophisticated and unrefined readers, showing that "formal education is not a prerequisite for intellectual culture" (Scrivener 1990, 120).[3] A partial explanation for Blake's obscurity lies in his attempt to undermine this class-based dichotomy, which his nineteenth-century critics did not acknowledge.[4] Indeed, as the alliance between the Jacobin middle-class intellectuals and the working classes then in formation broke down, an important segment of Blake's audience splintered.[5]

My aim, however, is not to speculate about an initial audience for *The Four Zoas*, but to connect Blake's moment of writing to the mid-Victorian recovery of his reputation, which enables the work of Ellis and Yeats.[6] Two brief transitional moves will take us from the 1790s to the age of Gilchrist and the Pre-Raphaelites: they involve Blake's first biographers and the early Victorian social crisis that stands behind the criticism of Gilchrist's mentor, Thomas Carlyle.

The biographies of Benjamin Heath Malkin and Allan Cunningham, while they open Blake's work to a wide contemporary audience, evince a certain anxiety about Blake's obscurity. In *A Father's Memoirs of his Child* (1806) Malkin identifies the causes that have "prevented [Blake's] general reception, as a son of taste and of the muses": these are sceptics and rationalist critics who unite against the "mystical philosopher," keeping Blake from "public notice" and his genius tied down "to the mechanical department of his profession" (Bentley 1975, 148). Malkin's picture of Blake as a simple if somewhat "touched" engraver colors Blake's nineteenth-century reputation; and his division of engraver from artist, without mentioning the economics of Blake's craft, blocks insight into the material conditions of Blake's isolation. Malkin does recognize, however, the generic form of Blake's prophecies, the "specimens in blank verse," where the style of writing is said to be "epic in structure" (Bentley 1975, 155). But he ignores their social content—Blake's artisanal Dissenting politics—and attributes their formal obscurity to Blake's "singularity," a theme picked up by Cunningham.

Cunningham's influential portrait of Blake in *Lives of the Most Eminent British Painters, Sculptors, and Architects* (1830), while "probably the most important factor in keeping Blake's name alive until Gilchrist's epochal *Life* in 1863" (Bentley 1975, 170), perpetuates the critical biases of Malkin. Blake's life of "dreaming abstraction" stamps his work with its peculiar beauty, but it also accounts for his "mysticism and obscurity." Cunningham courageously grapples with the prophecies, but he finds that *Urizen* surpasses "human comprehension" and that *Jerusalem*'s "crowning defect is obscurity" (Bentley 1975, 179, 182). His favorite work, *Songs of Innocence,* embodies Cunningham's curious mix of Augustan and Romantic presuppositions about what is "natural and touching" as opposed to "wild and mystical" in poetry. Yet Cunningham's critical assumptions, while in part adopted by Gilchrist and the Pre-Raphaelites, must pass through the agitated social atmosphere of the early Victorian period before reaching Blake's mid-century champions.

The social order that emerged in post-Napoleonic Europe underlies the second transitional moment in Blake's early reception, as shown in the work of Carlyle and Ruskin, two alembics of the mid-Victorian Blake. Rapid industrial expansion in Britain in the 1820s brought not only great prosperity but an unstable market, benefiting some while exploiting and impoverishing others, especially small tradesmen, farmers, and wage-earners (Beales 1969, 41). Such changes registered in the political arena, where the old governing class of hereditary landlords sought to contain the threat of the rising middle classes. Fortunately for Britain's ruling elite, tragically for its working classes, the crisis of 1929–32, which revived the old demon of revolution, was exorcised by the Reform Bill of 1832. The bourgeois-aristocratic consensus, however, faltered with the crises of the late thirties, and from the cauldron of social unrest arose Thomas Carlyle, brandishing his gospel of work and hero-worship.

The crucial element in Carlyle's—and the early Victorian—social solution is sincerity and the importance of being earnest. In Carlyle's analysis, what needs reforming is not the economy, but the moral life of the nation. The motto for *Past and Present*

(1843)—"ernst ist das Leben" (from Schiller)—is directed not simply at "Old Leisure" or the aristocracy, but at the working classes, whose whole *duty* lies in sincere work. The middle classes fare no better; but from their ranks come the morally upright industrial captains, those rough heroes, who will guide Britain through present as others have through past crises. These Carlylean emphases on earnest character and hero-worship do not escape the Scottish sage's protege, Alexander Gilchrist, who hailed his mentor as the "noblest influence of his time" (Gilchrist 1969, 2:373).

Bentley observes that Gilchrist is heavily influenced by "the governing spirit of the time." More specifically, Gilchrist drew from Carlyle two related principles: that history was made by solitary geniuses and that the genius achieved heroic stature by the sincere pursuit of his aim.[7] Gilchrist found this view exemplified by Blake's life and work.[8] Blake's earnest sincerity, it turns out, derives from his "solitary" engraver's life and his equally individual strain of thought, which produce a "style *sui generis* as no other artist's ever was" (Gilchrist 1969, 1:3). Blake's singular heroism, however, also guarantees his poor reception: "He neither wrote nor drew for the many . . . rather for children and angels" (1:3). Gilchrist here takes Blake at his word that children elucidated his visions better than adults, a view that confirms Blake's odd "singularity."

While Gilchrist's *Life* sets out to qualify Cunningham's portrait of the "insane genius," Blake's moral piety does not protect his prophetic writings from the charge of obscurity. Gilchrist cannot bring himself to call these works *poems,* yet he praises them for their enthusiasm and moral fervor. Enthusiasm, though, has "been kindled into overmastering intensity" as Blake's untutored genius has abjured the "guidance and control of intellect and will" (Gilchrist 1969, 1:227–28). Certain lines glow with "plenary inspiration," indicating the "devout and earnest spirit in which Blake wrote," but the result is incomprehensible: "dark oracles" and "morbid analogy" (1:227–29). *Jerusalem* is "not unsuggestive of prophecy," but in trying to manifest "inward notions" in formal signs, Blake courted the impression that he was mad. "Does not a prophet or hero always seem 'mad'," Gilchrist asks rhetorically; but he finally cannot absolve the prophecies from incoherence. *Milton,* he concludes, "equals its predecessor in obscurity" and, exasperated, he directs us to Swinburne for guidance (1:241–42).

The input of Swinburne and the Rossetti brothers into the "Life" represents an anti-Carlylean departure in Blake's Victorian reception. They glean their critical assumptions from Ruskin, although they drop his moral aestheticism, preferring to regard art as an autonomous practice, divorced from early Victorian social concerns.[9] Their hatred of industrial capitalism and evangelical ideology no doubt conditions their version of Blake as an anti-social "aesthete." And even though their involvement with the earnest Gilchrist's *Life* tempers their Pre-Raphaelite tone, the Rossetti-Swinburne collaboration brings to bear "purposes and modes of apprehending Blake which, unlike Gilchrist's, were not primarily moralistic or didactic" (Dorfman 1969, 6).

Swinburne's *William Blake: A Critical Essay* (1867) intensifies Gilchrist's portrait of Blake as an exemplary hero: "No man ever lived and labored in hotter earnest" (Swinburne 1970, 85). Blake earns the title of great artist because in him above all other men, "the moral and imaginative senses were so fused together as to compose the final artistic form" (Swinburne 1970, 298). What Swinburne means here is that Blake's *life* was heroic even if his art suffered lapses in structural design. Swinburne ultimately demotes Blake's work for both its formal obscurity and its social aesthetic. It is fine that Blake pursued moral-social improvement: "But if the artist does his work with an eye to such results . . . he will too probably fail even of them. Art for art's sake first of all, and afterwards we may suppose all the rest shall be added to her . . ." (Swinburne 1970, 91).

The art-for-art's-sake axiom becomes the slogan of fin de siècle England and thus serves as an important link between the Pre-Raphaelite and Ellis-Yeats moments of Blake's reception. Swinburne's criticism is not simply Pre-Raphaelite or *symboliste*. But he takes the epigraph to his *Essay* from Baudelaire and adopts two fundamental principles of nineteenth-century French aestheticism: first, art's autonomy from social and political considerations; second, the "superiority of the formal perfection of art to any other kind of value" (Hough 1961, 189). In turning to Swinburne's study of Blake's prophecies, then, we should underscore the character of his historical moment, marked by the deepening alienation of the Romantic artist, forced into the defensive posture of the aesthete guarding his art from the utilitarian values of the philistine marketplace.

Swinburne, like Baudelaire a Romantic poet in the era of high capitalism, champions the lyrical genius of Blake while lamenting the formal infractions of the prophetic books, with "their impenetrable mistiness, the obscurity of confused wind and cloud" (Swinburne 1970, 11). Like Swinburne, though, Blake is a religious rebel who believes in "holy insurrection," in "divine revolt against divine law," which unites the human and divine by resistance to God (157). If justly apprehended, this belief (Blake's mystical evangelism) can account for Blake's formal difficulties, "the wildest bodily forms in which he drew forth his visions from the mould of prophecy" (151). While he hints at the genre of Blake's longer works, Swinburne argues that Blake unfortunately lacks a sense of mimetic structure, particularly in *Jerusalem,* that "excursive and all but shapeless poem" cloaked in "the repellent haze of mythological form" (159, 164). And crucially for my argument, Swinburne finds that Blake's "character and training" cause this formal obscurity, for Blake was not "educated in any regular or rational way," as T. S. Eliot will reiterate in his influential essay on Blake.

As he delves deeper into *Jerusalem,* Swinburne revels in the "sands and shallows of prophetic speech" and extols Blake's "epic style." But classical scruples curb his praise. For there is one thing a writer certainly must not play with: "the material forms of art" (194–8). Swinburne elicits the right gloss for *Jerusalem*—"Allegory address'd to the Intellectual Powers"—but imposes his own classical assumptions on Blake's prophetic forms, which he claims break the rules too radically: "the laws and the dues of art it is never permissible to forget" (35). In effect, Swinburne's formalist critique, coupled with the "heresy of instruction" he shared with Rossetti, signals where he distorts Blake into an image of the déclassé rebel aesthete.[10] Blake retains his heroic stature as an "evangel of bodily liberty," but he loses points for his artistic obscurity. Swinburne's pantheist Hellenism muzzles Blake's Hebraic strain and, despite his libertarian ethics, Swinburne concludes: "art and poetry are in no wise given for the sustenance or the salvation of men in general" (36).[11] We glimpse here what Walter Benjamin defines as the romantic withdrawal of the art-for-art's-sake writer, who, like Baudelaire, is described as "an agent of the secret discontent of his class with its own rule" (Benjamin 1976, 104).[12] This withdrawal is completed by Yeats, whose willful obscurantism exceeds the bitter and enforced isolation of both his Victorian and Romantic predecessors.

II

By the time E. J. Ellis and W. B. Yeats inaugurate the public reception of *The Four Zoas,* the Romantic withdrawal of the fin de siècle artist is commonplace: "a puzzling novelty in the forties" but an "accepted orthodoxy in the nineties" (Hough 1961, 182). Scorning any interest in the social dimensions of Blake's writing— a "false idea . . . nowhere supported in Blake's works"—Ellis and Yeats center attention on one major area: the mystical contexts and symbols that underpin Blake's myth. While they regard *The Four Zoas* as Blake's literary masterpiece, their key contribution lies in the section entitled "The Symbolic System," a system that Yeats says is both the signature of Blake's genius and the guarantee of his sanity. Yeats also declares that two principal causes have prevented an understanding of Blake's work: "The first is the solidity of the myth, and its wonderful coherence. The second is the variety of terms in which the sections of it are named" (Ellis and Yeats 1893, 1:viii). The myth's coherence hinges on its relation to the tradition of mysticism, while its various terms are explained by Yeats's philosophy of symbolism. Identifying symbols, Yeats argues, is necessary before we can interpret Blake's paradoxes as "sequences of inexorable symbolic logic and not as confusion" (1:415–16).

In "The Necessity of Symbolism," the opening segment of "The Symbolic System," Yeats elevates mystical symbols over poetic metaphors because the former can be woven into a complete system (Ellis and Yeats 1893, 1:238). Completeness or totality is crucial: but like Swinburne before and Eliot after him, Yeats bewails Blake's lack of formal religious training, claiming (with no trace of irony) that had Blake been a Catholic of Dante's time he would have been "well content with Mary and the angels" and "less obscure because a traditional mythology stood on the threshold of his meaning" (Yeats 1961, 111).[13] The fourfold vision, it turns out, coheres by virtue of Swedenborgian correspondences, not by Blakean imagination. Yeats chastizes previous critics, especially the "one-eyed" Swinburne, for misreading many difficult passages, which Yeats considers incomprehensible only to those unfamiliar with Swedenborg's method (Ellis and Yeats 1893, 1:4).

Blake's fourfold vision, then, is only partially Blake's, an assumption that distorts Yeats's interpretation of *The Four Zoas*. The problem, in my view, is that Yeats yokes the epics together in his analysis, a move repeated by Frye and the myth critics. It turns out that the most fundamental text for the fourfold vision comes from *Milton*, plate 34: in the only diagrammed plate in Blake's epics, Yeats zeroes in on the "Four States of Humanity" depicted "in its Repose," a condition, significantly enough, that produces the "Fall" in *The Four Zoas*. As Deborah Dorfman astutely observes, this passive sense guides Yeats's view of Blake's four states and insinuates itself into his reading of *The Four Zoas* (Dorfman 1969, 211). In an important section on the poem, the "Story of Urthona in the *Book of Vala*," Yeats offers a plot summary based on Los's story, told in many "symbols" or correspondences, which are the "various names" that have concealed meaning from previous critics. That is—and this is Yeats insight as well as his folly— to be able to follow Blake's changing symbols, and to trace through them the single thread of narrative belonging to the story of Los, or Urthona, is to be able to "read all Blake's Prophetic Books as records of one great Myth" (Ellis and Yeats 1893, 1:370). Yeats grasps that the zoas are facets of each other, and that since Los-Urthona is closest to Albion's fourfold unity, he passes with Albion through "changes that cause him to become all the zoas in succession" (1:360). This insight posits Yeats on the threshold of understanding Blake's narrative practice in *The Four Zoas:* that what occurs in later Nights "is actually an elaboration of what was told early." But Yeats is not after narrative insight; he is after the "one great Myth" that Blake's system approximates.

As Yeats's analysis shows, the multicolored lens of fin de siècle Romanticism distorts the 1790s contexts that inform *The Four Zoas.* And as he admits, his immersion in magic, Rosicrucian lore, Jewish Kabbala, Blavatskian spiritualism, and Irish myth permeates everything he says about Blake and *The Four Zoas.* In discussing Night VIII, for example, Yeats identifies the symbol of the Polypus as "the eating cancer of analysis" that is adjoined to "the rock of belief in matter" (Ellis and Yeats 1893, 1:368). This antimaterialism, while ingrained in the fiber of Yeats's thinking, forms part of the ideological heritage he acquired from nineteenth-century Romantics. As a writer for the *Occult Review* put it, Blake is the "one great English mystic, whose thought is so singularly congenial to the temper of the present age" (quoted in Dorfman 1969, 226). Belief in matter may lead to materialism, especially of the dialectical kind, which Yeats flirted with but turned against while working on Blake.[14] Indeed, the problem with his precursors, Yeats discloses, is that they are not "Romantic" enough:

> I saw . . . that Swinburne in one way, Browning in another, and Tennyson in a third, had filled their work with what I called "impurities," curiosities about politics, about science, about history, about religion; and that we must create once more the pure work. (Yeats 1965, 112)

The pure work, the static artifact of Byzantium, freezes the active flames of Blake's Eden, replacing Blake's dynamic narrative of self, society, and cosmos with the idealized perfection of mystical tradition. Blake's revolutionary impulse, linked with his artisanal aesthetic, has, once again, dropped from the picture, to remain buried until the 1930s.

Ellis and Yeats's critical assumptions dominate the early modern reception of *The Four Zoas*, with two important qualifications: T. S. Eliot's essay in 1920, and the adoption of Blake by the academy after World War I.[15] Eliot's criticism bears directly on this history: it promotes both a "metaphysical" tradition that the academy adopts, with new critical slogans and methods, and a distinctly "literary" theory of culture based in the "Latin traditions," against which he judges Blake's formal and philosophical weakness (Eliot 1972, 155–56). In one sense, Eliot sees more clearly than others into the class determinants of Blake's obscurity. The "humble engraver," blocked from traditional education by a "manual occupation," is privy to a peculiar "honesty" (earnestness) that, unfortunately, inclines him to believe too strongly in his own philosophy. "[D]eprived of the advantage of culture," Eliot writes, Blake ends up with "formlessness"; and his "supernatural territories" reveal not only a lack of impersonal reason, common sense, and scientific objectivity, but a "meanness of culture." What Blake sorely lacks is the "Mediterranean gift of form," a phrase that inverts, with conscious impunity, Blake's denigration of "Mathematic" in favor of "Gothic" form. Indeed, Blake's radical sensibilities are measured against a Burkean "framework of accepted and traditional ideas." As with Swinburne and Yeats, Eliot devalues Blake's Hebraic strain—decidedly "not a Latin virtue"—in order to explain, without excusing, his obscurity.

Although not directly influenced by Eliot, D. J. Sloss and J. P. R. Wallis's interpretation of Blake is deeply affected by this complex cultural moment. On the one hand, the chaos surrounding World War I disrupted the publication of their edition of Blake, which, while complete in 1912, did not appear until 1926. On the other hand, Sloss and Wallis absorb, paradoxically, both the scientific and the metaphysical presuppositions of the early twentieth century, which taint their view of the formal obscurity and social content of *The Four Zoas*.

Sloss and Wallis focus on *The Four Zoas* as their area of expertise. While their realistic and respectful tone helps advance discussion of the poem, particularly regarding the characters of Tharmas and Enion, their philosophic assumptions reduce the value, as they distort the object, of their approach. A revealing statement appears early in their analysis, following a jab at Blake for not being a "formal thinker" (a lack, they say, which hurts his reputation as "a philosopher"). They decide that Blake's aesthetic appeal lies in isolated passages, whose contribution to knowledge, sadly, is not only "slight," but obscured by the arbitrary symbols in which Blake's ideas embodied themselves. Without Yeats's thoroughgoing "System," Sloss and Wallis turn to the positive science of the day to penetrate "the capriciousness of [Blake's] material." They write: "By a quaint irony, it comes about that his symbolism is only interpretable with safety by the method of 'modest inquiry' that he so vigorously repudiated" (Sloss and Wallis 1926, 2:125). But by a less quaint irony, the Sloss and Wallis method helps produce the errors it purports to find: they argue that their examination shows the gaps and loose ends in Blake's work and "discovers the limitations of his speculative and logical faculties" (Sloss and Wallis 1926, 2:125). But the kind of unity and clarity Sloss and Wallis demand are not what *The Four Zoas* offers. In effect they disallow the poem to speak on its own terms. The first critic to attempt such a reading is S. Foster Damon, who recognizes that Blake's symbols are, at bottom, *literary* rather than esoteric.

But this is not completely true. While Damon's *William Blake: His Philosophy and Symbols* (1924) is widely held to have founded the "modern" study of Blake, primarily because it approaches his work as *literature,* Damon incorporates the biases of the perennial philosophy method. Blake's reputation as painter and poet is secure: but this is not enough, for Damon must crown him "philosopher," or provide a basis for getting at his philosophy through a "rational explanation of Blake's obvious obscurities" (Damon 1958, xi,ix). Eliot may be the hidden force driving Damon to rescue Blake as a philosopher. But Damon's Blake, the singular, "sincere, enthusiastic mystic," resembles Gilchrist's eccentric, who Damon calls "a type which is never in tune with the times" (13). As he believes that "the key to everything Blake wrote lies in his mysticism," Damon, like Yeats, must "complete" Blake's philosophy to make sense of his work.

But, paradoxically, since Blake "never lost his grip on this world," it must be the future that he addressed. And since *The Four Zoas* was "never intended for the public," it must be the "New Age," the age of Damon and Yeats, that provides the proper receptive ground for this mystical epic. Damon does point to the generic mold of *The Four Zoas,* repeatedly calling it an "epic," but he does not pursue the point nor engage with poetic content. His

major concern is with the obvious obscurity of the poem, generated, for him, by Blake's needless "repetition" and his fear of
formal allegory (164 n.1). Thus, while he finds the poem structurally "flawed," mainly by "obscure transition passages," Damon says
"it has one of the greatest plans in all literature" (164). This assumption enables Damon to analyze *The Four Zoas* with some hope
of comprehending it. But, again, the mystical system is pursued
with such a vengeance that the poem gets left behind. As with his
predecessors, Damon nurtures an animus against the dreaded
"materialism," which he claims is not only his and Blake's enemy,
but Adam and Jesus' as well (150). Thus Damon's important work
also distorts the poem in the interests of academic mysticism.

III

The second major phase of *The Four Zoas'* twentieth-century
reception builds its case in reaction to the mysticism of the first.
As early as 1927 Helen White claims that Blake is not a mystic
"in any sense that means anything," and John Middleton Murry,
Jacob Bronowski, Mark Schorer, and David Erdman support her
judgment. These critics restore to Blake studies the political and
economic contexts of late eighteenth-century England and show
how they shaped the social and formal concerns of *The Four Zoas.*
The emergence of Marxian categories in the study of Blake, cata-
lyzed, in part, by the economic crisis of 1929, aids in this recovery.
But the mystical and revolutionary sides of Blake retain their
complex relationship in this period's criticism, as the works of
Murry and Milton Percival demonstrate.[16]

Murry's *William Blake* (1933) and Schorer's *William Blake: The
Politics of Vision* (1946) offer the first sustained readings of *The
Four Zoas* independent of the perennial philosophy approach. Yet
Murry is constrained to admit that the whole process of Blake's
work *"begins* with the mystical experience" (Murry 1964, 377);
and Schorer says that while Blake favors and treasures "the social
man," he sees society in individual terms (Schorer 1959, 268).
Both critics write trenchantly of Blake's difficult psychology, but
where Murry locates the formal obscurity of *The Four Zoas* in
Blake's personal history, Schorer explains it as a feature of
Blake's age.

Focusing on the narrative, Murry recognizes that in *The Four
Zoas* there are many versions of the "fall from Eternity" and dis-
cerns two basic patterns. One, the division of zoa from emanation,

describes the "apparently irreparable division" between the sexes; the second, the conspiracy between Luvah and Urizen, depicts, not simply English-French politics, but the inward division of the emotional and rational faculties. Murry asserts that the "criss-crossing and interweaving of these two themes" is what makes the "myth" of *The Four Zoas* so puzzling. And while the poem evinces Blake's psychic acumen and social compassion, its "victory" is not a formal one. The poem primarily records Blake's struggle for a new vision and so requires a new form. Murry concludes that while *The Four Zoas* is the most deeply engaging of all Blake's prophecies, it remains the "travail of Blake's final rebirth," a struggle that clears the way for the engraved epics (Murry 1933, 219).

Schorer, on the other hand, argues that Blake's narrative problems are part of his "curiously mixed" tradition of religion and politics (Schorer 1959, 262). As Schorer sees it, Blake conflates three antithetical traditions in *The Four Zoas:* millenarian Dissent, Enlightenment progress, and internalized Romantic apocalypse. Blake's work is obscure because he tries to resolve inherent difficulties by a purely "imaginative solution," despite his commitment to social history (Schorer 1959, 266—68). Schorer thus finds Blake's plunge into the psychic terrain of Man too deep and complex for clarity of expression. In one of the most incisive paragraphs written on the poem, Schorer observes:

> Yet the proliferation of characters, the splittings, the reproductions, the dislocations, that are so bewildering, even the confusions of identity whereby one character suddenly becomes another . . . all these serve rather to remind us of his insight than express it . . . as poetry, it was disastrous to take this way of showing that states of mind, involving the whole being, are in constant state of flux . . . appearing now in one form with one activity and function; and now in another form with a subtly or utterly different activity and function. The possibilities are both too vast and too complex for form. (Schorer 1959, 290)

Subsequent criticism has only begun to grapple with this challenge. But Schorer's work, despite its reliance on new critical, or what Blake would call "Mathematic," standards of form, has opened the way for Erdman's full recovery of the revolutionary political contexts that saturate *The Four Zoas.*

Erdman's *Blake: Prophet Against Empire* (1954) expands the approach opened by Murry, Bronowski, and Schorer by pursuing historical allegory into the texture of Blake's poem. Erdman concedes that his single focus on historical details partially reduces Blake's multilayered narrative, but he insists that history offers the surest ground of evaluation. Opposing both Yeats's mysticism and nineteenth-century historicism, Erdman tracks political history in the form of *The Four Zoas*, claiming that Blake's narrative difficulty derives from the push and pull of political events between 1797 and 1804:

> It [this political history] seems to have delivered a direct shock to the symbolic consistency and frail narrative frame of Blake's epic. And the strange Peace of Amiens would not only catch him off guard but upset the entire seventh act of his celestial drama. . . . . In *The Four Zoas* he seems to have allowed his tune to be called by events unfolding as he went. (Erdman 1969, 294)

Ever points of contention, Blake's two Nights VII, with his revisions in general, support Erdman's provocative criticism that Blake's socio-historical focus *causes* his formal obscurity.

In a compelling chapter (chapter twenty-one), Erdman argues that in 1802 Blake saw in the Peace of Amiens a "providential resolution" to the British-French (Urizen-Orc) war and that he revised *The Four Zoas* to reflect a "predestinarian emphasis," replacing Night VIIb with VIIa and writing a "meeker" opening to Night IX. More contentiously, Erdman declares that these revisions indicate Blake's passive submission to fate, a temporary lapse of energy and ambition, and even political compromise. Under the delusory hope that a lasting peace *had* been established, Blake succumbs to Romantic utopianism:

> [T]he revisions of *The Four Zoas* made in this spirit seem virtually to remove the central theme of struggle from the epic. They suggest that no kind of social or psychological revolution is necessary but submission. . . . It is this tentative removal of the social dynamic that causes Blake to founder, as Frye puts it, on the approaches to the apocalypse. (Erdman 1969, 380)

Erdman's "formal" critique turns on his conception of Blake's abandonment of the realist aesthetic embodied, for him, in *The French Revolution*. Erdman complains that in Night IX Los, the prophet, does everything *for* Albion, "the people," who without participating bear no responsibility for change. From his own Marxian perspective, under siege in the cold war atmosphere of the 1940s and 1950s, Erdman cites Blake for abrogating his prophetic duty, for confusing a symbolic apocalypse with its social communication. And, perhaps justly, he charges Blake with the fallacy of thinking that a change in his own mind is "equivalent to, if not the cause of, a change in international relations" (Erdman 1969, 381). Erdman knows better. But what his empirical approach does not account for is that Blake's internalized apocalypse shares an anticapitalist sensibility characteristic of Romantic thinking from Blake's age to our own.[17]

IV

With the work of Northrop Frye and the myth critics we enter the central phase of Blake's twentieth-century reception. Frye's *Fearful Symmetry* (1947) consolidates the major positions of its critical predecessors. Starting from the aestheticism of Yeats and Damon, Frye adds the literary formalism of Eliot, mixes in his own "higher critical" religious training, and concocts a structural study of Blake grounded in mythic archetypes. As Frye has it, literature "does not reflect life, but it doesn't escape or withdraw from life either, it swallows it" (Frye 1964, 80). And it is from Blake, Frye says, that he learned how literature contains life, although his archetypalism extends back through Blake to the Bible.

Three basic presuppositions underlie Frye's syncretistic approach. One is that the biblical imagination sees the world in purely poetic terms; it humanizes the world by transforming it into a single form with the mythic outlines of Creation, Fall, Redemption, and Apocalypse. The second assumption emerges from the first: the poet carries the prophetic burden of recreating this mythic outline, of preserving its "inner imaginative structure" against historical pressure (Frye 1976, 803). By recreating the structure of a myth, the poet retains its meaning rather than replaces it with an allegorical or conceptual substitute. The only way to ensure that the poet recreates rather than replaces a myth is by Frye's third postulate: the hypothesis of a "verbal universe" or "total order of words" to which each myth (or literary work) belongs. Only within a comprehensive mythology can each myth maintain its original shape, reflecting the biblical *mythos*, not the writer's changing historical situation. Dante, Tasso, Spenser, Milton, and Blake all fit within this encyclopedic system because no historical event, or social context, can exhaust the far goal of time projected by the mythology. Frye criticizes *The Four Zoas* precisely because it blurs, or fails to follow in a coherent fashion, the biblical structure or *mythos* he outlines.

Frye's mythic assumptions are featured in his account of what he calls the "Orc Cycle," the cyclical strife between the forces of rationality (Urizen) and passion (Orc) that turn the "fallen" wheel of history. The problem becomes a *narrative* crisis with the two Nights VII and how they and Night VIII relate structurally to Night IX. Frye faults *The Four Zoas* for not clearly indicating whether Orc or Los is the true apocalyptic agent in the poem, a fault detected by Sloss and Wallis. Reading backward from *Jerusalem*, Frye knows that Los *should* be the agent because Orc, a "mere" revolutionary power—"heat without light"—can only portend, not produce, the apocalypse. The poem fails because it refuses to sever history and eternity. Frye wants to know how the Second Coming can be more than just another temporal rebirth of Orc, more than another false revolutionary dawn. Or, as Frye asks of Night IX: "Has Blake's Ode to Joy any inner logic connecting it with the rest of the work beyond a purely emotional requirement of allegro finale?" (Frye 1969, 308). In other words, Blake has not given us an imaginatively coherent account of "how we get from eighteenth-century Deism to a Last Judgment through the power of Los, not Orc" (309).

Blake's coherent account, according to Frye, appears only in the engraved epics, where Los (now the cosmic-formalist aesthete) grasps the total form of history. Only Los understands that history evolves as a single archetypal form, a *mythos*, that supplies life with a containing framework. History as an ongoing revolutionary struggle (Orc's fate) cannot provide the sense of an ending: only an individualized apocalypse can provide it. Once this becomes clear, Frye writes, "the missing link in *The Four Zoas* between the vision of contemporary Deism at the end of Night VIII and the beginning of the apocalypse of Night IX is supplied" (Frye 1969, 323). And since Los provides this link in *Milton*, Frye is prompted to argue, in agreement with Murry, that Blake could not finish *The Four Zoas* because he "realized he was thinking in terms of another poem altogether" (269). By trying to drag history with him into the apocalypse of *The Four Zoas*, Blake allegedly slips out of the biblical scheme and entangles himself in the Orcian folds of the revolutionary process, thereby producing the formal obscurity of the poem.

While most subsequent Blake criticism is indebted to Frye, in one form or another, four major studies of *The Four Zoas* inherit Frye's presuppositions and stretch this third moment of *The Four Zoas*'s reception into the 1970s. Other studies depart from Frye's brand of mythic structuralism, but the work of Harold Bloom,

Morton Paley, G. E. Bentley, and Mary Lynn Johnson and Brian Wilkie build a consensus that dominates interpretation of the poem between 1960 and 1980.

Bloom and Paley inhabit distinct critical spaces along the Frye continuum—Bloom not yet swerving his mentor and Paley crossing the master's insights with Damon and his own Berkeleyan idealism. Both critics, however, adhere to Frye's Romantic humanism, placing ultimate trust in individual vision (or Los) over the messy collective struggle of history (embodied in Orc). Both also focus on the structural problems with Blake's two Nights VII, where the key social and formal issues are most concentrated. They locate the poem's structural flaw in Blake's "quite unaccountable" (Bloom) late revisions, especially in his Eternals and the related Lamb, Council, and Seven Eyes of God (Erdman's *deus ex machina*), which are superimposed on the basically Lambeth form of *Vala* (Paley 1970, 161). For Bloom, the Eternals are an "afterthought, and are never in *The Four Zoas* integrated into the mythic structure" (Bloom 1970 206). For Paley, the Eternals, along with the additions of Tharmas and Urthona, allow Blake to describe the "regenerative role of the imagination" more clearly than in the Lambeth myth, so that the Seven Eyes become "a construct of history showing the way out of the dilemma of recurrence" (Paley 1970, 135). With Frye, both Bloom and Paley, seeking peaceful passage from Nights VII to IX, argue that Orc's wrath in VIIb collides with Los's embrace of Urthona's Spectre in VIIa and disrupts the poem's coherence. But they differ as to how Blake resolves the problem.

Bloom asserts that Blake's formal problem is endemic to Romantic writing per se, then and now. Blake's difficulties in aligning social and psychological insights are "prophetic of the difficulties so often met and so infrequently mastered in the major poetry of our times" (Bloom 1963, 244). The solution: "In action, the poems progress toward ever deeper internalization" (Bloom 1971, 81). Bloom, even more suspicious of historical allegory than Frye, declares that the "dialectical encounters" of the poem, while they "illustrate" the "suffering condition of mankind," occur "utterly *within the self*" (Bloom 1970, 209—his italics). Similarly, Paley insists that history must be "abrogated," not because of universal suffering, but because this suffering periodically issues in Orcian wrath. Paley's solution, the superimposition of regenerative "light" over cyclical "heat," also occurs within the self: "Christianity translated the periodic regeneration of the world into a regeneration of the human individual . . . history can be regenerated, [but only] by and through the individual believer" (Paley 1983, 129). Paley draws on Blake's Felpham experience, his "re-conversion" to Christianity, in order to account for the inward turn of Blake's *Four Zoas* revisions. But ultimately the historical residue from *Vala* is too thick and forces Paley to conclude that Blake's Felpham revisions do not obviate his formal obscurity. By trying to merge history into the Apocalypse, Blake fails to "escape from historical consciousness," the "nightmare of recurrence," and it costs him the coherence of *The Four Zoas.*

Paley's analysis of *The Four Zoas* owes as much to G. E. Bentley as to Frye. Bentley's *William Blake's Vala or The Four Zoas* (1963) along with Wilkie and Johnson's *Blake's Four Zoas* (1978) offer the first book-length monographs on the poem, although they represent singular approaches within the receptive moment opened by Frye. Bentley anchors his unique but thorough analysis in textual history rather than esoteric, political, or biblical contexts; Wilkie and Johnson provide a night-by-night commentary that sticks closely to the "consensus of Blakeans" established by Damon, Murry, Frye, and Bloom.

Bentley's aim, like Paley's after and H. M. Margoliouth's before him, is to trace the metamorphosis of *Vala* into *The Four Zoas,* an aim consistent with Frye's emphasis on the poet's "total myth."[18] He uncovers three stages of composition: 1797 to 1802, when Blake began revising *Vala*; 1803 to 1805, when Blake's Felpham "conversion" compelled him to recast and expand the later nights; and 1805 to 1810, when further revision forced him to abandon the poem. Blake's interminable need to revise gets under Bentley's skin: he astutely marks how the changes, especially "The Council of God," reveal a "profound shift in the meaning of Blake's myth and symbolism," but he is rankled because the revisions lack cohesion. One understands why Bentley, after spending tedious hours and expending Herculean labors disentangling the manuscript, complains that Blake's revisions are "haphazard and indiscriminate" and "positively disrupt the flow of the narrative" (Bentley 1963, 178–79). But, perhaps avoidably, Bentley's formalist assumptions prejudice his account. His bias surfaces when he proclaims that "the nature of Blake's prophetic style" undermines the poem's narrative's coherence as much as his "inconsistent patchwork revision" does. More telling, Bentley finds the same flaws in *Milton* and *Jerusalem,* and concludes: "When the sequence of parts of a continuous narrative is obscure and of legitimate alternative interpretation, the result is a major failure" (Bentley 1963, 191). Despite his seminal contribution to Blake studies, Bentley too judges *The Four Zoas* by a foreign code.

Wilkie and Johnson share Bentley's critical assumptions, but their professed aim, to provide an introductory study, softens their judgment even as they praise the poem's *imaginative* success. While usefully opening Blake to a wider audience, they virtually bracket the poem's social content and belie its structural difficult-ies. With Bloom, the authors believe that, on first reading, the poem requires a visceral response, based on the analogy of read-ing one's own dreams. But while we are assured that Blake's "psy-chodramatic method" includes social, political, and religious meanings, and while local insights, and the emphasis on personal involvement, fulfill the book's modest aim, *Blake's Four Zoas* oper-ates, quite intentionally, within the individualist parameters of Frye's critical perspective. One of the "radical" messages of *The Four Zoas*, we are told, is "that to look at things in a new way makes all the difference," a theme developed extensively by Donald Ault (Wilkie and Johnson 1978, 6). Significantly, neither Erdman's prophet, Schorer's visionary republican, nor Bronowski's artisanal rebel make it into Wilkie and Johnson's "consensus." A revolt against this state of affairs ushers in the latest moment of Blake's twentieth-century reception.

V

The titles of Jackie DiSalvo's *War of Titans: Blake's Critique of Milton and the Politics of Religion* (1983) and Donald Ault's *Narrative Unbound: Revisioning William Blake's "The Four Zoas"* (1987) suggest their respective critical orientations. Both writers approach *The Four Zoas* from decidedly postformalist positions and open a new moment in the poem's reception. Both also bring something of the international post-1960s renaissance in literary theory to bear on their study of Blake. DiSalvo, however, deploying Marxist, femi-nist, and psychoanalytic methods, takes her questions from the political history Blake inherits from Milton's age. Ault addresses the narratological issues raised by Blake's "radically subversive text," preferring to mix phenomenology, deconstruction, and phi-losophy of science into his own brand of reader-response criti-cism. Both critics retain elements of previous approaches to *The Four Zoas;* but their sophisticated methodologies mark a significant departure from, and prevent an innocent return to, former procedures.

DiSalvo's book builds on the contextual approach of Schorer and Erdman, although she fuses key concepts from Joseph Anthony Wittreich's "prophetic" criticism into her socialist-feminist methodology. She extends Erdman's focus back into the prehistoric "matrilineal" beginnings of European culture, excavating political history in those biblical and Near Eastern mythologies that Frye reads as primordial archetypes. She then correlates the history of the myths with the social situations to which they respond and, exposing the discrepancy between them, heralds the reclamation of a "revolutionary apocalypse" in Blake. DiSalvo argues that Blake sets the orthodox "Genesis-Milton tradition against a (more radical) countermovement which similarly conflates Milton and the Apocalypse" (DiSalvo 1983, 14–15). Blake, as Wittreich holds, inherits the Miltonic mantle of revolutionary poet-prophet; but for DiSalvo, an "ideological breakthrough" allows Blake to see Milton's residual orthodoxy as a reflex of class prejudice. Milton champions the "bourgeois individual" over the plebeian sectaries, but Blake's own plebeian roots enable him to become the "prophetic challenger of Milton's religion and politics" (DiSalvo 1983, 23).

Marxist historicism helps DiSalvo redress distortions in the mystical and archetypal approaches, especially regarding the issues of form and content in *The Four Zoas*. She illustrates, for example, that Night VIIa, seen typically as depicting a breakthrough in Blake-Los's individual consciousness, actually contributes to "the contemporary advance toward a historicist view of society and culture of which *The Four Zoas* itself is the greatest literary product" (DiSalvo 1983, 49). Night VIIa, she explains, is a far more dialectical conception than critics acknowledge and, in fact, *does* connect coherently with Nights VIII and IX. In fact, she argues, VIIa completes the psychological with a social breakthrough. For when Los and Urthona's Spectre embrace, individual poetic will (Spectre) is harnessed to a radical, popular vision (Los), for Los functions as Albion-England's guardian of communal values. The Los-Spectre embrace, then, leads quite logically to Night IX's apocalypse because it reveals that Urizen's world is fallen, not eternal (as orthodox Christianity contends). Urizen's social order and contemporary bourgeois institutions are contingent on the community's mystification about its origins. Once these institutions are unveiled by the artisan prophet as forms of this world, they become subject to radical transformation: that is, to revolu-

tionary apocalypse. DiSalvo concludes that this utopain reclamation of commonwealth prophecy coincides with a "class-conscious
historical vision" emerging in the 1790s.

Where DiSalvo grounds Blake's prophetic project in the "political clarity of the common man," Ault denies that any ground
whatsoever supports *The Four Zoas* (Ault 1987, xvi). His Blake
motto—"The Eye altering alters all"—affiliates his "perspectival"
approach with the methods of both Wilkie and Johnson, and Frye,
who also insist on the primacy of perception. But Ault aims to
make his account of Blake "fundamentally incommensurable with
previous criticism" (Ault 1987, xviii). He does so by refusing to
settle for *any* reducible content, claiming that the poem's—or
more properly the narrative's—tendency to continually alter its
focus *is* its meaning. To regard any aspect of the text as marginal
is to reduce it, or make it commensurable, with the critic's own
limited perspective.

Ault defines his (and Blake's) project as a "perspective ontology"
designed to expose the false coherence of Newtonian metaphysics.
Newton assumes, according to Ault, two spurious conditions: that
there is a single unified world underlying massive conflicting empirical data; and that this world exists outside of, or prior to,
human perception. Blake's *The Four Zoas* denies these assumptions
and replaces them with the fundamental axiom of *Narrative Unbound:* "that the way something is perceived constitutes its being
or reality" (Ault 1987, 3). Ault locates his perspective ontology in
the act of reading—"a primary place where [the] human being
originates and can be revised" (5)—but instead of assuming even
the reader's extrinsic being, he asserts that the *Four Zoas* narrative
actually brings the reader and text into "mutual existence" (22).
The "circular interconstitution" of reader, text, and narrative is
embodied in Blake's interminable process of revising *The Four
Zoas,* which enables him to challenge readers *not* to suppress contradictory details and retreat into repressive "Newtonian" certainty. The link between revision and reading underpins Ault's
intrinsic method: "The poem's most fundamental reference," he
claims, is "to the forces against which it is constantly struggling,
'Single vision & Newton's sleep'" (25).

Against Bentley's charges of *The Four Zoas*'s incoherence and
Blake's loss of control and purpose, Ault counters that the poem's
unfinished state is an index of Blake's compositional strategies
rather than of his formal weakness. And where Bentley finds that
Blake's inconsistent revisions result in a "tragic failure," Ault finds
that the revisions become not simply what Blake does to the text,

but what the "text does, through the agency of the narrative, not only to the reader, but to itself" (Ault 1987, 4). That is, Blake's revisions have the power to pull the reader into their own "ground" of transformation precisely because they do not suppress the loose or incommensurable details that guarantee the narrative's "being." In fact, since Blake intentionally challenges the reader with his "technique of incommensurable frameworks of explanation," Ault asserts that "the accumulation of details does not *exemplify* but actually *constitutes*" his critical argument (Ault 1987, xxiv). The poem's "being" inheres in the gaps and lacunae of the narrative, which undercut both the formalist concept of poetic unity and the historicist notion of external reference.

Ault developed his elaborate perspective ontology in the 1970s, between Frye's fading milieu and the approaching poststructuralist storm in the academy. In the 1960s, social pressures fractured what remained of the New Critical consensus; and disillusionment following the political conjuncture of 1968 brought historical criticism into disrepute. Both intrinsic and extrinsic theories of meaning came under attack for presuming any kind of unity, whether within the text or between the historical moments of late and early industrial capitalism. While Ault disclaims that deconstructive principles—"*il n'y a pas de hors-texte*" and the like—initially influenced him, the academic climate already was forecast by the Yale critics' appropriation of Derrida and his attack on "objectivist" metaphysics. Ault's introduction to the first four "regions" of analysis—"Subverting Origin and Identity"—signals the poststructuralist paradigm that informs his approach to *The Four Zoas*.

This brief look at Donald Ault's rigorous, thorough analysis cannot possibly do justice to what is, without doubt, the closest reading of *The Four Zoas* to date. It stands as a major challenge to subsequent work on the poem and as a fitting (non)conclusion to its relatively short reception history. As for Ault's aim to make his criticism incommensurable with previous studies, I believe he has accomplished something of his task, even though his perception ontology places him squarely within the individualist boundaries of traditional Blake criticism. And by ensnaring himself in the fashionable terminology of the deconstruction moment, he invokes its debilitating skepticism.

A more therapeutic approach is offered in Paul Youngquist's *Madness and Blake's Myth* (1989), which resurrects a topic that Frye thought he laid to rest. "Though Blake did not succumb to the madness so often imputed to him," Youngquist says, "*The Four Zoas* gives ample evidence that he had an intimate acquaintance with its fundamental symptoms" (Youngquist 1989, 112). While Youngquist concentrates, with Ault, on the "discontinuities and schisms" of the poem, he distinguishes his approach from both the poststructural and Marxist positions, which he believes reduce Blake's artistic individuality to a critical system. In an age when notions of mental and artistic unity are under siege, Youngquist, with a certain historical logic, reactivates the "Dangerous Blake."[19]

Youngquist opts for an "empirical method" that he claims is neither clinical nor biographical, but phenomenological, one that gives "full credence" to Blake's experience in the world. He finds, however, that Blake differs from the human norm because he takes his visions literally and values the inner over the outer world. That is, when the world blocks his inner vision—as with the cold reception of his Lambeth works or Hayley at Felpham—Blake "splits" his experience in two. Youngquist avers that Blake masters his anxieties, but "at the expense of the world" (Youngquist 1989, 36).

Youngquist locates this "epistemological rupture" as the key to Blake's poetic development, which comes between the writing of *Vala* and *The Four Zoas*, his most "autistic" poem. Seeking "refuge from unbelief," from the perils of living a visionary life in a rationalist world, Blake develops a mythology that records the shattering of his personality, a myth of "madness" that resembles the dynamic of schizophrenia. Youngquist argues that both "enact the dissociation of a human whole, the proliferation of competing complexes, and the therapeutic effort, perhaps dubious, to achieve a new unity." In this effort, Blake discovers his "great subject": the "politics of consciousness," or the war among fragmented psychic agents for control over the whole (Youngquist 1989, 42).

The centerpiece of the book is section three of the chapter on *The Four Zoas* titled "Schizophrenia and the Ancient Man." The gist of Youngquist's commentary lies in showing that Blake moves the poem beyond a sexual to an artistic crisis. Blake shifts focus from Urizen and Vala to Los and Enitharmon through the crucial medium of Urthona's Spectre. Los retains the conviction that Albion's "autism" must end, but caught in a struggle between reason and inspiration, he is driven mad (123–26). Yet Los's tendency toward psychic withdrawal is counterbalanced by the Spectre, who, while he succumbs to abstraction, can initiate regeneration "when allowed to combine his desires with another" (129). Seeking a "common psychic ancestry," the Spectre merges with Los and Enitharmon, linking fantasy and reality so that through him, Blake refrains from "substituting an autistic world for the real one" (131). This victory over madness comes, disappointingly for Youngquist at the price of the poem.

With Murry, Frye, and Paley, Youngquist argues that Blake's late revisions are "the fruits of some conversion" which, in his view, turn the poem away from "wholly human answers" to psychic suffering and toward "a religious healing" (132). While sensibly demanding that we face changes in the poem's symbolism openly, Youngquist exaggerates Blake's later "revisions" as a form of Orwellian "double-think." Thus the Divine Vision, Council of God, and Lamb function as a "compensatory restitution of sanity," as part of a grand artistic defense against the "pathological potential" of visionary experience. Interesting, certainly, but not innocent of reducing Blake's poem to system. In fact, he argues that Blake's revisions convert the poem "from an oracle of psychological revolution to one of spiritual prophecy" (133) through the *deus ex machina* of religious transcendence.

This division of psychic and spiritual, revolutionary and prophetic, stems from Youngquist's faith in clinical method. He reduces the four zoas to secular characters and, with Ault, devalues the spiritual perspective of Blake's symbolic beings. Youngquist plays another poststructural card in his assessment of Blake's Jesus. He contends that by providing a center around which Blake organizes Albion's fragments and by offering "the one authentic proof of a collective identity," Jesus closes the "open vistas" of *The Four Zoas* into a "system." This lapse into the transcendent makes the poem finally "uncredible in the purely psychological terms" of Blake's "original myth."

The view that Blake's original myth is purely psychological remains open to debate. It does, however, situate Youngquist's probing analysis not only within the poststructural and idealist paradigms, but within the Romantic ideology, which prefers a politics of consciousness to political revolution and communal prophecy.

VI

This sketch of the poem's critical reception should indicate the need for collective effort on *The Four Zoas*. In the following chapters I draw on many of the positions outlined above, although in blending the diverse methods of Frye, Erdman, DiSalvo, Ault, and others I cannot say that my synthesis avoids their pitfalls. But I subscribe to Schorer's postulate that Blake's difficulties, and ours in studying him, derive from his "disinclination to separate the events of an individual life from those of its society and the cosmos" (Schorer 1959, 262). This "triple doctrine, cosmogonal, historical, and psychological, in a single symbolism," brings to the fore the problems of literary form and social content that attend the reception of *The Four Zoas*. It may also caution us to remain alert to the plural meanings in any given passage of the text, meanings that are, paradoxically, rhetorically connected but also often logically incompatible.

The poem's substantial achievement lies primarily in the way its experimental composite form delivers its powerful content. Blake's "epic" exceeds the boundaries of its difficult, problematic structure because it treats form both as meaning and as a means to individual and social liberation. I do not, I believe, simply invert formalist assumptions about unity. Nor do I hedge the problem of formal incoherence. I try various critical approaches that direct attention to the contexts, both intrinsic and extrinsic, that readers must engage to participate in Blake's visionary epic theatre.

Content and form need not perfectly align for a work to have impact. If a work lacks formal perfection, it can create an impact through sheer power. Its meaning can reside in the force that links content and form, reverberating beyond the confines of artistic structure. I agree with Erdman that history is the force that disrupts the narrative structure of *The Four Zoas*, but I do not devalue the poem for this disruption. I think, rather, that the link between content and form can become a "call" toward the social situation in which the work is created and received. I call this the *kerygmatic* meaning of the narrative.[20]

A secular appropriation of the theological concept of *kerygma*, the "proclamation" of the Gospel narratives, provides a more comprehensive critical approach to *The Four Zoas* than those offered by formalist, historical, or deconstructionist theories alone. It emphasizes a transaction between text and audience as the basis of an engaged and participatory approach. *Kerygma* points to the historicity of a text, its call for an existential commitment by its readers. The meaning of such texts lies partially in the transformation of word into act that marks their reception. Blake seeks to convert his audience, but not to any religious position. He expects readers to make his text their contemporary, although the method of appropriation remains their own. As Donald Marshall puts it:

Kerygma is that force in a story which goes beyond its internal structure to bring it into the human context in which the narrative is exchanged as part of a dialogue. Through this force, a structure that is generated out of history returns to history. The time that is closed in plot is opened in the *kerygma*. (Marshall 1982, 82)

A critical application of *kerygma* enables us to treat *The Four Zoas* as a dynamic interplay between force and form, as a rhetorical construct and a medium between readers and their social situations. From this perspective, a light may penetrate the dark glass of *The Four Zoas's* obscurity and lead us out of its mighty labyrinth.

2

The Uses of Obscurity: *The Four Zoas* in Eighteenth-Century Literary History

The principal charges which have been urged against this poem, and which in some degree may have affected its popularity, are the dark tints of its painting; and the obscurities which . . . retard the progress of the reader. With respect to . . . these objections, it must be admitted that, in the work before us, the great poet of Christianity offers no flattery to the passions; and, conscious of the demands and dignity of his subject, is less careful to please than to improve; to conciliate than to impress and awe.
—Richard Edwards, Advertisement to *Night Thoughts*

That which can made Explicit to the Idiot is not worth my care. The wisest of the Ancients considered what is not too Explicit as the fittest for Instruction because it rouzes the faculties to act. I name Moses Solomon Esop Homer Plato
—Blake, Letter to Trusler (23 August 1799)

No one has ever charged Blake with being too explicit. And at times it is hard to distinguish between his strategic and his unintentional uses of obscurity. Yet the difficulties that burden the reception of *The Four Zoas* derive as much from the poem's generic casting, and the traditions and contexts that it summons for interpretation, as from its vexing manuscript status or Blake's idiosyncratic mode of literary creation.[1]

One unlikely context is the long descriptive poem of the eighteenth century, a neglected but seminal area of study for *The Four Zoas*. Of special importance are those poems that Wordsworth deemed "composite orders," mixed-genre works like Edward Young's *Night Thoughts* and William Cowper's *The Task* that defy tradition and create their own formal standards.[2] *The Four Zoas* is one of these "composite orders." Yet Blake builds into his poem a critique of his eighteenth-century precursors. While Young's text is the most crucial, Blake also targets James Thomson's *The Seasons* and Alexander Pope's *An Essay on Man,* works that form with *Night Thoughts* a distinct tradition of Anglican apologetic poetry. I believe that even though *The Four Zoas* eludes and frustrates traditional generic classification, it culminates as it inverts the long poem of eighteenth-century Christian apologetics.[3]

Two developments in the late 1790s point to Blake's close relation to the apologetic tradition while writing *The Four Zoas.* One is the debate spurred by Paine's *The Age of Reason* and the other is the fate of Blake's work on Young's *Night Thoughts.*

In 1797, as he completed his earliest version of *The Four Zoas* (entitled *Vala*), Blake was preparing a colossal series of watercolor drawings to illuminate Young's popular poem. When the art market crashed and the Young project failed, Blake salvaged the work by co-opting proofs from his *Night Thoughts* designs for use in *Vala:* he inserted his own text into the blank space reserved for Young's poem and on the verso side of the proofs. The relationship between the poems, however, goes beyond material proximity into regions of style and genre.

When the bookseller Richard Edwards published a volume presenting the first four of Young's nine "Nights," with forty-three engravings by Blake, he attached an "Advertisement" that in effect apologized for certain difficulties in Young's text. While praising its original structure, he confronted the criticism that affected the poem's reception, namely the "dark tints" and "obscurities" that occasionally disrupt comprehension. Edwards argues that the dark tints are intentional: "the great poet of Christianity . . . is less careful to please than to improve" (Essick and LaBelle 1975, v). He finds it harder to vindicate Young from "the imputation of obscurity," although he enlists the "sublime" theory of Robert Lowth when he admits that "a studied and ambitious brevity of expression" could be the source of both vigor and obscurity.[4] What Edwards does not realize is that Young's "uneven sublimity" comes from the heady mixture of generic systems in his work.[5] Young attempts to vindicate the ways of the Anglican God, the God of natural religion, while he champions the visionary Saviour of revealed religion. The rift between the two systems comes to the surface over the meaning of *creation,* as the furor over Paine's *Age of Reason* suggests.

Paine's work, published in two parts in 1794–95, incited a number of orthodox responses, but Bishop Richard Watson's reply, *An Apology for the Bible* (1796), provoked Blake's angry retort. Despite his lifelong hatred of natural religion, Blake here sides with a Deist against a bishop because the latter offers a tepid, "lukewarm" defense of revealed religion. Neither Watson nor Paine possesses what Blake calls the "Everlasting Gospel," but Paine, in the best Dissenting manner, condemns where the bishop apologizes for the corruptions of Christianity. Paine's restatement of the Deist position, which uncovers the faultlines in the apologetic debate, can serve as an introduction to the historical sketch that follows.

Paine argues that since religion is one with reason and nature, revealed scripture can lay no claim to being *the* original religion. "Are we to have no word of God—no revelation?" Paine asks rhetorically, and he answers as the arch-Deists John Toland and Matthew Tindal answered: "THE WORD OF GOD IS THE CREATION WE BEHOLD." It is only the "Scripture called the creation," insists Paine, that speaks universally to all nations and peoples because it avoids the "obscurity" of that fabulous theology that "puts the whole orbit of reason into the shade" (Paine n.d., 37). As we will see, the authority of the creation rests on the rationalist argument from design: the "structure" of the universe, revealed by the mathematical principles of natural philosophy, offers the surest guide to religion and morality (Paine n.d., 183–84). This argument is validated by no less an authority than Isaac Newton, whose influence on the long poem of eighteenth-century Anglican apologetics rivals that of Milton himself.[6]

I

While the argument from design dates back to Plato's *Timaeus* and Cicero's *De Natura Deorum,* it was refurbished by Christian virtuosi in the seventeenth century and received scientific confirmation from Newton, who encountered the theory at Cambridge during the Restoration.[7] Newton uses the design metaphor in both his science and theology, in the *Principia Mathematica* (1687), which sets the stage for the collapse of Milton's epic cosmos, and in his "Treatise on Revelation." At the conclusion to the "Treatise," Newton cautiously asserts that it is *not* God's purpose to make revelation "Perspicuous . . . as a mathematic diagram," yet he articulates a formula held in common by all Christian rationalists: that truth lies in "the wisdom of God in the contrivance of creation" (Manuel 1974, 123–24). In the General Scholium to the second edition of the *Principia* (1713), Newton writes that the perfect "system of the sun, planets, and comets" can only proceed from "the counsel and dominion of an intelligent agent and powerful Being." We know God, he insists, "only by his most wise and excellent contrivances of things" (Newton 1966, 2:546).

This last phrase resounds in the work of the Boyle lecturers, who, after the appearance of the *Principia*, carry Newtonian natural philosophy into the debate on revealed and natural religion. Separating Creation from Fall, the Newtonians in effect displace God from the human sphere of history to the mechanical realm of nature. The die is cast by Richard Bentley, the first Boyle lecturer, who claims to demonstrate providence by the order and harmony displayed in the universe: the argument from design proves that creation was effected by a rational agent. Newton, corresponding with Bentley during the lectures, praises him for using the *Principia* in such a forum: "When I wrote my treatise about our system," Newton opens his first letter, "I had an eye upon such principles as might work with considering men for the belief of a Deity" (Thayer 1974, 46). The key phrase, one that echoes throughout the exchange of letters, is "contrivance or design," which points to a creator well skilled in geometry and mechanics.

After Newton and the Boyle Lectures (1691–1732), the historical ground shifts fairly rapidly, undermining the biblical cosmos while preparing for those "substitute textual formations," *The Seasons, An Essay on Man,* and *Night Thoughts.* The crisis in Protestant culture, stemming from the seventeenth century, is in part resolved by the Low Church faction of moderate Anglicans, who, with the influence of Newtonian science, institute a liberal Christianity that assures the survival of Anglican ideology into the coming century. Once the Protestant succession was secured in 1714, Margaret Jacob asserts, "that stability preached by Newtonians increasingly became a political reality" (Jacob 1976, 269). The liberal wing of the Anglican establishment consolidates its power between 1680 and 1720, when the concepts of mechanical science make their way into the common language of philosophers, preachers, literary journalists, lecturers, and coffeehouse wits. Poets such as James Thomson, Alexander Pope, and Edward Young were weaned in this atmosphere:

> The poets were elaborating what they found in the standard physicotheological handbooks, and so the progression is a natural one, from the ideas formulated by the theologians and scientists in the seven-

teenth century to the popular compendiums and finally into literature.
(Jones 1966, 20)

The two most popular handbooks, John Ray's *Wisdom of God in
the Creation* (1691) and William Derham's *Physico-Theology* (Boyle
Lectures for 1713), help spread Newton's theological influence,
which reaches its height in the 1720s, as the various kinds of
rational theology gain ascendency over orthodox Anglicanism.
The creation becomes a model for a stable polity, as God is manifest not only through the laws, order, and harmony of nature,
but, by analogy, through the law of right reason within. Such
presuppositions about the rules and design of creation translate
also into aesthetic terms: art and beauty reflect the rationality and
regularity of the universe.

II

In the midst of this cultural ferment, an unknown Scotsman
arrives in London in 1725 and, by 1726, begins tutoring at Watts
Academy, a center for the popular study of Newton's philosophy.
James Thomson's intense interest in Newtonianism—"an interest
that profoundly affected the whole direction of his thought and
the nature of his poetic imagery"—dates from his employment at
Watts (Grant 1951, 58). Thomson announces his presence by writing a poem of great scope and ambition: *Winter,* the first poem of
The Seasons, brings him immediate fame and is compared favorably with the "sublime" poetry in *Paradise Lost.* The composition
of Thomson's long poem, however, is interrupted by Newton's
death. Thomson's response, *A Poem Sacred to the Memory of Sir Isaac
Newton,* praises the scientist for demonstrating God's providential
creation from design: "our philosophic sun," he writes, "from
motion's simple laws, / Could trace the secret hand of Providence, /
Wide-working thro' this universal frame" (lines 14–16).
    In *Spring,* Thomson dilutes the Miltonic sublime with a bland
confidence in the design argument. He deploys the chain or scale
of being, as Pope does in *An Essay on Man,* although he more
closely resembles the Boyle lecturers, who offer rational proof
that the "God of Seasons" has designed, "with such perfection
fram'd," the whole "stupendous scheme of things."[8] Climbing the
great "scale of being," Thomson marvels at how the "whole creation round," by "swift degrees," works up through an empirical
love of nature, through the ethereal rapture of an "enthusiastic

heat," to the experience of "Deity" (*Spring*, lines 893–904). This heat, of course, is "inform'd by reason's purer ray," for reason is what exalts the "brute creation," enabling it to perceive the invisible hand that "wheels the silent spheres" (*Spring*, lines 863–64 and 895–995). While he provides a humanist link between natural and artistic creation, Thomson makes clear that the "system" created by the scientist is greater than those imagined by poet and prophet (*A Hymn*, lines 119–21).

Unlike Milton before and Blake after him, Thomson finds evidence of providence within creation, within the frame of nature, rather than within the believer or within history. Thomson is no mere Newtonian. Along with the ill-fated Richard Blackmore's *Creation* (1712), *The Seasons* contributes to a countermovement that breaks down the infinite spaces of Newton's universe in terms of human needs, a movement still going strong in *The Four Zoas* (Lindsay 1978, 113). Yet despite an electic use of Milton, Shaftesbury, Longinus, and Renaissance humanism, Thomson remains an Anglican apologist: he is "Intent, to gaze / Creation thro'," as he says, and from that "*round Complex*" to conceive of "THE SOLE BEING" who both "spoke the Word, / And Nature circled" (*Summer*, lines 1127–30). Ultimately, Thomson supports Newton's system and the great chain of being with the argument that the grandeur and regularity of the heavens demonstrate divine power. Using metaphors that Blake subjects to severe scrutiny in *The Four Zoas*, Thomson celebrates the "Round / Of *Seasons*, faithful; not excentric once: / So pois'd, and perfect, is the vast Machine" (*Summer*, lines 1927–30). Although he is not a slavish Newtonian, Thomson finds in the mechanistic movement of nature the evidence of a deity whose creation guarantees universal order.

Blake's eccentric narrative of *The Four Zoas* may seem as far removed from Thomson as from Pope's *An Essay on Man* (1733–34)—"the poet's ambitious attempt to translate fashionable philosophizing into pleasing verse" (Gay 1973,2 13). But the importance of the *Essay*, which represents a midpoint in the apologetic tradition I am sketching, is that it not only engages *Paradise Lost* but draws the counterresponse of Edward Young's *Night Thoughts*.

An Essay on Man proved to be one of the most influential poems of eighteenth-century apologetics.[9] Despite Pope's disavowal, the *Essay* captures the Deist as well as the liberal Anglican creed: both emphasize that reason and order are at the center of creation. As a man completely of his age, Pope does not question the rationality of creation: nature works by the formal principles of harmony and proportion, symmetry and balance. These principles, furthermore, by underwriting the structural design of the universe, inform both the system of Pope's ethics and the dynamic form of his heroic couplet. With its neoclassic tension of pattern and antithesis, Pope's poetry manifests the order that is a fundamental attribute of creation (Battestin 1974, 79).

The influence of the *Essay* also derives from Pope's rewriting of *Paradise Lost* in the Augustan idiom of the time. Pope alludes to Milton's reworking of Genesis through a number of generic signals: his opening stanza presents a garden, forbidden fruit, temptation, and a vindication of God's ways to Man; his second stanza begins "Say first!" and introduces a story about irreligious pride and religious humility, about creation and how it is violated and restored. Pope also places Milton's belief in the "great Hierarchal Standard" at the core of his poem. But he does replace Milton's visionary enthusiasm with Locke's more scientific epistemology—"What can we reason but from what we know?" (1:18)—and he avoids the sublime regions of Milton's flight above the Aonian mount. Indeed, he moves further away from Milton than does Thomson: In Pope's version of Christian humanism, the Hebraic strain is curbed rigorously by classical decorum.

While Blake follows his precursors in the line of Christian humanism, he and Pope occupy polar positions on the rational-visionary spectrum of this tradition. For Pope, the originating act of history is the divine fiat of Genesis, God's command to "Let there be light: and there was light." (Pope wittily reveals the Newtonian cast of his thinking in his epitaph: "Nature and Nature's laws lay hid in night: / God said, *Let Newton be!* and all was light.") But what Pope celebrates as the ordering power of the divine word, Blake interprets as the restricting agent of eternal death: creation prescribes bounds, limits the infinite, and gives form to primal matter. Again, we are simply at opposite ends of the apologetic spectrum. In *An Essay on Man*, creation is a *concordia discors* of harmonized elements, centered by the metaphor of the chain.

> Vast chain of being, which from God began,
> Natures aethereal, human, angel, man,
> Beast, bird, fish, insect! what no eye can see,
> No glass can reach! . . .
> Where, one step broken the great scale's destroy'd:
> From Nature's chain whatever link you strike,
> Tenth or ten thousandth, breaks the chain alike.
>
> (1:237–47)

The chain runs from the cosmos to society to the mind; when

any link snaps, the whole metaphysic breaks down. Contrast Blake's *The Four Zoas,* in which the chain functions as a repressive ideology, not as a guarantee of metaphysical order: "The Prophet of Eternity beat on his iron links," terrified "at the Shapes / Enslavd humanity put on he became what he beheld," beating the "Links of fate link after link an endless chain of sorrows" (53:22–24, 28). What remains a heresy to Pope becomes an awful reality to Blake.

The greatest distance between Pope and Blake comes in their views of what we can call the *social relations of creation,* in the application of the *concordia discors* concept to society. For Pope, the divine Creation established a paradigm for order in the social and moral regions of the scale: political discord could be reconciled by the "Music of a well-mix'd State" (3:294). Since "Order is Heav'n's first law," it follows that "Some are, and must be, greater than the rest, / More rich, more wise" (4:49–51). That is simply the great hierarchal standard. But a profound change separates Pope's view of this standard from Milton's: the Fall has been completely removed from the picture, and with it the sense of something acutely wrong with society. Pope denies the contradictions that Blake will highlight. In *An Essay on Man,* Pope asserts that since God and nature "link'd the gen'ral frame" and made self and social interest the same, then "Whatever IS, is RIGHT" (4:145). In *The Four Zoas,* Blake laments these very conditions: for him, whatever is, is WRONG.

Here, however, we come to another turn in the history. For Pope's art of creation is nurtured in the polite world that it serves, in part, to legitimate (Stephen 1955, 109). Besides a cardinal assumption of neoclassical aesthetics, Pope's emphasis on the rational setting of bounds could only spell disaster for a tradition of epic poetry transferred by Milton, who brought the heat and enthusiasm of biblical prophecy to bear on the classical form. As Pope's contemporary Thomas Blackwell mused, if the "very nerve of the Epic Strain" is the marvelous and wonderful, "what marvellous things happen in a *well-ordered* State" (quoted in Bate 1970, 49). For Pope, the work of art possesses a creative power analogous to God's; but it is the ordered, harmonious, refined "finished object," as Martin Battestin puts it, that "elicits comparison with the divine creation" (Battestin 1974, 91). When we get to *The Four Zoas,* the unruly creative *process,* not the polished object, bears the true signature of artistic integrity.

III

We can gauge the beginning of this turn in Young's *Night Thoughts,* which announces a countermovement of religious feeling "inaccessible to rational proofs or disproofs" (Gay 1973, 9). Young's poem directly counters the deistic stance and rationalist bent of Pope's *Essay.* Rivalling Pope's work as one of the century's most popular poems, it was published in the 1740s, the decade of Methodist Revival, of Richardson's *Pamela* and Fielding's *Tom Jones,* of Akenside's *Pleasures of Imagination,* William Collins' odes, and Bishop Robert Lowth's *Lectures on the Sacred Poetry of the Hebrews.* The 1740s witness a change whereby nature becomes associated with feeling rather than with mere reason: as Young's protagonist puts it to his libertine opponent: "to feel is to be fired; / And to believe, Lorenzo! is to feel" (Young 1970, 58).

Young's title, *The Complaint and the Consolation,* points to its generic status as Christian argument. John Butt places it in "a tradition of Christian apologetics which set out to confute" atheism and Deism (Butt 1979, 83). Young's central contention is with Pope's idea of creation, with the chain of being. Pope, of course, regards the chain as static and humanity's place in it as fixed. Aspiration and pride are sins. Young, on the other hand, emphasizes the incompleteness of creation and praises the complex strivings after immortality that define human nature. Humanity is not simply one link in the chain, but the crucial link, the locus where creation can become redemption. We have moved one step closer to *The Four Zoas.*

Yet Young displays his Anglican credentials in Nights VI and VII, where he refutes infidel doubt in futurity and immortality. The prefaces to Nights VI and VII feature the language of apologetics, as Young offers "proof" and "some plain arguments" as to the "being of God." Nature is the first proof, but it is a nature seen only in relation to human beings. It is a nature in figure: "Nature revolves, man advances; both / Eternal, that a circle, this a line / That gravitates, this soars." The aspiring soul in effect *demonstrates* its own divinity and ascends by zeal and humility, distinctly human traits in the scale of being, an idea which takes Young beyond Pope and Newton toward Blake: "The mind that would be happy, must be great. . . . Extended views a narrow mind extends" (Young 1970, 266). Human discontent is a divine impulse that God implants in his creatures to lead them to the infinite.

Paradoxically, like both Milton—"ah, could I reach your strain!"

(16)—and the Boyle lecturers, Young seeks to balance the claims of inspiration and reason, of revealed and natural religion. While the two systems tear at the fabric of his narrative, Young insistently defends the superiority of revelation, particularly in the proto-Blakean Night IV. Entitled "The Christian Triumph," this Night attacks Pope's rational faith in ordered creation and places the "key" to salvation in the sacrifice paid by Jesus's death: "that mighty hinge" on which all civil and religious progress turns (Young 1970, 168). Young offers a vivid, if undecorous, image of Christ's healing hand bleeding in the heavens: "There hangs all human hope!!!," he exclaims: "that nail supports / The falling universe!!! that gone, we drop!" (57). Christ's resurrection is "proof supreme" of immortality. As he meditates on the resurrection, Young heats up, "rapt by this triumphant theme," to soar with Milton "above the Aonian mount":

> Oh the burst gates ! crush'd sting! demolish'd throne!
> Last gasp of vanquish'd death! shout earth and heaven!
> This sum of good to man, whose nature then
> Took wing, and mounted with HIM from the tomb!
> Then, then I rose; then first humanity
> Triumphant past the crystal ports of light
> Stupendous guest!
>
> (Young 1970, 61)

This visionary humanism anticipates Blake, as does Young's waxing on his theme, that "men" are equal to angels: "They sung creation, for in that they shared," Young writes. But he speaks of "Creation's great superior, man," whom Christ redeems, and whose spiritual life is based on more than the argument from design: "Redemption! 'twas creation more sublime" (65–66).

The difficulty, however, is that Young depends on the great chain of being to support his visionary enthusiasm. He declares that nature is ordered by "neat gradation," that its "scale" ascends "unbroken upward" to God, and that even when the series breaks apart and reason "tumbles from her scheme," the scheme is supported by the concept of analogy, the logical counterpart of the design argument and "man's surest guide below" (132–33). Young's hesitating advance toward Blake, however, occurs when he moves back toward Milton's prophetic narrative, to Books XI and XII of *Paradise Lost*, where Michael instructs Adam in the art of visionary exegesis. Young's narrator grabs his nephew, the doubting Lorenzo, and they "mount" into flight, where they view a new creation: "Creation widens! vanguished nature yields! . . . art prevails! What monument of genius, spirit, power!" (135).

This more sublime creation unhinges natural religion from its rationalist moorings. Even while Night IV ends by acceding to the agents of reason, Young moves closer to the Blakean themes of *human* divinity and recreation. Humanity, a "terrestial God," alters the very nature of the creation: "How changed the face of nature! how improved!"; it transforms into another "scene! another self!" where former times and "fair creation are forgot!" (67). Defying the watchdogs of neoclassical decorum, Young challenges those "quietists" who "in homage to the skies" may find his Christianity unreasonable: "Think you my song too turbulent? too warm? / Are passions then the pagans of the soul? / Reason alone baptized—alone ordain'd / To touch things sacred—oh for warmer still!" (71). Young rejects "lukewarm" religion, especially when his melancholy mood is on, or when he ponders this "dark incarcerating colony" of earth that divides him from immortality. Yet, ultimately, Young refuses to separate the claims of reason and faith; the rest of *Night Thoughts* reiterates the apologetic doctrines of Night IV. He does take back some of his enthusiasm, but not his central belief that "Nature is Christian." Blake will probe Young's core belief until the fault lines of the apologetic topography are starkly exposed.

IV

Between Young and Blake the historical ground shifts again, as the forces of industry and trade, unleashed earlier in the century, begin to alter Britain's social and political landscape. In cultural terms, we enter the age of sensibility and pre-Romanticism, fueled by the poetry of bardic nationalism and the breakthrough in Christian apologetics associated with the German "higher critics" of the Bible. While too complex to be caused by one individual, these movements are sparked in some measure by the work of Bishop Robert Lowth, whose lectures, delivered in the 1740s and translated into English in 1787, help restore respect to "oriental," especially biblical, literature and aid in the recovery of Milton's prophetic legacy. These developments put eighteenth-century apologetics on the road to the internalized creation of Blake and the Romantic poets.

Lowth is that miracle of rare device who combines an enlightened sensibility with prophetic passion, drawing on secular criticism while setting biblical poetry on an emotional basis that the Romantic poets could share (Drury 1989, 70). He alters the context in which the apologetic poem is constructed by striking at the neoclassical presumption that Old Testament prophecy could not measure up to classical literature. As a classically-trained Oxford theologian, Lowth is not a little anxious about his topic, but he studiously balances the claims of reason and revelation. That is, he views Isaiah through the spectacles of Cicero.

Lowth first seeks an apology for prophetic creation through a psychological approach to literary style. For him, style is not simply diction or imagery, but sentiment and a "mode of thinking." Isaiah especially reaps praise for passion and elegance, for despite the "obscurity of his subjects," he achieves a surprising degree of "clearness and simplicity" (Lowth 1829, 176). Isaiah excels in all the classical "graces of method, order, connexion, and arrangement," although Lowth makes this important disclaimer, which relates directly to Blake:

> Though in asserting this we must not forget the nature of the prophetic impulse, which bears away the mind with irresistible violence, and frequently in rapid transitions from near to remote objects, from human to divine. (Lowth 1829, 176–77)

This psychology of prophetic creation is buttressed by a historical argument. While he seeks "perspicacity" in figurative language and warns against seeking "to demonstrate what is plain by what is occult," Lowth shows that the Hebrew writers draw on communal *topoi* to mitigate obscurity. Deploying the art of "allusion," the Hebrew poets require an antiquarian knowledge of past cultures to be understood. In Lecture 25, Lowth describes the Bible as a kind of grand relic that reaches the modern era in fragments: "We at present possess only some ruins," he insists, "notwithstanding the obscurity that antiquity has cast over them" (Lowth 1829, 212). By Lowth's time, developments in historical philology showed that familiarity with ancient customs and events could restore clarity to imagery that otherwise might seem hopelessly obscure.

To further clarify the nature of prophetic creativity, Lowth adds a rhetorical explanation to his psychological and historical ones. He admits that the "primitive" quality of Hebrew poetry was maintained late in their literature, when other nations had moved on to less figurative modes. But they did so, Lowth argues, because this style, the parabolic or sententious style, possessed uncommon "force and authority" over the minds of its auditors:

This obscurity is not indeed altogether without its uses: it whets the understanding, excites an appetite for knowledge, keeps alive the attention, and exercises the genius by the labour of investigation. The human mind, moreover, is ambitious of having a share in the discovery of truth. (Lowth 1829, 202)

Lowth carefully distinguishes the obscure rhetoric of scripture from mere allegory; he speaks of a "sublimer kind of allegory" that eschews the obvious and rouses the faculties, as Blake's does. Indeed, Blake invokes the Lowthian equation in his letters to Butts (6 July 1803), in which he describes *The Four Zoas* and *Milton* as a "Sublime Allegory," and to Trusler (23 August 1799), in which he follows Lowth in choosing Solomon's "enigmatical composition" as one of his "ancient" models. Lowth's insight into this text applies to *The Four Zoas;* "Solomon, after the manner of the oriental sages, meant to put to trial the acuteness of his readers" (Lowth 1829, 82).

The uses of obscurity become even more important when structure is at stake; for the Hebrew writers indulge in the liberty of "frequent digressions" and juxtapose events or objects in succession "without any express marks of comparison" (220).[10] In effect, the rhetorical and historical arguments converge, for structural complexity comes as much from the disparity between biblical and neoclassical culture as from intrinsic difficulties in the texts. Lowth further contends that the sublimity of Hebrew prophecy is obscure because prophecy anticipates what by nature eludes full clarity—the future. Although when first divulged, prophecy is "impenetrably obscure," the course of events gradually removes the veil. In fact, poetry describes events in a "manner exactly conformable to the intention of prophecy; that is, in a dark, disguised, and intricate manner; sketching out in a general way their form and outline" (92). Again, the rhetorical and psychological dimensions combine: it is the reader's function to search out historical and symbolic allusions and "share in the discovery of truth."

Lowth occupies a crucial place in the history of British apologetic literature, and not only because he advances the historicist study of culture or recovers the biblical "sublime," but because he clears the ground for the internalized creation of the Romantic poets. Lowth argues, with Young, that poetic creation does not imitate a nature already given or "out there," but that it mirrors nature's organic processes. Where a traditional schematic supported Pope's creation, such order broke down by midcentury, and with it the aesthetic norms that sustained the poetry of neoclassic culture.

V

Blake, along with the other Romantic poets, inherits a cosmological system in collapse, a "creation" that lacks traditional sanctions.[11] This collapse has drawn various explanations, but many point to a common feature: what Arthur Lovejoy calls a "temporalizing of the great chain of being" (Lovejoy 1965, chapter 9). Lovejoy finds a nascent evolutionary conception in Young's *Night Thoughts,* but he believes that the old static cosmology, in particular the argument from design, "broke down largely from its own weight" (Lovejoy 1965, 243–45). This insight is corroborated by the French historian Michel Foucault, who argues in more complex fashion that in the "Classical age," the *episteme* or configuration that maintains coherence from the Renaissance to the mid-eighteenth century is "ruptured" by a new force: "a profound historicity penetrates into the heart of things" and imposes upon them a new order, one implied by the "continuity of time" (Foucault 1973, xxiii). For Foucault, the old cosmology is separated from what he calls the "space of order," yet it remains "doomed to time" (Foucault 1973, 220). More incisively, Foucault points to a displacement which "toppled" the whole of Western thought, as "representation" lost the power to provide a foundation for the "links that can join its various elements together" (Foucault 1973, 238–39). These ruptured links of the great chain can be found only in "fragments, outlines, pieces, shards" of what once was visibly present in the rational design of creation.

Foucault's terminology may conceal his work's kinship with the Anglo-structuralism of Northrop Frye, who also speaks of a "mutation" from mechanism to vitalism ("the organic structure of being") that posits us on the doorstep to Romanticism. Although they make for strange bedfellows, Frye and Foucault share certain assumptions about cultural changes in eighteenth-century Europe. Both emphasize primitive and subconscious elements: Foucault contends that the "links" of coherence become submerged, "deeper and more dense than representation itself" (Foucault 1973, 239); Frye explains, in more narrowly aesthetic terms, that where writers put the emphasis on the "original process" of creation, qualities of "subconscious association take the lead, and the poetry becomes hypnotically repetitive, oracular, incantatory" (Frye 1963, 133). This new subconscious element, as Lowth suggests of Hebrew prophecy, binds writer and reader instead of separating them, as in neoclassicism. Frye agrees and locates the "primitive" quality of the age in the writer's identification with his or her subject and reader: "In Collins's *Ode on the Poetical Character,* in Smart's *Jubilate Agno,* and in Blake's *Four Zoas,* it attains its greatest intensity and completeness" (Frye 1963, 137). As the old cosmology deteriorates and the links of the chain are eroded, the poets are forced to interiorize creation, no longer having recourse to a rational, scientific order of nature.

The "new" creation of the Romantic poets contains a temporal as well as a subjective component, which implicates not only the poet but his age in the act of creation. That is, creation is bound to the conditions of its telling and precludes an eternal, transcendental perspective. This insight is expressed by the German higher critics of the Bible, whose English reviewer, Alexander Geddes, was known in Joseph Johnson's circle when Blake fraternized with the group. Although Geddes takes us from strictly Anglican apologetics—he is a Catholic Jacobin sympathizer—his texutal analysis of biblical narrative bears centrally on Blake's version of creation in *The Four Zoas.*

In his "Fragment Hypothesis" Geddes contends that the canonical biblical books derive from "unreliable base texts" whose authenticity has been compromised in translation (McGann 1986, 306). The Bible, in effect, is an unstable text—and Genesis, as well as the entire Pentateuch (Geddes heretically concludes), is *not* the work of Moses. Like Paine, who comes to similar conclusions, Geddes was vilified by the orthodox apologists for his theory; but Blake, with less of a reputation to uphold, draws a further conclusion. The so-called J and E sources are separate strands of a layered narrative that is not seamlessly and eternally sealed, but "produced" in stages over centuries. The Creation, as Blake will dramatize it, is tied inextricably to its composition history.

Blake focuses in particular on the most treasured of the apologetic themes: the Genesis Creation. Seizing on the disparity between the two Creation stories, Blake uses their "composite" form to suggest that the entire Bible is governed by the tension generated between the divergent themes, subjects, and styles of Genesis.[12] Blake conflates the different versions to highlight the contradictory nature of his material. He exploits the fact that by combining the two stories, the Genesis authors undermine a consistent linear ordering of Creation. Blake constructs his *Four Zoas* narrative on the model of the biblical cosmogony, but he problematizes his source, repeating the Creation in various frames, depicting it from multiple perspectives, to indicate its "fallen," i.e., time-bound status. As Blake will dramatize it in *The Four Zoas,* the Creation is, simultaneously, the Fall: every story of creation, every cosmogony, inscribes the temporal, and thus finite, perspective of its teller.

Bringing these "higher critical" insights to bear on Blake's unfinished *Four Zoas* manuscript may be like spearing fish in a barrel. But they do expose the hidden metaphysical assumptions that attend traditional versions of the Creation. In this they resemble, and anticipate, the method of deconstruction.[13] But I believe that Blake's Dissenting artisan background, coupled with his democratic sensibility (radicalized by the French Revolution), leads him to write a prophetic narrative that hastens as it foregrounds the collapse of the long poem of eighteenth-century Anglican apologetics. Blake's fragmented poem, in this view, owes less to its undecidable textual intentions, its subversion of its own origin and identity, than to changes in the republic of letters. The dissolution or exhaustion of the epic genre—since *Paradise Lost*—encourages a search for what Fredric Jameson calls "those substitute textual formations that appear in its wake," formations that rivet attention on the breakup of the old order even as they embody the contradictions of the new one (Jameson 1981, 146). Blake's narrative records the broader conflicts in his culture, especially the struggle between biblical and scientific creation in the religious poetry of the eighteenth century.

Protestant apologetics does not, of course, exhaust the contexts of *The Four Zoas,* nor of the long poems that inform its literary history. But in spite of Blake's tremendous range of allusion, I believe that a central organizing principle of the narrative remains operative, no matter how many contexts and traditions are summoned for interpretation: that is, to pit the prophetic and rationalist versions of Creation on a collision course, and to keep *repeating* the collisions, night after night, frame after vexing frame, until the day of intellectual battle "closes" in Night IX. The uses of obscurity lie in challenging readers to participate in this cultural battle, in moving them to transform the old order, with its designer creation, so that a new, more human creation can emerge.

3

Plotting the Fall: Creation Narratives in *The Four Zoas*

Men can do nothing without the make-believe of a beginning. Even Science, the strict-measurer, is obliged to start with a make-believe unit, and must fix on a point in the stars' unceasing journey when his sidereal clock shall pretend that time is Nought. His less accurate grandmother Poetry has always been understood to start in the middle; but on reflection it appears that her proceeding is not very different from his; since Science, too, reckons backwards as well as forwards, divides his unit into billions, and with his clockfinger at Nought really sets off *in medias res*. No retrospect will take us to the true beginning; and whether our prologue be in heaven or earth, it is but a fraction of that all-presupposing fact with which our story sets out.

—George Eliot, *Daniel Deronda*

WHILE harking back to Milton, Blake does not swerve his eighteenth-century precursors: he transmutes their most cherished theme of creation, refusing, even more radically than Milton, to separate Creation from the Fall. In the *Four Zoas*, Blake adapts the two Creation stories from Genesis, the so-called J and E strands (Urizen and Los's creations in Nights II and IV).[1] But within this larger, overarching pattern, he sets the various creation narratives of the zoas and emanations on a collision course. Through his composite artistry, Blake deploys the prophetic narrative strategies of repetition, juxtaposition, and allusion to bind each creation story to the fallen conditions of its telling. In effect, Blake filters creation through each speaker's divided consciousness, internalizing, as he arrests, the fragmentation of eighteenth-century poetic cosmology.

Creation emerges from the dynamic interaction of the four zoas, emanations, and their offspring, whose stories constitute, in effect, the cosmic "origin" of *The Four Zoas.* But these figures also make up the larger "being" of Albion, who has fragmented into a fluid cast of characters. Since the zoas and emanations incorporate aspects of each other, experience each other as introjections and incomplete identities, each version of the creation-fall intersects the others. The story of Albion's self-division gets told and retold from many conflictual perspectives. No one seamless retelling is possible: no single account takes priority. In Helen McNeil's apt formulation: "Repetition and variation replace linear narrative: several versions of the same event or slightly different versions of the same type of event can coexist without damaging the truth of any given version" (McNeil 1970, 354). Blake's rhetorical strategy is clear: he designs his narrative to force readers to participate in the creation, to experience the fall, making recreation necessary.[2]

The first retelling of the fall does not occur until Los's emanation, Enitharmon, sings her "Song of Vala" in the middle of Night I. But the opening episode, the bitter exchange between Tharmas and Enion, manifests all the key narrative elements repeated later. All versions contain at least two basic, but interrelated, perspectives: that of Albion "falling" for Vala and/or of Albion abdicating power because of a Urizen-Luvah conspiracy. The reason why Albion falls, or why there is a creation, must be gleaned from the narrative versions themselves, riddled as they are by the pressures and contingencies of the moment.

Night I

No amount of editorial labor can untangle the textual mess of Night I of the manuscript. These pages resist traditional notions of coherence and structural unity; their many revisions, insertions, scribblings, and erasures ensure that interpretation remains tentative. Nonetheless, the first Night is crucial to an analysis of the entire poem, and without pretense to have it all figured out, I enter the labyrinth.

"Begin with Tharmas Parent power." The narrator launches the poem with Tharmas's simple but passionate cry: "Lost! Lost! Lost! are my Emanations Enion O Enion / We are become a Victim to the Living" (4:8–9).[3] The narrative plunges, *in medias res,* into a dialogue about alienated human needs, out of which the characters construct the poem's setting. Tharmas claims that he and Enion are victimized by the other zoas, the "living creatures," whom *his* emanations have abandoned. In the next moment, however, the division is manifested in more explicitly gendered terms, as Tharmas complains: "The Men have recieved [*sic*] their death wounds & *their* Emanations are fled / To me for refuge" (4:15–16; my italics). The refuge, Tharmas's bosom, supplies the material from which Enion weaves the cosmos, marred from its inception by the torments of male-female love and jealousy.

Torment might best describe what Blake means by creation. The two major events of Night I—Enion's weaving the circle of destiny and her generation of Los and Enitharmon—are produced from Tharmas and Enion's quarrel. The real difficulty, however, both with these characters and the poem's opening episode, is that Tharmas and Enion are defined only in relation to each other. *Her* alienation—"I am . . . a Shadow in Oblivion"—induces *his* sense of loss. Their mutual blame and recrimination reveals a flawed rationality at the heart of the poem's creation: "Why wilt thou Examine every little fibre of my soul? . . . nought shalt thou find in it / But Death Despair & Everlasting brooding Melancholy" (4:29–33). From its opening, *The Four Zoas* signals its generic relation to the graveyard tradition of Young's *Night Thoughts* and the melancholic underside of Christian rationalism.

Enion uses Tharmas's fibres to weave a "tabernacle" for the spiritual (ungenerated) emanation, Jerusalem, whose absence is symptomatic of Albion-Urthona's fragmentation. As Enion weaves Jerusalem a covering from her own bosom (Tharmas said Jerusalem was in *his* bosom), Tharmas groans among his "Clouds" and reaches down to turn the "circle of Destiny" (5:8–11). Paradoxically, when he sinks into the sea, Tharmas discharges the bodily fibers that Enion threads into her "filmy woof," which becomes Tharmas's Spectre. The narrator then observes that this spectrous woof begins to "animate," to take on a will of its own, and that Enion weaves it into "the Circle of Destiny" (5:24).[4] The poem's setting, its universe, exists both prior to and after Enion weaves it into (external) being. This narrative paradox may court the charge of obscurity, but it underpins Blake's cryptic method.

Blake inserts numerous additions that qualify, in a prefigurative direction, the poem's defective creation.[5] One marginal passage introduces a host of symbolic names that figure importantly throughout the poem. We learn that in conjunction with the generated cosmos, a place called "Great Eternity" houses the redemptive "Lamb of God," who creates a refuge called "Beulah," where the "Daughters of Beulah" create "Spaces" to keep "sleepers" from falling forever into "Eternal Death," a condition of bleak negation that every character fears (12:4; 18:9; 20:15; 21:12).

Thus far, then, the narrator tells us that Tharmas turns the Circle of Destiny, that Enion weaves the Circle out of Tharmas's Spectre, and that the Daughters of Beulah create the Circle to keep sleepers from falling into Eternal Death. Further, in a move that anticipates the actions of Los and Enitharmon in Night VII, the Daughters perform the merciful act of embodying spectres through songs and forms of vegetation. However, the Spectre of Tharmas bewilders them. In a further paradox, the narrator says they regard the Spectre as "Eternal Death" and, in fear, close the "Gate of the Tongue" (5:38–43). The obscurity of their decision can be mitigated by grasping Blake's use of allusion: as Young had shown, fear of death not only betrays a lack of imagination but stifles articulation. As the Circle of Destiny is completed, the narrator personifies it as a "Frowning Continent" where Enion appears, "Terrified in her own Creation." She sits viewing her "woven shadow" in a parody of Miltonic contrition, what the narrator calls an "intoxification" of repentence and contrition.

Enion, however, embodies the Daughters' emanative potential *in* creation. As she says, her fear "shadows" her over, "drives [her] outward to a world of woe," where she trembles "before her own Created Phantasm" (5:52–3). Enion cannot hide behind the Gate of the Tongue, unlike the Daughters of Beulah: she must generate, or externalize, what ails her. In a bitter exchange, Enion speaks the language of lamentation and woe, while Tharmas answers in tones of domination, declaring,

> This world is Thine in which thou dwellest that within thy soul
> That dark & dismal infinite where Thought roams up & down
> Is Mine & there thou goest when with one Sting of my tongue
> Envenomed thou rollst inwards to the place whence I emergd
> (6:13–16)

Despite Tharmas's cruelty, Enion contributes to this fallen creation. Guilty and seeking to "weave a Covering" for her sins, Enion murders Tharmas's "Emanations." In a few pages we have come, so to speak, full circle. And as soon as she confesses this murder, Enion copulates with Tharmas, repeating (generating?) the woes of the opening dialogue. Aghast at their "creation," the narrator marvels to see "a bright wonder that Nature shudder'd at / Half Woman & half Spectre" (7:9–10). The birth of this hermaphroditic Spectre is repeated compulsively, in various guises and contexts, throughout *The Four Zoas*.

In the ensuing births of Los and Enitharmon, Blake brings his narrative strategies of juxtaposition and repetition more visibly into play. As Tharmas's Spectre mingles with Enion's Shadow, Enion's children "draw" from her spectrous life as she did (does) Tharmas's, repelling her into "Non Entity" (a variant of "Eternal Death") while awakening in her "pangs of maternal love" that, according to the narrator, "rehumanize" her. Blake links nadir and ascent, death and prefiguration: for while Los and Enitharmon repeat the scorn of their parents, they bear responsibility for the narrative's ultimate turn toward regeneration (for visual confirmation of this turn, see my commentary on the drawings).

To announce this ultimate turn, Blake displays prominently three important prophetic signals. First, his narrator relates the birth of Los and Enitharmon abruptly, adapting a standard adverbial marker from Milton and James Thomson, "Till": Tharmas mingles with Enion simply "Till with fierce pain she brought forth . . ." (8:1). Second, in an equally abrupt transition ("Then Eno"), Blake introduces the female figure who presides over the entire poem and who transforms the dimensions of fallen time and space. Eno expands history—she "drew it out to Seven thousand years"—and opens infinity within "atoms of space," thereby inspiring her sisters, the Daughters of Beulah, to keep providential watch over the newborn couple. Despite their lack of vision at this stage, the Daughters bear witness to the *crypsis* of prophetic form: "They saw not yet the Hand Divine for it was not yet reveald" (9:9–18).

Third, repetition plays as crucial a role in Los and Enitharmon's lives as in their parents. As soon as Eno creates nine moony spaces and opens "windows into Eden," the children mimic the behavior of their parents, driving males and females away in jealousy (9:30). They both also weave "mazes of delight" and enjoy Beulah as a pastoral refuge. But while she repeats Enion's fallen female tactics, Enitharmon lacks her mother's generative force: she "had no power to weave a Veil of covering for her Sins" (9:29). Blake's narrator implants an allusion to Vala, the emanative power of the poem's erased title, for this statement precedes Enitharmon's attack on Los and her creation narrative. In anger and scorn, she says to Los: "Thou in indolence reposest holding me in bonds / Hear! I will sing a Song of Death! it is a Song of Vala!" (10:8–9).

Enitharmon's song at the Feast provides the first narrated version of the creation-fall in *The Four Zoas,* and her terms—"indolence," "repose"—inform every major account. Her version, however, is marked by the exigencies of her quarrel with Los, whom she chastises for taking a lax attitude toward family dynamics: "if we grateful prove," she reasons, they "will withhold sweet love, whose food is thorns & bitter roots" (10:5–6). More importantly, Enitharmon repeats her parent's fallen behavior as she reads Los's indolence and repose into her vision of Albion's "initial" plight.

> The Fallen Man takes his repose: Urizen sleeps in the porch
> Luvah and Vala woke & flew up from the Human Heart
> Into the Brain; from thence upon the pillow Vala slumber'd.
> And Luvah siez'd the Horses of Light, & rose into the Chariot of
> Day
> Sweet laughter siezd me in my sleep! silent & close I laughd
> For in the visions of Vala I walkd with the mighty Fallen One
>
> (10:10–15)

While introducing Luvah and Vala, Enitharmon dissimulates her actions as Vala's in an effort to conceal that she *repeats* Vala's story in her own. Enitharmon has ulterior motives for doing so: she needs to divert Los's attention from their parents, who stand as proof of their generated nature, and get him to acquiesce in her scheme of domination. Thus, while Enitharmon implies an identity with Vala by relating her tale "in the visions of Vala" and by having Albion ask "Why dost thou weep as Vala," Los recognizes the temporal lag in her account. Allegedly recounting the traumatic event that triggers the plot, Enitharmon actually relates this event after Albion has fallen, so that her version cannot be primary.

Two events follow that seal the belatedness of Enitharmon's account. First, at its conclusion, Los "smote her upon the Earth twas long eer she revivd" (11:3); second, in revenge, Enitharmon calls on Urizen for protection (11:22). Both events, the violence and subsequent conspiracy with Urizen, attend later accounts, including Albion's in Night II, which like the others begins with the ramifications of an act that no zoa or emanation can situate accurately in the past. The primordial event of the creation-fall can only be constituted by its repetition in their tales and actions. In the words of Leslie Brisman, Enitharmon's "song is a history of the present state—a tale of the genesis of the tale and, as such, an extraordinary victory over the priority of the past" (Brisman 1978, 235).

In the next version, the "Demons of Waves" offer a political analysis of the "birth" of Luvah from Enitharmon (14:6–16:13). The complex historical meaning will be addressed in chapter five: at this point, I want to focus on narrative repetition. In terms of Blake's prophetic strategies, the Demons' narrative *repeats* a motif that attends each version of the creation: the compulsion to domi-

nate (built into the chain of being). The Demons, fearing Luvah
as if he was present—"Thou fierce Terror"—ask a new figure, the
"Spectre of Urthona," to "smite" Luvah because they believe that
he, Lucifer-like, bears responsibility for drawing them all down
from "heavens of joy into this Deep" (16:9–12). Tharmas, however,
dwells in the deep, and his emanation, banished to the margin
of nonentity, is compelled to sing one of her several haunting
lamentations, which invariably rivet attention on what is lacking
in eighteenth-century apologetic poems—the human cost of creation: "This was the Lamentation of Enion round the golden Feast /
Eternity groand and was troubled at the image of Eternal Death /
Without the body of Man an Exudation from his sickning
limbs" (18:8–10).

The Demons' account, and Enion's lament, elicits the narrator's
thematic statement about externalized creation and links previous
versions of the fall to the final one of Night I, by the Messengers
of Beulah. They clarify the Urizen-Luvah conspiracy theory cryp-
tically expressed by Enitharmon (10:10–13), but their audience,
the Council of God in "Great Eternity," demands an account of
("our brother") Albion's sickness. The Demons teach us that the
Urizen-Luvah plot makes sense only in relation to this other major factor in "creation": Albion's "repose," which allows the zoas
to usurp unity and enslave the spiritual (or collective) emanation,
Jerusalem, referred to as "The Emanation" (21:31; 22:5). The
Messengers recall the moment when creation becomes fall, a moment that returns us to the poem's opening dialogue.

In the fullest, yet still cyptic, version of Night I, the Messengers
explain that when Urizen-Luvah contest for power, Urthona divides, Enitharmon flies to Tharmas, Enion murders and hides
her, so that Urthona's "spectre fled / To Enion & his body fell"
(22:2C–28). This "spectre," like the shadowy female form lodged
in Enion's bosom, informs both the opening segment and the
Demons' account. Blake's plotting, then, slowly illuminates this
spectrous creature, who manifests the creation-fall only through
the zoas and emanations' variant perspectives.

This complex principle of prophetic narrative underpins
Blake's peculiar, pseudo-Gnostic, cosmology.[6] The Messengers, in
telling how all the zoas and emanations fall into "an unknown
Space" ("Ulro" or the "Circle of Destiny"), identify Albion with
his zoic and emanative "children." In an apt image, they state
flatly: "The Mans exteriors are become indefinite opend to pain"
(22:40). They further relate that Jerusalem is enslaved, though in
cosmic terms, "scatterd into the indefinite," suggesting that in its

most basic form, creation manifests what was never meant to appear: Albion's, the Eternal Man's, inner life. Creation is projection: "His inward eyes closing from the Divine vision & all / His children wandering outside from his bosom fleeing away" (19:14–15). Projection leads to generation, to externalizing and dividing the collective "Emanation," later identified as "Liberty," and she is "Lost" from the opening moment.

Night II

Blake repositioned the creation account that opens Night II (Albion's commissioning of Urizen), which appeared initially as the opening of *Vala*. Deploying the prophetic strategies of repetition and juxtaposition, Blake adjusts these narratives to highlight their conflicted perspectives on creation. While the two beginnings elude definitive analysis, Night II functions more clearly as Blake's version of the first Genesis Creation, the so-called E or Elohist strand.

As Night II begins, Albion abdicates his dominion (his control) to Urizen, hoping that Urizen can arrest the fallen creation by building the "Mundane Shell," a variant of Enion's "created Phantasm" described in Night I. Albion's abdication speech, however, belies what motivates his lapse into division:

> Turning his Eyes outward to Self. losing the Divine Vision
> Albion calld Urizen & said. Behold these sickning Spheres
> Whence is this Voice of Enion that soundeth in my Porches
> Take thou possession! take this Scepter! go forth in my might
> For I am weary, & must sleep in the dark sleep of Death
>
> (23:2–6)

As in Night I, we catch the creation in process for the "sickning Spheres" provide both an ontological setting and a psychological motive for Albion's call to Urizen. Like Enion, Albion tries to defend against his sickness by projecting it into the universe. What Urizen encounters points to Albion's psychic state, for Albion's "Sons," or zoas, have turned their (his) "Eyes outward to Self," implying that Albion's "body" manifests his internal condition. Urizen enters the "indefinite space" that Albion has externalized and shrinks in horror at "Eternal Death" (23:14). Moreover, Urizen is powerless to resist repeating this fallen activity; for when he constructs the mundane world, his helpers' (Reuben and Levi) sense organs "roll outward" so that "what is seen within is seen now without" (25:23). The image accurately describes both the Urizenic manner of building and the result of Albion's projection—actually coterminous events.

Blake's bold juxtapositions enable him to conflate his epic openings and interrogate various accounts of creation, especially Urizen's rationally-designed cosmos. Enion's lamenting "Voice" not only induces Albion's abdication, but fuels Urizen's construction of the Atmospheres, the Hall, the Altar, and the Temple. Most importantly, Urizen finds that building the Mundane Shell cannot muffle Enion's cry of discontent.

But Enion and Tharmas are absent throughout Night II, replaced by their "children" Los-Enitharmon and Luvah-Vala, whom Urizen exploits in his creation. Using symbolic instruments that will figure later in the plot, Urizen first seals Luvah-Vala in the "furnaces of affliction" and then erects his universe on "golden Looms." Blake's narrative pacing is typical: we hear, simply, "Then siezd the Lions of Urizen their work" as they build pyramids in the "deeps of Non Entity," deeps that the "Sons of Urizen" "measurd out in orderd spaces" with compasses (28:25–32). This mechanical precision, however, is buttressed by the labor of "female slaves" that the "Architect divine" employs, an image that foregrounds the human cost of creation.

At the same time, Blake critiques Urizen's world-building through the imagery of weaving, albeit in a different way than Enion's woven creation in Night I. Urizen's "Looms" bear industrial "spindles of iron" that eagles use to weave the "warp & woof" of the atmospheres, the "woven draperies" or "universal curtains" that hang on golden hooks. But these "strong wing'd Eagles," these Boyles and Newtons, open broad paths until the "weak / Begin their work; & many a net is nettted" (29:16). Urizen uses these nets to trap human desires, binding or "condensing the strong energies into little compass" (30:5), an image that is central to Blake's critique of rationalist or "mathematic" creation.

Repetitions follow. Urizen becomes astonished and confounded when he sees his emanation, Ahania, or "Her shadowy form now Separate" (30:45–46), and like Tharmas-Enion and Los-Enitharmon, drives the males away from her in torments of love and jealousy. As we move from pages 30 to 31, the narrator informs us that although Ahania comforts Urizen, they now have "two wills" and intellects, not one, "as in times of old" (30:48). One of many references to an ancient pastoral paradise before the woes of "creation," this passage not only reverts to Tharmas and Enion's division, but leads to another thematic statement about the "Lamb of God," Blake's complex symbol of visionary creativity.

The Lamb symbolizes a perpetual kind of "creation" to counter the dissolving, transitory creation of Urizen's "natural" world. Once the Mundane Shell is constructed, the narrator informs us that Urizen's sons, like the Messengers of Beulah at the end of Night I, "beheld Heaven walld round / They weighd & orderd all & Urizen comforted saw / The wondrous work flow forth like visible out of the invisible." This description is followed by a passage that points to Blake's version of the *felix culpa:* "For the Divine Lamb," the narrator informs us, "Permitted all lest Man should fall into Eternal Death" (33:8–12). While a deconstructive critic would not privilege Jesus or the Lamb, Blake needs this figure to counter Newtonian tradition. As with Young's indecorous "nail" that supports the "falling universe," Blake's Lamb preserves prophetic hope in redemption by containing "Eternal Death" in a body. Blake's brilliant irony is to turn this point into a critique of the great chain of being: "Thus were the stars of heaven created like a golden chain / To bind the Body of Man to heaven from falling into the Abyss" (33:16–18).

Blake is sowing prophetic seeds for later actions: the chain of jealousy figures importantly in the second Creation account, mirroring Genesis 2:4, that comes in Nights IV–V. In Night II, once Urizen completes his Mundane Universe, Blake brings Los and Enitharmon back into the narrative. They retain the fallen but potentially redemptive force of visionary imagination—as Urizen in a deist vein mockingly points out in Night I (12:25–29). Yet the Spectre invades them as well. Enitharmon has cut a deal with Urizen. Thus Los and Enitharmon, in despair, decide to "plant divisions in the Soul of Urizen & Ahania / To conduct the Voice of Enion to Ahania's pillow" (32:5, 34:3–4). After hearing Enion's cry, Ahania beholds her "in the Void" of Urizen's creation, and "never from that moment could she rest upon her pillow" (36:19). Enion's moving lamentation—"I am made to sow a thistle for wheat"—closes Night II and triggers Ahania's version of the creation-fall in Night III.

Night III

Ahania's sisterly compassion for Enion marks a redemptive moment that, anticipated by the Lamb of God in Nights I and II, is nullified by Urizen's defensive reaction in Night III. In her tale, as Harold Bloom comments, "Nights I and II are now being retold" from another perspective. As with Enitharmon's version in Night I, Ahania's story is conditioned by the present situation, in which she seeks to allay Urizen's massive anxiety about his creation. As in Young's *Night Thoughts,* the central themes are prospects for the future and immortality in a mortal world.

Ahania asks Urizen to rejoice in his creative efforts, but he fears "futurity darkning present joy," repeating a motif from the Night I opening. Like Tharmas, Urizen "darkens" as the light around his crown is "obscured . . . in thick clouds" (39:11 and 38:1), because he hears of his demise by "that Prophetic boy" "born of the dark Ocean" (38:6, 2). Ahania tries to convince him to "Leave all futurity" to the "Eternal One," but Urizen doubts all things "visionary," including Jesus "the soft delusion of Eternity" (12:25). He *knows* that his oppressive creation, like Satan's plot in *Paradise Lost,* will redound upon his head. But the logic of his creation is that he must reap the torment he sows.

Ahania begins her account by repeating a strange image from previous versions while adding crucial new information: Blake's art of *crypsis* at work. Echoing Night I, she opens: "The Darkning Man walkd on the steps of fire before his halls / And Vala walkd with him in dreams of soft deluding slumber" (39:15–16). While the second line introduces the formal or ostensible cause of the fallen creation—Vala's separation—the first line reveals the repetitive nature of his "origin," for Albion is "Darkning" when Vala walks with him. To complicate matters, Urizen hovers above Albion and Vala, his splendor already faded, which suggests his complicity in dividing Albion into male and female. Yet the sexual or gendered division—Vala's separation—implies a perceptual division, a falling-off from mental activity and a succumbing to the "soft deluding slumbers" that, paradoxically, inaugurate the poem's plot. As she launches her account, Ahania uses the techniques of juxtaposition and abrupt transition, moving to a seminal description with only "then" as introduction.

Then Man ascended mourning into the splendors of his palace
Above him rose a Shadow from his wearied intellect
Of living gold, pure, perfect, holy; in white linen pure he hover'd
A sweet entrancing self delusion, a watry vision of Man
Soft exulting in existence all the Man absorbing
Man fell upon his face prostrate before the watry shadow
Saying O Lord whence is this change thou knowest I am nothing

And Vala trembled & coverd her face, & her locks. were spread on
   the pavement

(40:2–9)

In her "Vision," Ahania informs us that Albion becomes "Idola-
trous to his own Shadow" precisely when he "turnd his back on
Vala" (41:4). She points to an inevitable conclusion: that Urizen
orchestrates the fall *as* he creates. He ensnares Albion with a guilt
that forces him to deny his own desire, embodied in both Vala and
Luvah, and to call on Urizen for help, although Albion, ultimately
indivisible from Urizen, bears responsibility for mental "weariness," for indolence and uncreative repose.
   Ahania presents Urizen's fallen creation from the angle of the
repressed in Night II. While the narrator is obsessed with the
human bondage (sealing) of Luvah and Vala in the "furnaces
of affliction," Urizen focuses on his geometry. Ahania need only
mention Luvah (dwelling in the cloud "above") and Urizen rolls
his "clouds in thick mists" of paranoid indignity. But Ahania is
compelled—"Prophetic dreads urge me to speak. futurity is before me"—and moans that "a dark lamp Eternal Death haunts all
my expectation." She explains: "Rent from Eternal Brotherhood
we die & are no more" (41:7–8). The voice of the emanation,
Enion, that sounds in Albion's ears ("porches") is the voice of both
Urizen and Tharmas as well. However you view it, the male severed from the female is a symptom of Albion's disunity. She tells
Urizen she "hears" Albion's "Voice," but it is actually Enion's
haunting voice "that soundeth in my [Albion's] ears." Sexual or
gendered divisions tear Albion apart, but Urizen anesthetizes him
with various substitutes for intellectual battle.
   Ahania condenses previous versions in the next section of Night
III, which concludes her account. Albion speaks through her and
repeats the woeful action of Night II when *his* own "mental" organs turn outward. Seeking to protect her counterpart, Ahania
relates that *Albion*, not Urizen, turns Vala and Luvah's "Ears outward" and shrinks their bodily organs "Till in narrow forms [they]
creep" (42:5). We heard in Night II that Urizen was responsible
for their reptilization, and in Night I we saw both Tharmas and
Enion turn into serpentine spectres. Now Ahania places the blame
on Albion, who drives his own zoas and emanations into the outer
world: "And the vast form of Nature like a Serpent roll'd between" (42:17). Blake's wry genealogy of nature hinges on juxtaposition and repetition, but as the multiple viewpoints are laid
out, a pattern begins to emerge.

Indeed, Ahania's vision dramatizes events so effectively that Urizen must come to terms with his responsiblity in the crisis or relive it. He chooses, of course, to relive it and compulsively repeats key incidents from earlier versions:

His visage changd to darkness & his strong right hand came forth
To cast Ahania to the Earth he siezd her by the hair
And threw her from the steps of ice that froze around his throne

Saying Art thou also become like Vala. thus I cast thee out
Shall the feminine indolent bliss. The indulgent self of weariness
The passive idle sleep the enormous night & darkness of Death
Set herself up to give her laws to the active masculine virtue
Thou little diminutive portion that darst be a counterpart
Thy passivity thy laws of obedience & insincerity
Are my abhorrence.

(43:2–11)

Urizen's blustering verbal onslaught exposes his own worst impulses, all of which he projects onto Ahania, expecially his "indolence" and "indulgence," as Albion projected his desire onto Vala. Plagued by anxiety about the future, Urizen feels dwarfed and becomes the very "self of weariness" he accuse Ahania of being. Albion had accused himself of the same weariness, just as Enitharmon accused Los: in each case, Ahania's version suggests, Urizen is the architect of accusation. Guilt is woven into the very fabric of creation, turning creation into a projection of internal strife, rather than a production of ordered reason, as the Christian rationalists would have it.

Urizen's response to Ahania's narrative establishes his responsibility not only for the flawed creation of the early Nights but for the ensuing action of the epic's middle Nights. Ahania's banishment is Urizen's light fading. When Ahania falls, the very contours of Urizen's world collapse: "The Bounds of Destiny crashd direful & the swelling Sea / Burst from its bonds in whirlpools fierce rearing with Human voice / Triumphing even to the Stars at bright Ahania's fall" (43:27–30). As Ahania cracks the bounds of Urizen's universe, the narrator details her fall in language that recalls the poem's opening, the birth of Tharmas's Spectre—"a blue sulphurous flame"—that becomes, in Blake's cosmic graveyard, a "universal groan of death." More crucially, from this groan "one like a shadow of smoke appeard" (44:14), whom the narrator identifies as Tharmas.

When Ahania falls, the event not only telescopes Urizen's fall

within her vision, but reenacts Tharmas's emergence in the opening lines of the poem. Urizen becomes Tharmas through the
Spectre just as Ahania becomes Enion through the Shadow
(44:21–22). Once Tharmas acknowledges his desperate need for
redemption, it is Enion, not the Lamb of God, who returns, re-
marking upon Tharmas's fall four times. Indeed, as Urizen's
"bounds are broken," Tharmas (or his "Voice") repeats the theme
of the poem's opening:" "hatred now began / Instead of love to
Enion" (45:10–11; 4:18–19). Enion's terrifying lament follows, re-
calling imagery of "Terror" and "clouds" from the opening dialogue. Both Enion and Ahania, earth mother and heavenly
goddess, find themselves banished to the abyss of male cosmology.
     Once Urizen's world collapses, Tharmas appears in the confu-
sion and floods the poem's universe, which compels him to tell
his version of the creation-fall in Night IV. Tharmas's version will,
however, instigate a decisive countermovement in the plot. For he
acknowledges his kinship with Urthona's Spectre, helps restore
Enitharmon to Los in the name of this old kinship, and enables
Los to "bind" Urizen's creation into a human body. In the middle
Nights, Tharmas and Los plan to rebuild Urizen's ruined world,
which is Blake's version of the second Creation story in Genesis.
Unfortunately, the binding of Urizen produces a series of catas-
trophes that further obfuscate while they gradually reveal the
(prophetic) meaning of creation.

Night IV

     Tharmas's return at the collapse of Urizen's Mundane Universe
is analogous to the biblical Flood, but in Blake's parabolic narrative style, this event seems to intersect the point in Genesis between
the two Creation stories. In this Night Tharmas and Los plan to
rebuild the poem's cosmos, but they retell and repeat earlier motifs (the birth of Los and Enitharmon), as in the biblical narrative,
where continuity between pre- and postdiluvial worlds is maintained by repetition of key cosmogonic events and tribal stories.
In *The Four Zoas*, however, Blake retains the liberty to juxtapose
events and motifs from the entire range of scriptural history, forcing his audience to take an active role in the plot's construction.
     A prime example of Blake's narrative freedom comes in the
opening exchange of Night IV between Tharmas and Los.[7] Tharmas commands Los and Enitharmon: "Go forth Rebuild this Universe. . . . A Universe of Death & Decay" (48:4–5). While the

command echoes the epic statement of theme (4:5), Los and Enitharmon boast that Urizen, not Tharmas, grants them power over
both Tharmas and Urthona, whom Los calls his "shadow" (48:20).
Los is in his spectre's power. This is proven when, enraged, Tharmas responds by reenacting the birth of the Spectre in Night I:
he tears Enitharmon from Los's side in a gruesome parody of
Eve's birth from Adam's rib. This event is depicted visually on
pages 46, 48, and 52, and provides a context for the Spectre of
Urthona's first account of the creation-fall (50:1–27).[8]

As in all versions, the Spectre identifies "repose" as a fundamental element (or weakness) of creation. The first thing the Spectre
remembers is Tharmas vacating or "fleeing from the battle,"
drawing the "Sons of Beulah" into his (Tharmas's) "vortex." Urthona's sons, apparently preparing forge and anvil for continuous
intellectual battle, also flee when they hear "symphonies of war."
But as they flee Urthona's side, the Spectre says that "pangs smote
me unknown before," pangs of separation that generate his
"counter part," whom he calls "Love" and names "Enitharmon"
(50:17). By nature, then, by a spiritual law of Blake's creation,
Enitharmon is born with Los or the Spectre in *divided* or exterior
form. She "breaks forth" from his loins as they "animate," and
the Spectre, like Tharmas in Night I or Urizen in Night III, pities
the "female pale & weak." Yet the males suppress their own divided, hence piteous and weak, aspects. As the Spectre reports,
both he and Enitharmon find themselves "issuing" (a key creational
metaphor) down the "bloody tide" into the phenomenal form of
a "blue obscure" shadow "from the breathing Nostrils / Of Enion"
(50:13–23). As these motifs and images attend other creation accounts, it must be *Albion's* repose that leads to internal collapse.

While the Spectre takes us back to Night I, to Los and Enitharmon's "birth" from Enion, his account encodes crucial information for later Nights. For the Spectre appeals to an ancient bond
with Tharmas, when Urthona protected Tharmas allegedly before the poem opens, as Tharmas lay "rotting upon the Rocks"
(50:24). This alliance is renewed in Night IV as Tharmas, claiming
that he will never see Enion (earth mother of creation) again if
Los does not "bind" Urizen, commands Los to take the "hammers
of Urthona" and "rebuild" the universe.

The creation that follows, Blake's second Genesis, is a bitter
critique of rational Christianity, of both its cosmology and its ethics. Taking the "chain of being" as his point of departure, Blake
exposes the human suffering suppressed in the ancient (Mosaic)

and modern (Newtonian) cosmologies. By merging the two Creation accounts, Blake alludes to the Elohist Creation while crossing it with the human story of Genesis 2:4. In a savage parody of Genesis's seven days of Creation, Blake has Los beat out links on the anvil that lash Enitharmon as a "chain of sorrow." However, Los's fallen "body," a creation repeating the errors of Urizen, holds out hope of regeneration, as Urizen's abstract cosmos is humanized. A limit is put to falling: creation is given temporal form. For Blake, the "Fall" must attend creation in order to activate the long, prophetic process of historical regeneration.

Abruptly shifting from fallen to regenerative creation, Blake inserts a passage on the "Divine Vision" that betokens the spiritual agency at work in Los's creation. Blake's biblical reference is the Lazarus story. Although the Daughters of Beulah again repeat that "Eternal Death is in Beulah," they humbly place hope for regeneration in the "Saviour" (56:1–7). For the Saviour can bear the torments of generation, "Luvahs robes of blood," the "limbs of Man vegetated," and redeem the "Human polypus" from "Eternal Death." How? In a sense, the *how* depends on readers who believe in this power—miracles are hindered by unbelief—as the Daughters do. Yet in another sense, redemption is built *into* the cosmos, and remains available to the spiritually alert, no matter where they find themselves within the cosmos.

Blake seals his *felix culpa* at the conclusion of Night IV, despite the nagging doubts that (in his honest way) he will not dispel at this stage of his revelation. Yet he signals clearly, for the "Saviour" puts ontological limits to fallen creation by establishing "Satan" and "Adam" within Albion's (i.e., "in every human") bosom (56:19–20). The very cosmos feels this redemptive act:

> Then wondrously the Starry Wheels felt the divine hand. Limit
> Was put to Eternal Death Los felt the Limit & saw
> The Finger of God touch the Seventh furnace in terror
> And Los beheld the hand of God over his furnaces
>
> (56:23–26)

Blake uses sublime "terror" against the "starry wheel" cosmology of orthodox apologetics, for Los the prophet feels the same "limit" as the wheels (as the indeterminate syntax of lines 245–46 suggests). Creation by design cannot put an end to *human* fallenness. By creating a body, Los holds out hope of reversal, not only of the external direction of creation, but of the rational argument for the preservation of Christianity.

Night V

In Los's creation, Blake interweaves different layers of his composite form: elements from the Lambeth prophecies of *Urizen* and *Los* are combined with additions and insertions written at Felpham. A key symbol tying both layers, and the middle Nights, together is the chain of being, Blake's "chain of jealousy," that emerges simultaneously with the binding of Urizen into a body. This chain metamorphizes into the central figure of Night V: the child of Los and Enitharmon that the narrator names "Orc," the temporal form of the zoa Luvah, whose oppression and aggression generates much of the "subsequent" action in the poem.

The birth of Orc is attended by a run of allusions to *Paradise Lost, Night Thoughts,* and the Bible, linked by the illustration that heads Night V. Blake's depiction of the biblical Nimrod, whom Erdman traces to Young's poem, recalls Milton's treatment of this figure in *Paradise Lost*. For Orc's birth is tied to Nimrod through the latter's situation at the beginning of Book XII, which, like the opening of Night V, hovers between the pre- and postdiluvian worlds. The "mighty hunter" in Young's text symbolizes death itself, although Blake, with wry humor, advances Young and Milton's treatment by making Nimrod (Orc) both a type of death and a political power that will oppose Urizen's domination. The drawing of Nimrod connects the war in heaven to human history, just as Orc brings zoic divisions to fallen time on earth.

Nimrod translates as "rebel" and functions as a negative type in both Milton and Young. Blake follows Milton in showing that Nimrod (Orc) disrupts the pastoral harmony of paternal rule; he is one "who not content / With fair equality, fraternal state, / Will arrogate Dominion undeserved" (XII:25).[9] Perhaps a first glimmer of the collusion, and ultimate identity, between Urizen and Orc, this passage also points to all divided zoic activity, which thrives on dominion. Blake draws Nimrod with a crown; and Milton's archangel says that Nimrod claims "second Sovranty," and that from "rebellion" derives his name, "Though of Rebellion he others accuse" (XII:36–37).[10] This typology of a second sovereignty plays off that of Noah in *Paradise Lost,* the "second source of Men," who provides a "second stock" from which Abraham produces the salvific "woman's seed" promised in the protoevangelium of

Genesis 3:15. Blake is more combative. His Nimrod becomes an Orc whose prophetic wrath forces Urizen to confront his role in the fallen creation. Blake chips away at Milton's "rational liberty," although Young retains it, and sets his typology in a more complex and syncretistic perspective than his precursors.

The narrative of Orc's birth repeats essentials from the Messenger's account of Luvah-Vala in Night I (22:15). Here, after the deluge, Los and Enitharmon shrink "into fixed space" (57:12) and simultaneously bind Urizen in "chains of intellect," until Enitharmon finds herself in labor. Her groans "drown" the music of the spheres and lead to this composite image: "The wheels of turning darkness / Began in solemn revolutions. Earth convulsd . . . Till" from Enitharmon's heart "a terrible Child sprang forth" (58:7, 17). As ever, Blake offers a double perspective: Orc can be a Nimrod or the apocalyptic Lamb of Revelation.

The demons respond to Orc's birth by recasting their narrative at the Feast in Night I (58:22–59:20). The identify Vala as the "lovely form / That drew the body of Man from heaven into this dark Abyss" (59:1–3), an accusation that repeats, with a twist, their earlier accusation that Luvah the "fierce Terror" drew them down into "this Deep" (16:9–12). Did Luvah or Vala make the zoas and emanations fall into creation? Blake's complicated account contains some cryptic clues. For the Demons prophesy another birth, of Rahab from Vala, that they say will produce a "rage" to "redound" on her "dark deceit." Another clue is the *Night Thoughts* resurrection drawing. In Milton Percival's view, Luvah-Orc is the "substance of the myth," its point of departure and return: "At the summit he is Christ; at the nadir he is Satan" (Percival 1938, 29). To grasp Orc's significance, readers must be able to negotiate the various contexts and frames in which Blake inserts his characters.

Moving beyond his eighteenth-century sources, Blake has Los and Enitharmon respond to Orc's birth by internalizing the chain of being. Blake's genius is to detail this process in ideological terms. The chain (of jealous being) enters the "limbs" of Orc as "fibres" that become "one with him a living Chain / Sustained by the Demons life" (63:3–4). While Blake alludes to classical (Prometheus) and biblical (Abraham and Isaac) myths in the traumatic scene at the "iron mountain's top," the treatment is distinctly his own. The chain, called "the bloody chain of nights & days," is said to be "Depending from the bosom of Los with griding pain" (60:20), a line that reiterates the "raping" of Enitharmon from Los's side in Night IV. Blake's drawings seal the point. Enitharmon, horrified, covers her ears; Los, with spiky sun-king crown, throws his hands to the sky in apparent despair. The narrator explains: not Los's "Consummation," Enitharmon's "death," Urthona's "strength," nor "all the power of Luvah's Bulls. . . . could uproot the infernal chain" (63:27–32). In Night V Blake exposes the psychic scars of the chain of being cosmology.

Night V shows the effect of Los and Enitharmon's creation. As they go to Golgonooza, their artisanal haven, to work against Eternal Death, Orc's counterpart Vala begins to "reanimate" in Enitharmon's heart. Enitharmon's heart gates later become a locus of redemption and catastrophe. They were left swinging open at the end of Night I and now offer glimpses not only of Ahania weeping in the void, or of the infernal chain of jealousy, but of "the rendings of fierce howling Orc" (63:10–16). In these fallen conditions, the stage is set for Urizen's reentry.

Despite his self-deception, Urizen cannot evade the coming confrontation nor delay the prophetic course of events his actions have set in motion: "If you go on So / the result is So." He understands this and, in half conscious fear, declares that he will explore "these dens & find that deep pulsation" of human suffering that shakes his universe ("caverns"). In an interesting line, he wonders, "perhaps this is the night / Of Prophecy" when Luvah—he cannot acknowledge Orc—has "burst his way from Enitharmon," or when a "globe of life blood" issues from her loins, forcing Urizen to face the suppressed contradictions of his cosmology. "Then," he muses, "love shall shew its root in deepest Hell." This line not only concludes the Night but takes us back to Night I—"O Enion thou art thyself a root growing in hell" (4:40)—sealing a connection between Enion's fallen state and Orc's rebellious pulsation.

Night VI

In this Night, Urizen encounters all the horrors of his fallen creation and decides to rebuild his universe, extending his new dominion using a "vast Chain" that drives Urthona and Tharmas into the rocks of Ulro, where Urizen meets Orc in Night VII.

As with Satan's journey over the "vast abrupt" in *Paradise Lost*, Urizen travels through the abyss guided by the "Divine hand," repeating the action of Night V from another perspective. Fearing futurity, Urizen again waxes nostalgic for the "climes of bliss" and, shocked at the misery he has perpetrated, decides to remodel the old cosmology. With pointed irony, though, one-uping the

Augustan wits, Blake has Urizen refurbish the ancient cosmos along modern rationalist lines, in fear of "falling" into the mechanistic vortexes he creates:

Stemming his downward fall labouring up against futurity
Creating many a Vortex fixing many a Science in the deep
And thence throwing his venturous limbs into the Vast unknown
Swift Swift from Chaos to chaos from void to void a road immense
(72:12–15)

In his portrait of Urizen's modern science, Blake combines the images in *Paradise Lost* of God circumscribing the world with his compasses and Satan paving the road from hell to earth. In effect, he implicates Milton the rational theologian with the Newtonians as agents of the new cosmology.

By manuscript page 73, framed by a crucial *Night Thoughts* drawing, Urizen binds "all futurity . . . in his vast chain" and gains a "New Dominion" in the process. In a stroke of apologetic genius, Blake describes the chain as a vast "Web," created, as is Orc's chain, from the soul of its bearer. The chain-web is secreted from Urizen's "mantle of years / A Living Mantle adjoind to his life & growing from his Soul." Unlike Los's earth-rooted chain, the web secrets across the vortexes and makes a new "tent of the universe" that unfortunately, but with a merciless logic—"for the Will cannot be violated" (74:31–2)—vibrates with anxiety. Blake celebrates the creativity required for such building, as Urizen expands his senses and tries to get his workers to open "within" into Eternity: "But they refused because their outward forms were in the Abyss" (74:2). His binding has worked too well.

Night VI presents Urizen's "chain of being" cosmology from his, not Los and Orc's, perspective. The chain we know has rooted into Orc's world and is contained in Urthona's dens; but in Night VI we get a series of prophetic juxtapositions that slowly, but inevitably, move the narrative toward direct confrontation with Orc. The narrator informs us that Urizen binds futurity in his great chain while he simultaneously laments the fate of Luvah: "Till" a "white woof" covers him and forms a giant web or tent. Urizen wanders as his web quivers with "torment," "Till" he comes to "the world of dark Urthona." Urizen, however, is compelled by spiritual forces more powerful than his sciences: "By Providence divine conducted not bent from his own will / Lest death Eternal should be the result" (74:30–32). Urizen continues to wander "till" he perches on Urthona's rock, from which he descends into the underworld, where Urthona's shadow ("a spectre Vast") denies him entrance, in accord with epic convention.

In the final act of the Night, Urizen, confronted by both Tharmas and Urthona's Spectre, withdraws into his "dire Web" in a marvelously calculated strategy. Dramatizing Blake's prophetic techniques, the narrator says abruptly: "Then Urizen arose," and as the rational cosmologist vibrates his web, Tharmas and Urthona flee, fearing absorption into Urizen's "net of religion." More tellingly, Blake has Urizen hurl comets at Urthona and Tharmas, and the "massy Globes . . . slow oerwheel" Urthona's squadrons, weaving the dire web and "preparing Urizens path before him" (75:25–34). Urizen's excellent command of mechanics enables him to outwit and overpower his opponents, and he draws blood from Orc. This first strike is important, especially in the context of the remaining Nights, when the revolutionary violence of late eighteenth-century Europe pushes more disturbingly into the poem.

Night VII

The two Nights VII in *The Four Zoas,* as every Blake scholar knows, contain such intractable structural problems that editors can only approximate a solution. The textual and critical debate is, perhaps, interminable.[11] We could admit that Blake did not wrestle his narrative into shape and leave it at that. Or we could go the deconstruction route and regard the gaps and lacunae of the manuscript as integral parts of the Night's narrative meaning (see Ault 1987, 327–33, 475–76). My solution, equally open to criticism, is to regard the unfinished narrative in terms of Blake's prophetic strategy, where the impacted layers of text can function rhetorically, as a part of Blake's design to harass readers into active engagement and reconstruction of the narrative strands. Acknowledging the subjective nature of such a choice, I base my reading on Erdman's 1982 text (with qualifications: see my Note on the Manuscript).

In Night VII the plotting of creation reaches a decisive turning point. Generation turns into regeneration, as portrayed in the creation account of Enitharmon's Shadow and Urthona's Spectre. The focus shifts from cosmic space to the biblical tree of temptation, although their version is prepared for by Urizen's journey through the void spaces of Night VI, a Night, according to Brenda Webster, that "repeats the original trauma of separation and fall"

(Webster 1983, 232). As he enters the inmost cave of Urthona's dens, Urizen engraves his code of morality in an iron book, the tablets of moral law: these "tracings" cool the flames of Orc "till underneath his heal a deadly root / Struck thro the rock the root of Mystery" (78:4–5; E 353). The root sprouts into the Tree of Mystery, Blake's symbol for religious mystification, and branches into the "heaven of Los," indicating the extension of Urizenic ideology into prophecy and, thus, Los's complicity in exposing Orc to further exploitation.

Urizen makes use of the chain and rock, although Orc exposes his hypocrisy in doing so. He intuits that Urizen's natural morality is a debased temporal strategy for reducing him to Urizen's will "by soft mild arts" of reasoning. Orc realizes that he is a "Worm compelld" to feed off of Urizen's natural morality because law or mystery restrains: "Art thou the cold attractive power that holds me in this chain / I well remember how I stole thy light and it became fire. . . . is this the triumph this the Godlike State / That lies beyond the bounds of Science" (80:38–42; E 356). Orc recognizes that Urizen's great system, his web, vibrates dangerously with the "torment" that will effect its own downfall. Fearing futurity, as in Night III, Urizen compels Orc and Enitharmon's Shadow to climb the Tree, which motivates the Spectre of Urthona's rescue attempt. The Spectre-Shadow dialogue that follows (83:4–84:42) brings us to the most perspicuous, if still partial, creation narrative in the poem.

The Spectre-Shadow account begins on a manuscript page (82) with a crucial drawing. An acrobatic female figure turns what looks like the circle of destiny, filled with eight stars ("Eyes of God"), that becomes a tamborine held by a sleeping woman on page 128. Erdman and Magno relate this image to a number of other moments in the poem: to the Tharmas-Enion dialogue of Night I; to the Saviour's naming the "limits" of Satan and Adam in Night IV, when the "Starry Wheels felt the divine hand" (56:19–23); to the end of Night VI, when Urizen "o'erwheels" Urthona's squadrons; and to Night VIII, page 104, the culminating image, when the "stars open as eyes" (Erdman and Magno 1987, 70–71). Blake's narrative art of *crypsis* finds its visual component in this image of creation-destiny slowly turning toward vision (open eyes).[12]

As with previous versions, Shadow and Spectre enact the creation-fall while they narrate it. For when Enitharmon's Shadow slides down the tree toward Orc winding his way up, she takes on those qualities of Vala that leads Urthona (and the other zoas) into temptation: the Spectre, watching the tree generate fruit, "prepard the poison of sweet Love" and "embracd / The fleeting image" (82:25–27; E 358). The Shadow responds with her version of the fall, which involves the "births" of Urizen, Luvah, and Vala, to which the Spectre responds on page 84, finishing what she "forgets." The dialogue leads to the Spectre's plot to bring Vala down to Orc, to destroy the body that he claims he created, and to "unite" with Enitharmon, fallen acts that ironically prefigure regeneration.

Enitharmon's Shadow recalls that when Albion the "Eternal Man" perceived or "sensed" Vala, he melted in a swoon of passion, begetting Urizen in the same instant. Albion "reveld in delight among the Flowers / Vala was pregnant & brought forth Urizen Prince of Light / First born of Generation" (83:11–13; E 358). This passage is the first time any zoa is said to be "generated," suggesting that Urizen's very creation as a separate being engenders the fall. Urizen, in effect, is *conceived*—both "thought up" and born—as the world of the poem emerges. Vala's presence, then, provokes Urizen's reaction (i.e., his birth), but in a typically Blakean construction, Urizen's reaction in turn creates Vala: as soon as he appears, the Shadow says, "Then behold a wonder to the Eyes / Of the now fallen Man a double form Vala appeard. A Male / And female" (83:13–15). This statement also makes clear that Luvah, Vala's male counterpart, does not exist in fallen or divided form either until Vala's mysterious (fabricated?) presence evokes Urizen's reaction. In short, Albion's encounter with Vala, with his own desire, issues in a Urizenic reaction that "begets" or produces the created world of the poem. At this point, the Shadow recalls how she and Los were born "enslavd to vegetative forms," but this painful memory is repressed and the Spectre must resume where she leaves off.

Urthona's Spectre supplies the clearest description of the creation-fall in the poem, although, as Donald Ault suggests, this is because the narrative itself undergoes a transformation that the repetitions help clarify. Rather than subverting Blake's prophetic narrative scheme, however, this transformation operates according to a cryptic logic, even if the Spectre cannot specify an actual beginning for the creation-fall. He simply alludes to a time when the four zoas lived each other's lives in "Universal Manhood." From Blake's perspective, the fictive nature of the creation actually makes it more "true" than Milton's more literal or Pope's more philosophic interpretations. The Spectre proceeds, quite simply, on the once-upon-a-time formula:

>   One dread morn
> Listen O vision of Delight One dread morn of goary blood
> The manhood was divided for the gentle passions making way
> Thro the infinite labyrinths of the heart & thro the nostrils issuing
> In odorous stupefaction stood before the Eyes of Man
> A female bright. I stood before my anvil dark a mass
> Of iron glowd bright prepard for spades & plowshares. sudden
>   down
> I sunk with cries of blood issuing downward in the veins. . . .
>   I sunk along
> The goary tide even to the place of seed & there dividing
> I was divided in darkness & oblivion thou an infant woe
> And I an infant terror in the womb of Enion
> My masculine spirit scorning the frail body issud forth
> From Enions brain In this deformed form leaving thee there
> Till times passd over thee but still my spirit returning hoverd
> And formd a Male to be a counterpart to thee O Love
> Darkend & Lost In due time issuing forth from Enions womb
> Thou & that demon Los wert born Ah jealousy & woe
> Ah poor divided dark Urthona now a Spectre wandering
> The deeps of Los the Slave of that Creation I created
>   (84:11–31; E 359)

The Spectre presents as clear an exposition of the precipitating moment as any one zoa or emanation can. Albion's "manhood" is divided because (?) of "the gentle passions making way," which then issue as a female entity—desire is externalized rather than fulfilled as soon as the "Man" becomes conscious of it. When exactly Albion becomes conscious of desire remains indeterminate: ultimately, no retrospect takes us back to the beginning; the origin of the creation-fall is simply the "all-presupposing fact" with which Blake's story sets out.

Enitharmon's Shadow and Urthona's Spectre want to destroy the old creation and fabricate a new one. The Shadow wants to punish Vala, whom she resembles, by subjecting her to Orc's rage, even though she does not (consciously) acknowledge that she knows Orc is Luvah. The Spectre affirms her plan, but only because he self-destructively wants revenge on Los, whom he resembles. The plan is to destroy "That body I created," says the Spectre, by forcing Vala to copulate with Orc (nature with revolution), which ironically will produce the worst horror in the poem: Rahab. The irony is offset, however, by creative providence. For despite their lethally distorted nature—the Shadow explains, rather humorously, that she is bound to the Spectre's embrace, "else be assurd so horrible a form / Should never in my arms repose" (83–84)—the birth of Rahab at least puts into consolidated form what has been externally created. The lines are drawn clearly enough that Los and Enitharmon can see to separate themselves from the "formless indefinite" that their Spectre and Shadow impose on existence.

The various strands of narrative now form a pattern. At the stitching of VIIa and VIIb, the consolidations begin to point to redemption. Blake heralds the turn by repeating the Lazarus myth in the new context, immediately before Erdman's arrangement of Night VIIa2, when Los embraces the Spectre and Shadow. The Los-Spectre, Los-Enitharmon exchanges that ensue move the poem toward internalized or Romantic creation (i.e. re-creation).

The Los-Spectre-Shadow dialogues feature key elements from the Genesis tradition, with Los and the Shadow of Enitharmon playing out the temptation scene. But not before the Spectre and Shadow "conferrd among the intoxicating fumes of Mystery / Till Enitharmons shadow pregnant" brings forth the "wonder horrible" that produces the bloodshed of Nights VIIb and VIII. She will be named Rahab and comes to symbolize natural religion, or Deism: even now she raves in Urizen's heavens, wreaking havoc on all the nations (96:30; E 361). According to Blake's cryptic strategy, however, she is identified at this point as "the nameless shadow" (91:19; E 363). She is a powerful mystery, associated with death, generation, and decay, and she makes Enitharmon and Los despair of regeneration.

But in a series of miraculous events, the Spectre enters Los's "bosom" and Enitharmon is said to tell "the tale / Of Urthona" (85:28–29; E 367), which follows the Lazarus story, where the Daughters of Beulah pit the rational demonstration of death, or the shadow's emergence into Urizen's world (95:1–2; E 367), against faith in the "Eternal Promise" of resurrection. The narrator informs us that "the tree of Mystery" enroots in Los's world, as we learned earlier, "But then the Spectre enterd Los's bosom Every sigh & groan / Of Enitharmon bore Urthona's Spectre on its wings" (85:26–27; E 367). Los then embraces the Spectre, who, however, informs Los that unity with Enitharmon cannot rationally be effected in the "mortal body," because Los is simply an "organ of life" and is continually created. Los responds with an important speech:

Los furious answerd. Spectre horrible thy words astound my Ear
With irresistible conviction I feel I am not one of those
Who when convincd can still persist. Tho furious. controllable
By Reasons power. Even I already feel a World within

Opening its gates & in it all the real substances
Of which these in the outward World are shadows which pass away
(86:4–9; E 368)

While Los's idealism is the key regenerative attitude, it is the uto-
pian goal, not the starting point, of the prophecy. He may experience grace, but, like Adam in *Paradise Lost*, his female counterpart
has other interests in the tree.

Blake expands his allusive range by conflating imagery from
Revelation and Genesis in the temptation scene. Enitharmon hides
"beneath Urizens tree," but eventually mingles with the Spectre
(in yet another narrative repetition) and sees the "Center opend
by Divine Mercy." Enthused, the Spectre commands Los to destroy
the Body, but Los refuses, stemming the endless cycle of creation-
destruction-creation that has characterized the poem's cosmogony. Instead Los labors at building his city of art, Golgonooza,
because he relies not on the proof of his senses, on empirical
evidence, but on inspiration and the evidence of things unseen:
"They Builded Golgonooza," the narrator informs us, "for beneath / Was opend new heavens & a new Earth beneath & within"
(87:1–8; E 368). But at this stage of the plot, Enitharmon is under
Urizen's power, and when she eats the fruit and despairs of life,
and Los urges her to keep the faith, she demands: "thou art
strong & mighty / To bear this Self conviction take then Eat thou
also of / The fruit & give me proof of life Eternal or I die" (87:20–
22; E 369). True to tradition, Los eats; but Blake alters tradition
by having the Spectre of Urthona comfort him in an act of brotherly love that allows Los to create, in turn, a body for the Spectre;
for "without a Created body," the narrator relates to us, "the Spectre is Eternal Death" (87:25–38; E 369).

These zoic acts of human sympathy offset the compulsively repeated acts of domination that characterize life in the poem so
far. They also break Enitharmon's heart. Fortunately, it is a break
that opens the gates to life within, where the Lamb of God is seen
bearing Luvah's garments of mortality. Creation is a matter of the
heart rather than the head, although Los's activity of continual
imaginative re-creation requires the cooperation of all the zoas
and emanations to redeem the "Universal Humanity."

Coda: Night VIII

Before creation-fall becomes fortunate in the apocalyptic reversals of Night IX, the narrative must consolidate its varied, an-

tagonistic positions. Although it does not contain a creation
account, Night VIII stages the final intellectual battle between
the narrative's contending cosmologies. Written later than other
sections of the poem, Night VIII shows the advantage of Blake's
experience in writing his engraved epics. It constitutes a veritable
symbolic history of natural religion to counter the natural histories of Hume, Gibbon, and other suspects rounded up in *Milton*
(plate 40) and *Jerusalem* (preface to chapter three). Night VIII
also presents Blake's case against the mystery or fertility religions
and clarifies the relation of the emanation or "feminine" in his
view of creation. While I believe that Blake remains an eighteenth-
century Christian apologist, he melts down both the orthodoxies
and heterodoxies of Anglican and Dissenter in the forge of his
prophetic workshop, exercising the divine arts of imagination.

The consolidations of Night VIII emerge when Urizen's cosmic
web collapses from the weight of its own contradictions. His creation is too "shapeless" (103:25; E 375), too mired in its own natural
processes, to be the work of redemptive spiritual agency. Blake
thus sets the natural and imaginative cosmologies on a collision
course: he sets the forces of Vala against those of Jerusalem, two
conceptions of the female, in a symbolic struggle over two kinds
of creation. Urizen's "Direful Web of Religion" collapses when
the "Shadowy Female" absorbs his "Sciences" into her indefinite,
transitory processes of change, decay, and death. This delusory
female principle dooms Urizen because he has "murdered" her
counterpart, the dying god of the mystery religions: Luvah, the
"source of every joy that this mysterious tree / Unfolds in Alleg-
oric fruit" (103:18–19). As the natural source of Urizen's sciences,
the Shadowy Female "branches" through his heavens, his cosmos,
in the power of Orc, the temporal Luvah whose function as the
suppressed source of joy is now exposed. Orc's liberation from
his "chains" becomes a central concern in Night IX: his painful
exposure in Nights VII and VIII continues as the Shadowy Female gathers "the fruit of that Mysterious tree till" (abrupt transition) Urizen becomes entangled in his own net.

Once Urizen is caught in his own contradictions, Los and Enitharmon resume their creative labors, weaving the spectres' bodies
to protect them from "Eternal Death," the ravages of abstraction.
As they labor at their forge and loom, a "Vast Family" appears,
"a Universal female form created / From those who were dead in
Ulro" (103:32–39). Redeemed by her labor, overcoming her jealous scorn of other females, Enitharmon names the family "Jerusalem," an act that both recalls the fragmentation of the poem's

opening and heralds the return of collective unity. More importantly, Enitharmon sees a unified male-female form: she envisions the "Lamb of God within Jerusalems Veil," a vision that offsets the externally created, delusory "Veil" associated with the "false" female, Vala. In sum, the two female principles, linked with their male counterparts, are finally delineated.

This delineation or clarification occurs on the crucial page 113 of the manuscript ("first portion"), inserted between the first and second "portions" of page 104 (on Blake's instruction). A late addition to the manuscript, this page is given over to the Sons of Eden, whose song to the Lamb announces the end of the cryptic process of Blake's prophetic narrative. The Sons repeat the word "Now" five times in five lines, signaling that the diverse narrative accounts are achieving *some* clarity.

Page 113 features not only the dramatic oppositions that drive the narrative, but a drawing that carries Blake's signature contribution to poetic cosmology. Los and Enitharmon *work:* they labor at forge and loom to house and clothe their creation, "Creating Continually" (113:4; E 376). Urizen manages his creation like a dark satanic mill owner. He allows Satan and the "Shadowy Female," now named "Rahab," to use his "spindles of iron" and to prepare "far different mantles," "webs of torture" that, like Urizen's net, cover the spectres from "head to feet" (113:19–21). Los and Enitharmon build the artisanal city of Golgonooza; Satan and Rahab design mills on the margin of Ulro, where the "Lake of Udan Adan" is formed from "the tears & sighs & death sweat of the Victims / Of Urizens laws. to irrigate the roots of the tree of Mystery." Blake counterposes the two creations: one is based on calculation and sustained by an accusatory morality; the other is based on imaginative empathy and sustained by compassion and forgiveness. For Blake, it is an error to separate creative design from emotional effect: creation and fall are indivisible.

The drawing concentrates the issues that have occupied both this and the last chapter. Laboring mightily under her task, a female figure pushes a circle, the Circle of Destiny, replete with open-eyed stars, off the page and out of the poem. Although the chalk shading no doubt suppresses a sexual scene, Los responds with an explicit revelation, written just above the figure's head and shoulders. The call and response of text and drawing offers a fine example of Blake's mature composite art. Repetition, juxtaposition, allusion are packed densely but clearly into a text that, in the best parabolic style, seeks to stretch the minds of its auditors. Erdman and Magno, building on the poetic details, establish the illustrative context in one of their finest passages:

> The wheel image is built up gradually. The spindle and reel of creativity busily supply the poor spectres of the dead, "Clothing their limbs With gifts & gold of Eden" (112–13). But the Satanic "Mills of resistless wheels . . . unwind the soft threads," and Vala's daughters, Rahab & Tirzah, reclothe the spectres with mantles of despair and veils of ignorance (17–21). It seems a hopeless context. No wonder that Enitharmon pushes with all her might; no wonder that we cannot see motion in the wheel. Laboring in the mill like a slave, she cannot see the Eyes—but we can. (Erdman and Magno 1987, 81)

It may be of small comfort to female readers that yet once more the women bear the brunt of both creation and redemption. But Enitharmon, if that is who pushes the circle, is oppressed by Vala and Rahab as well as Urizen and Satan. In other words, there are two creations, two kinds of creating, and they both contain male and female components.

The more revealing point concerns the relation of the narrative strategy of repetition to the different creations. For Blake, anybody can be redeemed if they accept the rigors of self-sacrifice. Even Vala, to whom Los speaks: "Hear me repeat my Generations that thou mayst also repent" (113:53; E 380). Los addresses Vala after the Lamb is crucified and discloses the transitory nature of external (i.e., mortal) creation. Yet Blake's narrative has not entered its apocalyptic stage, as Ahania still pines for Urizen: she "Saw not as yet the Divine vision her Eyes are Toward Urizen" (108:7; E 383). But a crucial change has occurred and, despite her lack of "vision," Ahania regains a sisterly connection with Enion that transforms their worship of abstract male and earthly female religions into an embrace of selfless cooperation.

In Ahania's lament and Enion's response, which close Night VIII, Blake also moves beyond his closest eighteenth-century precursor, Young and his graveyard school. For Ahania, addressing the "Caverns of the Grave," creation is "Eternal Death." She asks her audience why they let kings and priests devour them and "the grave mock & laugh at the plowd field," where death is "goddess & queen" (108:15–18). For Ahania, "universal death devours all" (109:8). In response, Enion identifies herself as "an Eternal Consummation" and as the "watry Grave" itself, but she no longer fears death: "A voice came in the night a midnight cry upon the mountains / Awake the bridegroom cometh I awoke to sleep no more" (109:21–23). The androgynous Lamb takes away her fear of sexual contact: "More happy is the dark consumer hope drowns all my torment," a major reversal from the opening pages. Out of compassion for Ahania, Enion explains:

> Behold the time approaches fast that thou shalt be as a thing
> Forgotten when one speaks of thee he will not be believd
> When the man gently fades away in his immortality
> When the mortal disappers in improvd knowledge cast away
> The former things so shall the Mortal gently fade away
> And so become invisible to those who still remain
>
> (109:29–34; E 384–85)

All the (t)errors of creation come about through externalizing what should never have appeared: the alienated human needs so powerfully recorded by Ahania. But Enion, as the first to project the internal cosmos, justly speaks the last word. Assured by the vision of the Lamb, she is no longer compelled into external or emanative life. If the males follow her example, then, in Harold Bloom's words, the possibility opens of a transformation of "natural repetition into human renewal." Then internalization could turn the woes of natural creation into the joys of imaginative recreation, and the prophetic text would accomplish part of its *kerygmatic* design.

4

Blake's Typology in Historical Context

No amount of historical explanation can make Blake out to be
other than a phoenix among poets; but if we put his work into
its historical and intellectual context, and alongside that of his
poetic contemporaries of the 1790s, we find at least that he is
not a freak without historical causes. . . .
              —M. H. Abrams, "The Spirit of the Age"

Blake mentions *types* infrequently, but so pervasive is his effort
to explain the hidden meanings of the biblical myths that he
introduces the traditional typological characters . . . with clear
prefigurative import. . . . The sweeping generality of Blake's
typological equation testifies to the central position that prefigurative structures occupy in his poetry.
              —Paul Korshin, *Typologies in England*

IN this chapter I sketch the crucial seventeenth- and eighteenth-
century religious debates that shape Blake's use of biblical typology. Blake's figural power, like his composite narrative artistry,
resists scholarly reduction to its sources. But his "phoenix" status
points to an important truth. That while the Dissenting artisan
poet-prophet is ever a vigilant defender of revealed religion, he
remains acutely, ironically, aware of the Enlightenment critique of
the Bible's prefigurative form and language. Blake's use of typology thus attains its full scope when seen in relation to the literary,
philosophical, and religious issues broached in chapter 2 and in
the present chapter, which sets up a sustained reading of typological history in *The Four Zoas* in chapters 5 and 6.

I

Blake is a spiritual artist and poet, a mental traveler who takes
seriously the bardic task of bridging past, present, and future.

This visionary ambition, coupled with his sense of prophetic vocation, serves a fundamentally affective aesthetic.[1] Blake challenges and, at times, harangues his readers to alter their perception, both of themselves as individuals and as members of a broadly-conceived "Christian" community. Despite his religiously unorthodox style and Enlightened impulses, Blake admonishes readers to "figure" their personal destinies within the universal history encoded in the Bible. The key to his prophetic rhetoric lies in *repetition:* the poet directs events as acts in a cosmic drama, acts that are repeated through "providence" or what Blake calls "spiritual agency." While this agency dwells with the bardic poet, who bears the moral-artistic burden of drawing biblical parallels to contemporary events, it must transfer to the readers, who in turn make the past their contemporary while lifting the present into the region of universal history.

This view of Blake's effort to write a "total" history has met much opposition of late, especially from critics affiliated with deconstruction theory. As Tilottama Rajan contends in her account of Blake's canon, Blake's intertextual structures qualify any claims "by the prophetic mode to provide a divinatory reading of cultural history" (Rajan 1990, 203). As Blake's use of organized juxtaposition arrests his "totalizing impulses," so his canon undercuts the unified biblical canon, which Rajan reads as a document of "cultural imperialism."

> In actuality, the Bible is not an eschatological narrative, but a collection of writings that inscribes the holoscopic impulse in an intertextual field. When we refer to it, however, we refer to an *editorial* activity supervised by the institutional church. This activity produces a cultural paradigm that typologically absorbs difference into unity. (Rajan 1990, 198)

This interesting if jargonistic passage takes its idea of canon formation from the eighteenth- and nineteenth-century historical criticism it studies. While Blake heard these arguments, he did not view the canon formation of the Bible as a totally repressive force or imperialist activity. In part, of course. But what we lose here is the sense of forming an oppositional body of inspired literature in the teeth of institutional or state repression. While Rajan (1990) rightly opposes typological reading as a way to silence other "codes," she misses an important point: that Blake utilizes the typological equation to set up expectations that he foils even as he appeals to them. Blake effectively re-appropriates the transgressive impulses of the biblical prophets and, by a deliberate recontextualizing of events, figures, and symbols from the Bible, transforms a literature used ideologically to oppress people into one that can serve as a means for their liberation. Blake's strategy is to juxtapose multiple versions of a history that readers must engage and negotiate for themselves.

Scholars conversant with Blake's use of typology call this historicizing activity a re-creation or "renewal" of the biblical types, and my discussion draws on previous studies.[2] Yet I want to reclaim typology as a fundamentally historical strategy in order to analyze Blake's complex treatment of history in *The Four Zoas*. My starting point is A. C. Charity's assertion that typology is "a way of regarding history rather than texts" (Charity 1966, 99).[3] Charity refers to scriptural and theological typology, but this approach must be qualified to comprehend Blake's peculiar practice. We need to consider the intellectual context in which, and against which, Blake works. Blake's strategies in *The Four Zoas* are not "the conceits of a warmed or overweening brain"—as Locke defines enthusiasm—but resemble those of other religious poets and biblical apologists of the late eighteenth century. Blake could not deploy conventional typology as his pre-Enlightenment forerunners could; even Milton, adhering to a kind of figurative literalism, did so in the face of what D. C. Allen calls "the intrusion of rationalistic methods into the study of the Bible" (Allen 1963, 39). In order to measure changes in prefigurative thinking brought on by the Enlightenment critique of the Bible, we need to look briefly at the old system.

Typology is not only an interpretive strategy but a method of constructing narratives whose events, paradoxically, are both realistic and symbolic. In his enduringly influential essay on typology, Erich Auerbach asserts that events become symbolic by either prefiguring or fulfilling other events, and that they retain their historicity even as they become figurative.[4] For Auerbach, the special nature of biblical typology resides in its capacity to provoke a reader's understanding of the past in the *present* moment: "The two poles of a figure," he writes, "are within temporality. They are both contained in the flowing stream of historical life, and only their comprehension, the *intellectus spiritualis*, of their interdependence is a spiritual act" (Auerbach 1984, 53). Traditional typology fosters the *intellectus spiritualis* that preserves history as realistic event as it interprets history as revelation (Auerbach 1984, 32, 68). Perhaps most appropriate to the faith of the Middle Ages, strict typology nonetheless contains the edifying kernal that even secular versions retain. The idea is to evoke a response—ultimately a committed response—"Go thou, and do likewise" is the existential command that infuses typological narrative with meaning.

Under the power of the figural system, then, historical events take on narrative shape, although a sense of the extratextual nature of typology persists in all conventional versions.[5] The poet must present past events in such a way as to trigger their typical or figural meaning. In effect, the figural strategist activates the past through the *kerygmatic* or transactive nature of prophetic rhetoric: readers must "witness" to the intrusion of spiritual agency within the text, within their own lives, and within history. They are called to *engagement,* to put self and society to radical decision, turning the dead letters of the past into living acts of understanding.[6]

II

The hundred years of biblical controversy between Milton and Blake determines the modern conception of this venerable, yet seriously impugned, strategy. While scholars identify the year 1700 as a seminal date in biblical exegesis, and while many agree that the hitherto seamless fabric connecting history and scripture is severed at this time (thus undermining traditional figuralism), a rent in this fabric starts during the Reformation.[7] Leslie Stephen points out that Protestant writers against Rome were "forging the weapons which were soon to be used against themselves. . . . Whatever, that is, was gained by reason was gained by Protestants" (Stephen 1962, 2:66). But reason, or the new rationalist orientation, did not cause the crisis in biblical authority, for the Renaissance inheritance of an immanent Christian humanism, derived from Nicholas of Cusa and extended by Ficino, More, and Erasmus, did as much to undermine tradition. Christ's humanity becomes the criterion for uniting the temporal with the divine, a unification that occurs *within* the worldly arena, not in some exclusive transcendent realm. This Christian humanism profoundly influenced later developments in cosmology, science, and history. Further, Christian humanism modulated into the distinctly Protestant "inner light" hermeneutic that Puritans opposed to papal authority, a hermeneutic that is but a small step from the *lumen naturale* of Spinoza and the Deists, who crowned reason king and wielded its authority against scriptural revelation (Allen 1963, 61).

Yet between Erasmus's humanism and Spinoza's "natural light," conventional typology (or figurative literalism) continued to flourish. Puritans saw their experience in the mirror of the Old Testament and, in the English civil war, pushed the historicity of the types to radical extremes. While Puritan and biblical typology are distinct—Paul Korshin offers the term "applied typology" for nonconventional uses—the sectaries' refusal to separate their history from scripture makes for a fairly literal figuralism. In Hans Frei's succinct explanation: "the divine author of the book is the same as the governor of the history narrated in it" (Frei 1974, 74). Accepting the rough date of 1700, Frei defines as "pre-critical" this insistence on narrative continuity between sacred and contemporary history, or between what he calls the verbal and ostensive components of the Bible.

By 1700, however, the unity of history and narrative, the founding assumption of biblical typology, breaks down under the onslaught of rationalist and empirical criticism. Frei helps explain this "eclipse" by showing how the standard of factuality, which informs the new science, subjects scripture to a foreign code of analysis. Facts, previously associated with the literal dimension of the text only, take priority over the "Word." Sacred and secular history lose narrative equivalence (with dire consequences for a theological view of history). The bearing this rift has on Blake's use of typology should not be underestimated, despite Blake's persistent and often defensive reactions against Enlightenment canons of taste and judgment.

A crucial ingredient of the Enlightenment critique is the superiority of reason as the ultimate criterion of truth. For centuries both reason and faith were accepted as valid modes of argument, yet by the late seventeenth century they clashed: "and the result for the intelligent man of modern times is that faith has been completely defeated by the superior artillery of reason" (Allen 1963, 2). This defeat was not the aim of seventeenth-century Christian rationalists. But such "men of latitude" as John Wilkins and Robert Boyle, who adopted the methods of the new science while professing orthodoxy, did raise doubts about the Bible's authority, which historical scholarship was showing to be riddled with inconsistencies.

The Christian rationalists were pious men who were not out to denigrate the Bible so much as to champion a more "natural" religion in accord with the new science. Yet from this new critical orientation arose philosophers such as Benedict Spinoza and Pierre Bayle, who developed a nascent historical criticism of the Bible. Bayle's *Historical and Critical Dictionary* (1697) performed one of the most damaging cuts in the fabric of sacred and secular history and supplied, according to Ernst Cassirer, "the real arsenal of all Enlightenment philosophy." Bayle argues that religion could be defended only on philosophical grounds, the "criteria of moral reason" (Cassirer 1955, 173). Yet Bayle, brandishing his sword in both directions, also attacked the a priori position of the rationalists, arguing that knowledge must be based on facts as they could be adduced from observation. Because of Bayle's insistence on "the pure concept of the factual" as an historical category, Cassirer regards him as "the originator of the ideal of historical accuracy," although he admits that facts themselves are the aim and end of Bayle's historiography (Cassirer 1955, 206).

As developed by English Deists such as John Toland and Anthony Collins, however, the insistence on historical factuality did undermine the figurative unity of the Bible. By demonstrating the existence of a purely secular history, the Deists altered the terms of the debate on scriptural truth. The towering presence of John Locke looms behind these developments. Yet it is not simply Locke's empirical method that bodes ill for typology, but his theory of language, which posits the elementary assumption that a proposition can have only one meaning, not two or more as the figuralists claim. Although the prudent Locke denied kinship with the irreverent Toland, who claimed he was Locke's disciple, Locke gave sanction for rejecting typology or prefiguration as a "crude anthropomorphism" because it did not adhere to what Hans Frei calls the "regular and intelligible rules of the natural use of language and thought."[8] Anthony Collins applied Lockean notions in his analysis of typology and short-circuited the literal and figurative unity between events; for an event or statement with two or more meanings simply breaks the linguistic rule that words refer to "the Operations of sensible Things." Collins writes:

> To suppose, that an author has but one meaning at a time to a proposition (which is to be found out by critical examination of his words), and to cite that proposition from him, and argue from it in that one meaning, is to proceed by the common rules of grammar and logic; which being human rules, are not very difficult to be set forth and explain'd. But to suppose passages cited, explain'd and argue'd from in any other method, seems very extraordinary and difficult to understand, and to reduce to *rules*. (Collins 1724, 51)

The ground has shifted beneath the typologists: an exegetical argument about the narrative meaning of events has become a philosophical argument about the "fact-claims" allegedly made in those narratives. A logical distinction abstracts the story from the reality it depicts, a distinction fatal to the figurative literalism of conventional as well as of Puritan typology.

III

In response to this challenge by historical critics, biblical apologists offered two fundamentally distinct arguments: first, that the Bible's ostensive reference (its history) *is* accurate and factual; second, that the Bible is only partially historical. This paradox of an event being *partially* historical drove the rational apologists to defend the Bible on factual grounds, where they played into the hands of Deists, freethinkers, and skeptics. The other group, nonplussed by such a paradox, shifted the terms of the debate once more, this time from empirical to cultural or mythological criteria of history.

Christian apologists who adopted empirical methods not only weakened their position, argues Peter Gay, but provided fodder for their enemies.[9] Leslie Stephen remarks that reasoning theists struck at tenets that they themselves held sacred. Hans Frei claims that apologists hurt their own cause by insisting that the Bible offered reliable history: they were too "akin to the mindset of their opponents, and all the more the latter's prey." Indeed, Coleridge saw that by embracing the principle of factuality, the apologists became their own betrayers: "the whole Bible," he says, looking back in 1832, "had been surrendered to the ridicule of its enemies."[10] With such apologists of the Bible, Blake's paranoia may seem more justified. Perhaps we can gauge the importance Blake attached to the Bacon-Newton-Locke triad when viewed within the eighteenth-century debate on typological history.[11]

Those apologists who defended the Bible on mythological rather than strictly empirical grounds proved more resilient against the opposition. Two basic factions deserve scrutiny in regard to Blake. One group consists of the "analogists" and antiquarians like William Stukeley and Jacob Bryant, to whom Blake professed kinship in his description of a lost painting, *The Ancient Britons.* The other group, known as the German "higher critics," anticipates Blake's own heterodox version of typology. J. G. Herder, an admirer of Bishop Robert Lowth, seems closely akin to Blake, especially in his interest in universal history and his opposition to Enlightenment rationalism. As G. H. Lewes states, "Herder had something of the Hebrew prophet in him, but the

Hebrew prophet fallen on deistical times" (quoted in Shaffer 1975, 32). These groups modify biblical typology in a secular direction and ease the pressure exerted by rational criticism on prefigurative language. Paul Korshin defines the change in terms of what he calls "abstracted typology": "typology abstracted from its traditional context but retaining some of its foreshadowing quality" (Korshin 1982, chapter five). The spirit of rationalism had won an important battle, but not necessarily the war, as Korshin suggests in his discussion of Anthony Collins:

> Collins had spotted the weakness in much typological argument—its proneness to imaginative connections without any evidentiary foundations for them. . . . The effect of his position, and of the Deist-inspired controversy, leads to a new movement to find the rational bases for typology. (Korshin 1982, 116)

This new movement is fueled by analogists and speculative mythologists who, ironically, adopt the methodology of the historical critics to enlarge, not reduce, the scope of typology.

Where Bayle could enlist the new travel and anthropological literature from Africa, Asia, and the New World against the distortions of ecclesiastical tradition, mythologues such as Stukeley and Bryant turned this method to their favor, expanding the range of biblical typology into universal history. As Bishop Lowth argued, the emergence of primitivism and orientalism changed the terms of the debate, because the Bible could now be favorably compared to other cultures. Rather than adversely judged by the canons of modern rationality, the Bible was praised for its bardic sensibility. A new appreciation of the historical bases of myth helped overrule deist objections to the irrationality of biblical history. Even so, while antiquarians in the Renaissance had reexamined the relations between pagan myth and Christianity, by the mid-eighteenth century a secular historiography had developed, challenging writers like Bryant not only to locate but to prove that biblical "types" inhabited the primitive history of non-Christian nations.

Bryant's *A New System: or an Analysis of Antient Mythology* (1774–78) offers a curious mix of antiquarianism, historical criticism, and figuralism. While rummaging among the linguistic arcana of ancient history, he links pagan and biblical myth through his analysis of the Flood—the founding event in his system—which lies scattered in the myths and languages of the distant past. To retrieve these myths, Bryant wields the tools of the new critical philology: he adopts the critical apparatus of the historians in defense of the Bible's primordial visionary history. Although Bryant's system is largely discredited by Blake's time, it fuels the mythopoeic imagination of Romantic poets and appeals to the antiquarian in Blake, who not only engraved an illustration of Bryant's Flood as a young man, but placed the "flood" at the center of the *Four Zoas* narrative. Indeed, Bryant's reduction of ancient history to biblical analogues is worked out in a language that makes Blake's obscurities look tame. Ultimately, what Blake finds most handy in Bryant's system is his methodological versatility, his two-way analogizing, which traces prefigurative structures from pagan types to biblical antitypes and vice versa, wherever the evidence (or spirit) leads.

In *The Ancient Britons,* Blake publicly champions Bryant's system against the "reasoning historian," affiliating it with his own visionary historiography. Indeed, Blake cherished his own poetry as "of the highest antiquity" and drew on Bryant's euhemerist assumption that "there was always covert meaning" in Egyptian, Greek, and Phoenician myths as a source for his own "mythological and recondite meaning" (Erdman 1982, 542). Bryant's assumption that myth is coded history connects antiquarian typology with the interpretive method of the higher critics. However, what distinguishes the higher critics (and Blake) from antiquarians like Bryant is the importance they attach to the interpreter's central role in situating past and present within the stream of universal history.

IV

The starting point of the higher criticism consists in sustaining a critical emphasis on historicity, on the realism of events, while introducing a crucial subjective element into the interpretive act. Advancing beyond the tactics of figurative literalism, the higher critics avoid reducing history to the empirical by raising the fact-claim of an event into the higher category of *understanding*.[12] This subjective process, however, requires the complementary act of reconstructing the event within its specific socio-cultural context, an act that Herder perfects in his concept of *Einfühlung*, which denotes the interpreter's emphatic submersion in the "life-spirit" of a culture's past. Herder proclaims that "you must enter the spirit of a nation before you can share even one of its thoughts or deeds," a proclamation that underlies the higher critical approach to history:

In order to feel the whole nature of the soul which reigns in everything, which models after itself all other tendencies and all other spiritual faculties, and colors even the most trivial actions, do not limit
your response to a word, but penetrate deeply into this century, this
region, this entire history, plunge yourself into it all and feel it all
inside yourself—then only will you be in a position to understand.[13]
(Herder 1969, 182)

This passage seems to parallel the historicism of conventional
typology. Hans Frei, however, counters that *Einfühlung* does not
restore the narrative identity between event and figure, but replaces this identity with the still referential development of the
past age's spirit or mythic consciousness. The ground has shifted
too deeply to facilitate a return to the Puritan faith in an unrup-
tured divine history—i.e., a "pre-critical" figuralism.

But the higher critics, in response to this shift, pivot from empirical to intellectual history, a move that favors an apology of the
Bible. Elinor Shaffer connects this reoriented hermeneutics to the
rise of Romanticism, claiming that both rely on the historian-
interpreter's imaginative "capacity to recreate . . . the experience"
of the past, or of what Herder deems the *volk*. Corroborating her
claim, and extending Herder's historicism, J. A. Ernesti's *Institutio
Interpretis* (1761) combines the "Romantic techniques of empathy
and recreation" with the empiricism of historical critics. Ernesti
writes:

He who desires to understand and interpret the books of the New
Testament, must, *first of all*, acquire some historical knowledge of the
author of each book; of the state of things existing when it was written
. . . of the particular history of its ancient versions . . . and other things
of this nature. (Ernesti 1827, 18)

These rather demanding philological qualifications nonetheless
make art "*the* instrument whereby empirical history is possible,"
for "only art can hold out the hope" that the past can be reenacted
in the historian's mind (Shaffer 1975, 86 quoting Ernesti's *Institutio*). A cross between an emergent secular historicism and a bud-
ding idealist philosophy produces the mythologized history of the
higher critics, who operate on the novel assumption that human
nature is *not* everywhere the same, that uniformity of culture and
religion is contradicted by the minute particulars of each nation's
folk spirit.[14]

While Blake expressed a similar antipathy toward Enlightenment uniformity, he resembles his German contemporaries most
nearly on the fact-claim issue. While the German idealists (and

Coleridge) had difficulty reconciling the rationalist and spiritual strands of their project, they (with Blake) intended to salvage revealed religion by deploying the new method of historicism: that is, reconstructing the past era from its own materials and reinhabiting its life-spirit.

Blake's place in the development of what Shaffer calls "a new form of history" has been largely ignored, mainly because of such pronouncements as the following:

> The reasoning historian, turner and twister of causes and consequences, such as Hume, Gibbon, and Voltaire: cannot with all their artifice, turn or twist one fact or disarrange self evident action and reality. . . . Acts alone are history. . . . His opinions, who does not see spiritual agency, is not worth any man's reading; he who rejects a fact because it is improbable, must reject all History and retain doubts only. (Erdman 1982, 543–44)

In the context of the debate under discussion, this passage indicates Blake's concern to find an inclusive place for history in his myth. He focuses on defining the "nature" of a historical event, a focus transferred to *The Four Zoas* as the thematic contention between faith and demonstration. Blake bases his method on "the evidence of things unseen" (Hebrews 11 : 1), or on what he calls self-evidence: "The man who pretends to be a modest enquirer after truth of a self-evident thing is a knave," he writes in the margins of Bishop Watson's *Apology*. "The truth & certainty of . . . Inspiration needs no one to prove it" (Erdman 1982, 613–14). According to Blake, the rationalist obsession with demonstrative evidence distorts the spiritual basis of typological meaning, and the apologists who follow such a method are "state tricksters" out to defend the established Church against the "Everlasting Gospel."

Blake's visionary historicism derives from his conception of a postbiblical stream of history where events repeat by a kind of providential compulsion. This conception, sanctioned by John's warning in Revelation—"seal not the words of this book"—is indebted also to the Enlightenment expansion of European history into world history, which preserves typological thinking as it alters its traditional orientation. Where Puritans and antiquarians privilege the Bible as *the* sacred book, Blake and the higher critics place the Bible within a temporal frame that includes "oriental" religions in general. The claim of the Bible to be the "origin and pattern of religious civilization," argues Shaffer, "was reduced to a moral and finally to a symbolic claim only" (Shaffer 1975, 56). This expanded view of sacred history changes the nature of historical repetition as well: for those writers who treat the Bible as "oriental" religion draw attention away from its alleged fact-claims and replace the criterion of accuracy with one of cultural influence. What repeats, then, is more than the event: the entire cultural milieu, the social context of the mythology (as both Herder and Ernesti proclaim), must be reenacted in the mind of the poetic historian.

Significantly, though, an emphasis on historical actuality remains crucial to Blake, his Romantic compatriots, and the German higher critics. Coleridge, the self-anointed conduit of the higher criticism in England, is more literal on this point than Blake, as he recalls Milton's strictures against tampering with the "truth" of holy writ. But as with Blake, Coleridge examines empirical history through the lens of imagination, so that an "extraordinary but typically romantic conjunction begins to emerge: primal historical fact can only be known through visionary eyes" (Shaffer 1975, 81). This Romantic validation of the historian as seer derives, in part, from early Christian experience of the Word as *kerygmatic* event. The urgent faith and vision of the apostles could, theoretically, be repeated or reawakened in contemporary readers. But as apocalyptic expectation wanes, such faith requires an imaginative leap into the past, a leap supremely enacted by the prophetic Romantic poet. Art or poetry becomes the model of historical reconstruction. With its "reader-oriented" affective aesthetic, prophetic poetry does not retell or simply chronicle historical events, but narrates them to induce a response. The response, of course, entails that readers understand not only the empirical details of the past age, but the past's contemporary significance. The fact-claim of the narrated event then is transposed by the higher critic into a spiritual-claim whose rhetorical power in moving the reader becomes more important than the event's factuality.

In effect, typological repetition neutralizes chronology and abandons causal links between events in favor of repeated type scenes. More radically than his contemporaries, Blake deploys nonsequential narrative strategies in order to suggest, or induce, the disruptive experience of visionary simultaneity. Yet we must see Blake in context: he is not a freak pursuing eccentric ideas in a cultural vacuum. Coleridge and Wordsworth also seek to transform history into "spots of time" that symbolize and absorb its *telos*. However, not even Romantic prophets can do away with a simulacrum of sequence: both Blake and Coleridge transform their narratives into a "visionary" series of epiphanic moments based on the logic of dramatic repetition. In *Kubla Khan* Coleridge links Jewish, pagan, and Christian religions by merging the holy cities of Jerusalem, Babylon, and Rome into the sacred city of Xanadu, a syncretism effected by the work of repetition and simultaneity rather than sequence. Blake develops his own peculiar mix of prophecy and antiquarianism, or what Michael Ferber describes as "left antiquarianism" (Ferber 1985, 49–52). His use of repetitive structures, however, bears relation to the narrative experiments of the English Romantics, who draw on the pathbreaking biblical criticism of the German higher critics.

V

Blake, at least in *The Four Zoas,* seriously attempts to redeem history by preserving rather than negating it. His mode of history is unashamedly symbolic; but the historicity of his narrative is inherent in the collective or intersubjective nature of his project. Blake shares this communal focus with such prophets as the thirteenth-century abbot, Joachim of Fiore, who also attempts to parallel individual and universal history.[15] Blake's goal, like Joachim's, is to coax and persuade readers to place the individual present within a revised collective past, a goal he personalizes in his hero, Albion, whose "anatomy" symbolically contains all individuals. Albion, the antiquarian giant, is asleep but would awaken if he (his members) would connect individual experience with the larger experience of the *volk* or nation. Peter Fisher comments pointedly:

> Universal history becomes the analogy of individual biography, and goes through the same phases until, at last, the . . . separate experiences which form the events of history become one common human experience in the vision of the Giant Albion. (Fisher 1961, 23)

The individual, then, achieves spiritual integration by linking personal and cultural histories and, after critical engagement with those histories, by sharing the "one common human experience" available to all. Blake thus reconstitutes the Albionic frame of history by turning individual conversion, the *intellectus spiritualis,* into a type or promise of collective conversion. Los's personal experience, while central, ultimately is not enough to effect a "Last Judgment," as events following the two Nights VII demonstrate. Los must await the ripening of the historical process guided by the "Hand" of an artistically-ordered providence that works through the zoas and emanations, Blake's spiritual agents of history.

Blake's peculiar brand of typological history challenges readers to understand their lives in public terms, and he embeds this challenge in narrative strategies meant to rouse the mental faculties into committed interpretation. *Commitment* is a key term and approximates the New Testament *kerygma*. This concept insures that history begins "in the middest," in the present, and that it retains a fundamentally ethical or edifying purpose: "Typology does not exist for the sake of interpreting the past. . . . . Rather, it is the past's meaning 'for us'" (Charity 1966, 98). Blake's "abstracted" typological narratives bring readers to the point of decision, forcing them to work through personal and historical crises by embodying those crisis in *narrative* events that repeat in order to be transformed. Poets and their readers must interpret these events as repetitions, of course, to transform them, and this act depends not only on the reader's immersion in the past, as Ernesti and Herder counsel, but on an analysis of contemporary history informed by a social hermeneutic.

This social focus can break the impasse that appears when individuals, such as demoralized Romantic prophets, ascribe a vicious circularity to history. In a cogent critique of Northrop Frye's modern adaptation of typology, Fredric Jameson argues that Frye distorts the biblical hermeneutic by collapsing the fourth or anagogic level of meaning into the third or moral level, which is concerned with individual experience and which Frye identifies with Blake's Albion, whom he considers the singular "body" of Man.

> The essentially historical interpretive system of the church fathers has here been recontained and its political elements turned back into the merest figures for Utopian realities of the individual subject. A social hermeneutic will, on the contrary, wish to keep faith with its medieval precursor in just this respect, and must necessarily restore a perspective in which . . . bodily transfiguration once again becomes a figure for the perfected community. The unity of the body must once again prefigure the renewed organic identity of associative or collective life, rather than, as for Frye, the reverse. (Jameson 1981, 74)

Blake keeps the collective faith, at least in *The Four Zoas*, where the narrative histories of the individual zoas and emanations merge, and Albion, collective humanity, regains his "ancient" liberty, Jerusalem.

Of course, without the reader's engagement in this process, Albionic "Man" cannot be actualized outside the text, a fact that keeps Blake's syncretistic vision from swallowing difference into unity. Blake places a burden on his readers that tests the limits of readability; for identity is no mere metaphysical assumption: individual identity is a relational concept in Blake. He requires an intersubjective response to his prophetic activity, for without it the private and public dimensions of time remain polarized, nullifying the special bond between ethics and history. While this ethical component may distort the brute contingency of the historical process, especially as secular historians conceive it, Blake contains history within an eschatological framework in order to subject it to human transformation. Blake in effect crosses the providential design of the Christian apologists with the secular historicism of Herder. The politically radical potential of this mixture is revealed by the millenarians of the 1790s, whose goal for history Blake shares even if he opposes their means of attaining it.[16]

Blake's unique place within the Christian hermeneutic tradition broadens this tradition's conceptual field while it illuminates his own narrative practice. Blake does not seek to bind his readers to a specific doctrinal or religious project, but rather attempts to inculcate the visionary habit of mind that can enable them to *refigure* their ways of seeing and being. If he must forgo figurative literalism because of the powerful Enlightenment critique of typological reasoning, Blake preserves the historicist kernal of figuralism even against his self-conscious fictionalizing of the Apocalypse. I believe that Blake retains a sense of democratic purpose, of revolutionary change, despite apocalyptic disconfirmations. In this he resembles his prophetic precursor, Milton, and his contemporary Joseph Priestley, who acknowledged that his millennial computations were wrong: "The greatest of all events is not less certain for being delayed beyond our expectations" Priestley said in 1804.[17] But Blake knew that the Apocalypse could not be empirically confirmed nor discredited, but only collectively affirmed; and if this affirmation is incumbent on the expanded vision of the individual prophet, it cannot be reduced to him. "Would to God that all the Lord's people were prophets" is not the hope of Moses alone, but of all genuinely prophetic poets.

5

Repetition and Simultaneity: Typological History in *The Four Zoas* Nights I–VIIa

For the Methode of a Poet historical is not such, as of an Historiographer. For an Historiographer discourseth of affayres orderly as they were done, accounting as well the times as the actions, but a Poet thrusteth into the middest, even where it most concerneth him, and there recoursing to the things forepaste, and divining of things to come, maketh a pleasing Analysis of all.

—Edmund Spenser

As we are stuck with chronology in living out clock-time, so are we with linearity in reading the text. Although he does communicate it, Blake cannot achieve simultaneity within the text. This apprehension must occur within the mind of the reader.

—Karleen Middleton Murphy

BLAKE situates the social and cultural changes afflicting eighteenth-century Europe within the larger span of Judeo-Christian and ancient history, a move so sweeping that it provokes charges of obscurity and incoherence. Yet as the last chapter argued, Blake's figurative project does not annul a secular practice and understanding of history. It responds with a "universal" plan: one that replays ancient "events" in the contemporary moment to activate the present meaning of the past. For Blake, historical events lie partly within the poet's mind; but they must be put into a shared form and re-enacted within the present if readers are to convert to a prophetic view of history that transforms the world.

At least conversion and transformation remain part of Blake's prophetic heritage. In this chapter I examine Blake's use of typo-

logical strategy in *The Four Zoas,* by which Blake seeks to induce
in readers an imaginative response to, and an active engagement
with, history.[1] This strategy aims at a paradoxical simultaneity of
reference that expands while it sustains the anticipatory pattern
of traditional typology. While Blake's poetic history is contami-
nated by figurality, as Paul de Man might say, its typological code
retains a referential function. This code, built on repetitive allusion and symbolism, creates an allegory of history that not only
stages a return to key cultural scenes and sources, but problematizes that return by mixing competing versions of those
sources. Blake's narrative history thus requires active interpretation: once readers grasp their participatory relation to that history, they can exit the textual workshop to spread the gospel of
transformation among their contemporaries.

Although Blake's figural excesses threaten to undermine his use
of typological structures—Korshin notices that Blake "is fond of
uniting type and antitype in the same text" (Korshin 1982, 311)—
a prefigurative pattern can, with accuracy, be discerned and
traced in the poem. Allowing for a margin of error in tracing
patterns of coherence in so disruptive a text, and without valoriz-
ing the typological at the expense of the other modes—tragic or
comic, pastoral or satiric—I offer the following overview: In Night
I, Blake reenacts the division of the Israelite monarchy in the
story of Luvah and Urizen, as told by the Demons in the Nuptial
Song and in the Messengers' version of the Fall; in Night II, he
relates the biblical Creation to Near Eastern fertility myths; in
Nights III–IV, he examines the Flood, stemming from Urizen's
expulsion of Ahania in Night III, which alludes to the Atlantis
deluge and to biblical history from Noah to the rise of prophecy
in Israel; in Nights V–VI, he explores the historical struggle between Law and Prophecy, which archetypal critics call the "Orc
Cycle"; in Night VIIa, Blake replays the Genesis temptation scene,
with the Tree of Mystery doubling as a cross for Orc's crucifixion,
which leads to Los's redemptive embrace of his Spectre and Emanation.

Night I

The Nuptial Song sung by the Demons attending Los and
Enitharmon's wedding feast (14:6–16:12) typifies the way Blake
conflates biblical and contemporary history. Beginning "Ephraim called out to Zion: Awake O Brother Mountain," the

Song encloses us in the geography of the Old Testament while establishing its contemporary context through imagery of labor, farming, cities, and palaces ruined in war. The allusions are ambiguous enough to point both ways: mills, barns, and palaces appear in both ancient Israel and modern Europe. Of particular relevance is the imagery of blood and battle, which David Erdman traces to the Napoleonic Wars: he identifies historical particulars in the Urizen-Luvah strife in terms of Nelson's defeat of Napoleon in the Mediterranean in 1798–99. While Blake's allusions need not be as specific as the Battle of the Nile in 1798, the Britain-France war undoubtedly informs the meaning of the Urizen-Luvah strife. The triumph celebrated in the Song, "explicitly that of Urizen over Luvah," or Britain over France, is credible in general terms. But since Blake's mills, palaces, and children nourished for slaughter refer both ways, to ancient and contemporary contexts, it will be best to supplement Erdman's approach not only with Frye's archetypal insights, but also with the social history of Old Testament culture excavated by Jackie DiSalvo.[2]

In the Messengers' version of the "Fall" that concludes Night I, Blake deftly blends allusions to biblical and contemporary European culture. Erdman finds military history in their version, but DiSalvo more usefully identifies the inception and division of the Israelite monarchy, which spans roughly from 1200 to 900 B.C. (DiSalvo 1983, 195). Earlier I sifted the Messengers' story for its Miltonic echoes; Urizen's departure to the "North" suggested a cosmological meaning (Lucifer-Urizen's conspiracy triggers the war that leads to the creation). Milton enables us to connect the cosmic war to Israel's division into northern and southern kingdoms; indeed, since Blake analogizes Israel's division with the division between Britain and its southern neighbor turned enemy, France, we get some sense of the method and range of Blake's poetic history.

Such multiple perspectives underlie Blake's strategy for approximating simultaneity in his narrative. When Urizen conspires with Luvah to sack Jerusalem and seize control of the kingdom, the meanings of *Jerusalem* begin to proliferate. Jerusalem represents not only the biblical Jerusalem of 1000 B.C. and, perhaps, 70 A.D., but also the contemporary eighteenth-century "heavenly city" to be built among England's dark satanic mills. The Messengers further report the destruction of these Jerusalems in the phrase "Shiloh is in ruins" (21:9). At Shiloh, Hebrew priests housed the Ark of the Covenant, until it was overthrown by the Philistines early in Israelite history, an event that led to the formation of the united monarchy. Erdman, for his part, interprets Shiloh as France's "tabernacle of Liberty," which he equates with Judah or the southern kingdom, and Jerusalem as the tabernacle or seat of British liberty in the north, both now in ruins. He concludes that the Messengers' speech (they are named, significantly for him, the "Ambassadors") is a "spiritual digest" of the failed peace negotiations of 1796–97 (Erdman 1969, 309). Again, the precise dating seems out of character with Blake's symbolic practice. But that the Messengers allude to eighteenth-century British-French relations by declaring that tyrants rule in the north and the south, and that the people therefore are left in a "fierce and hungring void," bears importantly on Blake's meaning.

Night II

With Urizen's construction of the Mundane Shell, however, Blake exhibits even more clearly his manipulation of typological history. In the first place, Night II retains traces of its initial function as the opening to *Vala*, dovetailing nicely with both the Messengers's creation-fall story and the Old Testament history that informs the conclusion of Night I. Albion abdicates his kingdom and symbolically links the divisions of his cosmos, his mind, and his political power under one narrative "event," a move that Blake effects by juxtaposing allusions to ancient Near Eastern and contemporary politics. That Lucifer's (Albion's) war or cosmic division foreshadows all subsequent wars Blake suggests through reference to Nimrod in the passage on the building of the Mundane Shell (25:32). Blake draws on *Paradise Lost:* Nimrod's rise to power is associated with Satan's war in heaven and ancient Israel's collapsing tribal unity. Milton's narrator tells us that after the Flood mankind shall dwell in peace for many years:

> till one shall rise
> Of proud ambitious heart, who not content
> With fair equality, fraternal state,
> Will arrogate Dominion undeserved
> Over his brethren. . . .
> A mighty Hunter thence he shall be styl'd
> Before the Lord, as in despite of Heav'n
> Or from Heav'n claiming second Sovranty.
>
> (XII: 23–24)

Because Nimrod functions as a Satanic type, "from Heav'n claiming second Sovranty," both Milton and Blake clearly link the war in heaven with political discord on earth—especially with the breakup of tribal culture and the onset of imperial monarchy in Israel. But while Milton clarifies the Old Testament allusion, Erdman sees in Nimrod's imperial aggression a modern reference, particularly in Nimrod's hounds (which he takes as a type of "King George's armies") and in the "ill-fated tower of Babel," which prefigures a similar "fate of discord and collapse for an unrepentant British empire" (Erdman 1969, 322). By conflating references to past and present figures and events, Blake demands that readers expand their historical horizons and engage in the making of history.

The second episode, the construction of the Mundane Shell (24:8–32:15), falls into three sections that comprise the historical strands Blake sews into the narrative. These sections include allusions to Druid myth, to Israel's sojourn in Canaan following its escape from Egypt, and to the building of Solomon's temple—all juxtaposed to eighteenth-century British history.

Druidism had been romanticized by Blake's time, primarily through the influence of William Stukeley, who, out of patriotic and antiquarian zeal, connected the Druids with the biblical patriarchs and both to a more ancient "British" religion.[3] Blake's narrator speaks of "Jerusalem's Children in the dungeons of Babylon," where they "play before the Armies before the hounds of Nimrod / While the Prince of Light" stands "on Salisbury plain among the druid stones" (25:31–33). Within the compression chamber of Blake's prophetic workshop, Urizen can occupy battlefields in both England and Babylon. The latter signifies the archetypal locus of war and oppression, although as Francis Wilford postulated (on what turned out to be forged evidence), Britain was the original seat of biblical history.[4] The point, however, is that the reader must discern an ancient pattern in the present situation.

> Groans run along Tyburns brook and along the River of Oxford
> Among the Druid Temples. Albion groand on Tyburns brook
> Albion gave his loud death groan The Atlantic Mountains trembled
> Aloft the moon fled with a cry the Sun with streams of blood
> From Albion's Loins fled all Peoples and Nations of the Earth
> Fled with the noise of Slaughter & the stars of heaven fled
> Jerusalem came down in a dire ruin over all the Earth
> She fell cold from Lambeths vales in groans & Dewy death
> The dew of anxious souls the death-sweat of the dying
> In every pillard hall & arched roof of Albions skies

The brother & the brother bathe in blood upon the Severn
The Maiden weeping by.

(25:7–18)

Adopting the tone and imagery of Revelation, Blake connects the "abominations" of Druid history with the desolating wars fought along the Rhine and the Severn in the late eighteenth century. Blake augments his typological equation of Druid, biblical, and British history with the imagery of industrial slavery that ties the brick kilns of ancient Babylon and Egypt to the sweatshops of the modern Babylon, England in the late eighteenth century. In Erdman's pungent phrase, "British commerce accompanied by the British sword is spreading Druid slaughter" (Erdman 1969, 330).

Jerusalem functions as Blake's archetype of liberty enslaved; but true to the historical base of his figurative system, the archetype must be situated within a particular milieu to activate interpretation.[5] Thus when Blake's narrator tells us that Jerusalem has fallen in ruins, he associates Israel's bondage in Egypt and Babylon with the industrial worker's exploitation in England. This association carries further resonance in Britain and Israel's divided monarchies; that is, in each monarchy's oppression of its people. Blake pursues this typology of oppression in the episode of Luvah and Vala sealed in the "furnaces of affliction" (25:40).

In terms of ancient history, Luvah's bondage recalls the practices of those natural religions of the ancient Near East that posed a threat to Israelite religion. Luvah appears as a dying god and Vala as his female counterpart or goddess, and together they promote fertility of land and of human sexuality. But their fertility rituals require blood-letting and suffering, natural and human sacrifice. Blake regards such sacrifice as the "Keynote of Druidism" and deplores the conjunction of sex and suffering in debasing human potential before an inhuman god, a conjunction he identifies with natural religion (Damon 1979, 109). He further associates the fertility cult with the historical alliance of priest and king, symbolized by Vala tantalizing Luvah, which enables Urizen to channel Luvah's passions in the service of war. In depicting Vala's evolution, which Harold Bloom calls "a natural history of natural religion" (Erdman 1982, 952), Blake's narrator traces her development from an earthworm to a jealous serpent of sexual love to a dragon of illusory nature, an all-powerful force that consumes both Luvah and Vala, reducing them to infants easily subdued by Urizen's priests. The natural power of Vala, in other words, is negated and then subsumed by the "restrictive morality of the Jehovah priestcraft" (Erdman 1982, 953). In short, Israel-England's (Albion's) sexual energy and labor power are usurped by the moral elite for purposes of profit, war, and social control. The final section of the Mundane Shell episode, the building of the Temple, throws these contradictions into sharp relief.

The Temple-building passage (30:8—32:15) ranges over Old Testament history from the rise of monarchy to Solomon's reign, roughly the period from 1200 to 900 B.C. During this period, when kings replaced judges as Israel's leaders, Hebrew assimilation of Canaanite culture became an acute problem. It was complicated by the threat of invasion from the Philistines, an Aegean people who settled on the coast of Palestine. In the middle of the eleventh century B.C. the Philistines stormed the hills of Ephraim, captured the Ark of the Covenant, and destroyed the city of Shiloh, fracturing Israel's tribal identity. In reaction, the Israelites elevated such warriors as Samuel, Saul, and David to kings; Samuel in particular played a central role in the transition from tribal confederation to united monarchy, although he opposed kingship on the Canaanite model (Albright 1963, 42). "The Philistine threat," writes biblical scholar P. J. Parr, "was probably the decisive factor in the emergence of a permanent political (but at first military) union of all Israel under a king—what historians call the united monarchy (or kingdom)" (Parr 1975, 896). Ironically, however, this transition signaled a "Canaanization" of Israel. For now a ruling monarchial elite, in imitation of its "pagan" neighbors, would assert a monopoly on the performance of religious rituals, a monopoly that reaches its culmination in the construction of Solomon's temple (DiSalvo 1983, 195–99). As Albright explains, the temple was not intended to be a place of public worship, but rather to be a royal chapel into which the palladium of Israel was brought "as a sign that the worship of Yahweh was thereafter to be under the special protection of the king" (Albright 1957, 193–94). As the temple was built next to the king's palace, it made explicit "the alliance between Yahwistic priesthood and the sacral kingship of the House of David, an alliance that to Blake's mind could only be ominous" (Sandler 1972, 38–39). Blake calls this ominous alliance "State Religion" and traces its etiology from Solomon's reign, back to Urizen the priest-king's creation of the universe, and forward to the Anglican state church.

That Solomon historicizes Urizen's mythological activity becomes clear when we consider his reputation for both wisdom and exploitation. Urizen is the zoa whose consort, Ahania, derives from the "Wisdom" figure of Solomon's Proverbs, especially proverb eight, where she dwells with the Lord "when he set a compass upon the face of the deep" (Proverbs 8:27), an allusion that recalls Blake's drawing of a Urizenic God on the frontispiece to *Europe a Prophecy* (1794). More importantly, though, Blake's narrator alludes to Solomon's temple when describing the construction of the "golden Altar" and the sacrifice of Albion's sons and daughters in the interests of war and commerce. Under Solomon's reign Israel established its first powerful standing army (I Kings 9:15–19) and built an elaborate copper refinery to supply parts for the chariots; further, Solomon's extensive and costly building operations and huge military establishment were financed, in part, by his elaborate mercantile and industrial enterprises, "such as caravan trade in the desert and naval expeditions in the Red Sea and the Mediterranean, and copper mining and refining in the Arabach" (Albright 1957, 291). Erdman's references to Admiral Nelson's Mediterranean campaigns are apt, particularly when these campaigns are seen as George III's (another debased archetype) attempt to centralize authority in the British monarchy and to neutralize dissent through patriotic appeals to "God and King," to state religion.

The "golden Altar" passage, however, focuses on England's exploited workers, a point that foregrounds Blake's narrative strategies of juxtaposition and repetition. "Severe the labor," the narrator reports, "female slaves the mortar trod oppressed / Of Terrible workmanship the Altar labour of ten thousand Slaves / One thousand Men of wondrous power spent their lives in its formation" (30:12–14, 39–41). Blake here seeks his contemporary reader's response: Solomon's use of enforced labor in the construction of his temple both anticipates and occurs simultaneously with the industrial buildup of Hanoverian England.

And Vala like a shadow oft appeard to Urizen
The King of Light beheld her mourning among the brick kilns
    compelld
To labor night & day among the fires, her lamenting voice
Is heard when night returns & the labourers take their rest

O Lord wilt thou not look upon our sore afflictions
Among these flames incessant labouring, our hard masters laugh
At all our sorrow. We are made to turn the wheel for water
To carry the heavy basket on our scorched shoulders, to sift
The sand & ashes, & to mix the clay with tears & repentance
                                                (30:56–31:10)

Erdman reads in this passage the sorrows of the most destitute laborers, the brickmakers, both male and female, endlessly laboring "among the brick kilns" that ring the outskirts of London in the late eighteenth century (Erdman 1969, 338). More suggestively, perhaps, Blake renders labor in the service of war in terms of the sacrificial rites common to ancient fertility religions, which make nature (Vala) Urizen's harlot and which build a temple of "secret lust" controlled by the state-supported priesthood. In effect, British workers, kept ignorant of the "secret" purpose of the goods they produce and "the immense machines they build and operate" (Erdman 1969, 338), are subjected to a dual mystification. They are deceived not only about the purposes of their labor (their human sacrifice) but about their sexuality. They are cheated of gratification by Urizen's morality, which instills repression in the name of God and King and rules by the double power of moral guilt and political force. Perhaps not expecting his readers to identify the precise historical equivalents, Blake urges them (and us) to connect Urizen's temple building to "types" in Old Testament and contemporary social history.

Nights III–IV

The historical force that disrupts *The Four Zoas* is allegorized as the tension generated by Urizen and Luvah, the mythic agents whose archetypal struggle is anchored in the temporal field of the narrative. The middle section of the poem clarifies this struggle, which occupied Blake in the Lambeth prophecies (1793–95). By tracing Orc's (the fallen Luvah) genealogy to Los, the "eternal Prophet," particularly in the context of the Old Testament, Blake suggests that Orc's revolutionary wrath is an outgrowth of prophecy: especially of Los's prophetic impatience with the priest-king alliance forged in the interest of a "united kingdom." Blake depicts Urizen's kingdom as a usurpation of a more ancient alliance, portrayed by the figure of Tharmas, the "parent power," from whom Los traces *his* lineage.

The Tharmas-Los-Orc line forms a prophetic opposition to Urizen's assumed power. It also discloses the reason-passion, master-slave antinomies that are Urizen's ideological tools for domination. While Luvah-Orc accommodates the tyrant by accepting his moral categories, Urizen's compulsive need to subjugate his and Luvah's children leads to the collapse of his world. The personal and social misery generated by the Urizen-Orc struggle is registered in Enion's lamentations that resound (in Albion's ears) throughout the poem. This emotional register is recorded not only in the celebrated lament that begins "I am made to sow a thistle for wheat," but in the revelatory line that precedes this lament: "Thus Enion wails from the dark deep, the golden heavens tremble" (34:100). Urizen's world, his "golden heavens," simply cannot be secure with such explosive pain as Enion's at its source. These heavens finally collapse when, in Night III, Ahania unwittingly exposes the contradiction of building a world at the expense of most of its inhabitants.

Blake manipulates chronology and the typological code most clearly in the episode of Tharmas's flood. This archetypal event issues from Ahania's expulsion into Enion's abyss and conflates allusions to the Atlantis deluge, the primal waters of Genesis, and the biblical Flood. Blake's strategy is based on his interpretation of the flood as a "type" of the Atlantis deluge, which, in turn, produces the primal waters from which creation emerges. Once again Blake seals the connection between Creation and Fall. When Urizen hurls Ahania into the abyss, she "falls" until "One like a shadow of smoke appeard" (44:14), one who then speaks to Enion: "Fall off afar from Tharmas come not too near my strong fury. . . . So Tharmas bellowd oer the ocean thundring sobbing bursting / The bounds of Destiny were broken & hatred now began / Instead of love to Enion" (45:6–11). The speech repeats lines from Enion's opening dialogue with Tharmas: the repetition returns us to the chaos of the poem's beginning. However, in a typically paradoxical move, Blake pushes the narrative forward as well. For Tharmas's flood inevitably recalls the biblical deluge— in both a covenant or what Blake calls a "Limit" is established which arrests the "Fall" and anticipates a redemptive turn. Blake approximates Jehovah's rainbow covenant with Israel in the pact that Tharmas and Los make to bind Urizen, eventually giving the "abstract horror" a local habitation. This pact offsets the priest-king alliance that produces the monarchy, and theocratic oppression, symbolized in the labor on Urizen's Solomonic temple.

As he opens Night IV, Blake underpins Los's binding of Urizen with Old Testament history. As Jackie DiSalvo has it, with Tharmas's flood we enter the "dark ages" of the ancient Near Eastern theocratic empires, narrated through the mehanism of the Orc Cycle. Rather too abruptly, however, DiSalvo shifts from the Flood to early Christianity, as she contends that "a waning of concrete historical reference" takes place in Nights IV and V (DiSalvo 1983, 222). But while DiSalvo's shift of emphasis can be supported by allusions in Night IV to the entombed Christ (the Lamb) and to the Lazarus narrative, a more abstracted typological approach enables us to read Old Testament history in the New Testament stories and vice versa. Blake's prophetic narrative strategies foster our ability to walk up and down the halls of time.

The Orc Cycle theory helps us trace the struggle between theocratic rule and prophetic opposition and supplies historical referents for the archetypal Urizen-Orc conflict. When Tharmas and Los ally to bind Urizen, the strife between them occurs largely in cultural and ideological rather than in strictly military terms. Of this struggle in its Old Testament context, Parr writes:

> The prophetic movement apparently was little encouraged by the united monarchy's third king. As son of the harem, Solomon had had little contact with the people of his realm, and he used many of them in labor battalions in his vast building programs. . . . By fostering social discontentment in such ventures, Solomon prepared the way for the disintegration of the united kingdom and the resurgence of the prophetic movement. (Parr 1975, 913)

The temple theocracy draws prophetic fire because it sanctions pagan worship of the king—and of a religious elite—and so enslaves the people. Amos, voice of prophetic indignation, is warned by the high priest Amaziah not to prophesy at Bethel, "for it is the king's chapel, and it is the king's court," to which Amos replies that he speaks there because the Lord commands him (Amos 7:13–17). An argument between Los and Enitharmon at the end of Night II alludes to a similar situation. Enitharmon declares allegiance to Urizen and boasts of her control over history, "the nine bright spheres" that contain the poem's temporal sequence (34:62), but this boast triggers Los's jealous resolve to "seek revenge" on Urizen. In effect, Los realizes that Enitharmon, prophetic "space," has been usurped by the Urizenic priest-king alliance.[6] But his Jehovah-like rage and machinations suggest an important point: the historical emergence of prophecy and prophetic wrath, depicted in the birth of Los's "son" Orc, suggests complicity between prophecy and monarchy, of Los and Urizen, in Israel's "fall" into social division. Blake puts the prophetic mode into question as a hermeneutic challenge to his readers.

Indeed, when Los binds Urizen he takes on those qualities of the priest that he seeks to humanize. He binds Urizen into a "Body of Death" that sets a limit to fallen life, although it is the lowest limit yet reached in the poem—the state that Blake calls "Ulro." The narrator recites the effects of this deadly repetition:

on the one hand, when Los binds Urizen and Enitharmon labors
with the "Terrible Child," the "wheels of turning darkness / Began
in solemn revolutions" (58:7–8). On the other, the narrator says
that in "terrors Los shrunk from his task" and that as he beats
the links of Urizen's chain, "Pale terror siezd the Eyes of Los"
and "he became what he was doing he was himself transformed"
(55:16–23). Neither heat nor light emanate from the organ of
prophecy: "all the furnaces were out & the bellows had ceast to
blow" (57:26–17). At this point another tragic cycle kicks in as the
terrible child of wrath reaches maturity.

Nights V–VI

Blake depicts the resurgence of prophecy in ancient Israel and
modern Europe through Orc's dramatic birth from Enitharmon's
"loins" in Night V. While Nights V and VI detail the emergence
of apocalyptic prophecy in ancient Israel, Blake challenges us to
expand our typological frame of reference. Since Orc's birth and
pubescent rise recapitulate the situation addressed in the Prelud-
ium to Blake's earlier poem *America*, readers are invited to interpret Orc's embrace of Enitharmon as "the historical birth of
modern revolution" (Erdman 1969, 307).

The song the Demons sing at Orc's birth, like their song in
Night I, recasts the creation-fall narrative in more clearly historical terms. In this new context, however, the narrator seizes on the
contemporary repetition of the ancient struggle: "But now the
times return upon thee Enitharmons womb / Now holds thee soon
to issue forth. Sound clarions of war" (59:17–18). But Los the
prophet does not bear his torment patiently, not "now" or in ancient times; "breathing terrible blood & vengeance," he lets "loose
the Enormous Spirit" (of Orc), opening the "furnaces of affliction" sealed by Urizen in Night II. Bloom identifies Vala here as
a self-destructive goddess of warfare who incites Luvah to don
the sacrificial robes of a dying god, a god "whose manifestation
is the Napoleonic wars" (Erdman 1982, 956). Erdman, supporting
Bloom, turns Vala's bow and arrows (59:5–8, 19–20) into cannon
and mortars, marshaling referents to the English-French war
(Erdman 1969, 353). Although they provide empirical clues, neither critic identifies the way that Blake deciphers the entangled
history of Europe by the figural code of prophecy.

In Blake's application of the figural view, the French Revolution
bears witness to divine pathos while English reaction appears as

the fearful and jealous "Urizenic" god. But, again, the two powers are implicated in the struggle, a point Blake visualizes in Orc's chaining to Urizen's "rock of Law." By opposing and repressing the Jacobin demons, the English angels side with legal restraint against passionate energy and, with the prophet's partial consent, censor the outpouring of righteous indignation. Los's "Eyes," after all, are blinded by "Terror" and he builds his city of artistic vision, Golgonooza, "in dark prophetic fear" of Orc. Once Orc reaches maturity, Los attempts to control him by binding him with "the bloody chain of nights and days" (60:19); but as with his binding of Urizen, Los becomes what he beholds and a chain issues from his own bosom into Urizen-Orc's rock. This complex of events induces W. J. T. Mitchell to ask: "Is Los' time a chain that binds from eternity or links us to it? Are the links the night-marish circle of compulsive repetition or the division of the night into 'watches' for a possible new dawn?" (Mitchell 1978, 137). The answer, paradoxically, is "yes" to both parts of the question: history moves compulsively toward tragic repetitions that, potentially, signal the morning or ripening of time. Regenerative potential survives in Los, in prophecy, however faintly. For Los possesses the spiritual agency that, combined with Tharmas his parent, becomes the fourth zoa who breaks the repetitive cycle of generation, of death and decay, reaction and revolt. Without Los's ability to discern visionary promise in the terrible revolutionary activity of Luvah-Orc, history would be irredeemable.

As he crosses into Night VI, Blake subtly refocuses his perspective on Old Testament–contemporary parallels. After the binding of Orc, the poem passes through a vortex along the B.C./A.D. divide as modern European history comes more clearly into view and ancient history recedes. DiSalvo contends that in Night VI "the frequency of Miltonic and contemporary allusions indicates that we have finally reached modern Europe" (DiSalvo 1983, 222). She also argues that Urizen's activity is a rebuilding of civilization in the Industrial era, a contention that Erdman supports by interpreting Urizen's journey through chaos as a survey of the "industrial inferno" of Blake's England (Erdman 1969, 373). But even if Blake sharpens his contemporary focus, he retains the prefigurative strategy, as the multiple historical echoes confirm.

Urizen's journey, based on Satan's prelapsarian trek through chaos, predates Genesis and thus suggests that Blake updates the dual time frame in *Paradise Lost*. By the freedom his abstracted typology has already established, Blake multiplies the "types" of Urizen's Satanic journey, especially Urizen's plan to rebuild his

Mundane World, cosmologically and economically, along rationalist lines, which recalls Urizen's building of Solomon's temple and
its analogues in the tower of Babylon and the pyramids of Egypt.

For example, as Urizen surveys the ruins of his world from
Night II, the narrator describes his journey as an "Eternal falling"
(69:20) through the extraterrestial void of Newtonian space. And
while exploring the void, Urizen encounters his and Luvah's children enslaved in a modern industrial hell that parallels the subjugation of Israel's children in the Babylonian and Egyptian
"furnaces of affliction." The long passage on page 70 (5–45) char-
acterizes the current state of Urizen's empire in terms that recall
his ancient oppresions. Children employed in the brick kilns are
working "in burning dungeons" while others are "lying on beds
of sulphur / On racks & wheels" as women are "marching oer
burning wastes / Of sand in bands of hundreds & of fifties &
of thousands" (70:18–21). Miners are described as "multitudes"
imprisoned in "the solid mountains & in rocks which heaved with
their torment," while in the cities workers become "dishumanized"
by the abject labor of war production. Poetic history to be sure,
but one not void of particulars.

Repetition, however, while it turns these particulars into a famil-
iar pattern, is not a law unto itself. Blake's conflations of time
require an endpoint toward which his whole typological strategy
aims and within which repetitions can be transfigured by visionary simultaneity.[7] A kind of providence thus guides his narrative
history: as Urizen falls the "ever pitying one who seeth all things
saw his fall" and provides him with "bosom of clay" that stems his
precipitous rush into nonentity. But the "ever pitying one" cannot
prematurely arrest history, and so Urizen must continually fall,
rise, and write his book of law and morality: "Time after Time
for such a journey none but iron pens / Can write And adaman-
tine leaves recieve [sic] nor can the man who goes / The journey
obstinate refuse to write time after time / Endless had been his
travel but the Divine hand him led" (71:41–72:2). In a sense, then,
a progressive principle operates within the repetitions, but only
if readers can discern a "Divine hand," or spiritual agency, in
their relation to history.

The key point, thus, lies in apprehending the historical nature
of Blake's providence, a view that scholars critical of *The Four Zoas*
often ignore, claiming that the Council of Eternals or Blake's Jesus
exist in a transcendent realm above history. But if the Blakean
equation of humanity and divinity is truly a staple of his thought,
then the "Divine hand" becomes a human power embodied in

the prophet's narrative vision. Blake vertically connects the two dimensions. Like the Italian historian of culture, Giambattista Vico, who situates providence within the movement of history, Blake shows that providence must work in and through the nightmare repetitions of temporal life (the Orc Cycle) to be at all effective. In his "demonstration" of providence, Vico ties Augustine's transcendent and miraculous agency to what Karl Lowith calls an ultimate frame of reference—"the universal and permanent order of the historical course itself" (Lowith 1949, 23–24).[8] Both Vico's *ricorso* and Blake's Orc Cycle are primarily and definitively historical phenomenon: Blake, of course, demonstrates that the cycle is also a cosmic recurrence, but one intimately related to the psychological and social life of "Man", and thus capable of human transformation.

The immanent nature of Blake's providence becomes clearer when we recognize that Night VI is still technically within a pre-Edenic time frame. Blake makes this point, as usual, through allusion: when Urizen, "By Providence divine conducted," alights on the "Peaked rock of Urthona," he imitates Satan's landing on Mount Niphates in *Paradise Lost*. The prelapsarian machinations of Satan are a "type" of Urizen's fallen stratagem in both the Old Testament and in contemporary Europe, a typology that, however skewed, places both cosmic and social repetitions within a narrative (and thus temporal) framework. As Urizen lands in Urthona's world, he overlooks not Adam and Eve in an innocent garden, but an Orc whose self-conscious hatred of this condition precludes any possibility of innocence despoiled from above. And if the garden is already spoiled, subsequent history is too, a point that underscores the irony of Urizen's attempt to reassert his theocratic authority in eighteenth-century England. Urizen chooses to build a "new" world on solely rationalist grounds and, like the Ancient of Days, fixes his foot on the airy space of the vortex. New science is old cosmology writ large: and written in terms that repeat the theocratic and legalistic oppression of David and Solomon.[9] Thus seeking to solidify order and evade change, Urizen sets his scientists and politicians to construct another world "where none should dare oppose his will himself being King / Of All & all futurity he bound in his vast chain" (73:19–20).

But true to Blake's immanent or dialectical conception of history, Urizen's obsessive rage for order once again subjects his "children" to social contradictions that threaten his rule.[10] Ironically, these contradictions force Urizen to secrete an ideology that entraps him within his own meshwork.

For Urizen lamented over them in a selfish lamentation
Till a white woof coverd his cold limbs from head to feet
Hair white as snow coverd him in flaky locks terrific
Overspreading his limbs. In pride he wandered weeping
Clothd in aged venerableness obstinately resolvd
Travelling thro darkness & wherever he traveld a dire Web
Followd behind him as the Web of a Spider dusky & cold
Shivering across from Vortex to Vortex drawn out from his mantle
    of years
A living Mantle adjoind to his life & growing from his Soul
(73:26–34)

Another irony is involved in Urizen's new effort at domination: by attempting to universalize his rationalist ideology, Urizen shrinks the "expansive orbs" or perceptual powers of everyone in his kingdom, rendering communication and real social stability, a stability based on communal vision, impossible. The social tensions that result, as they accumulate and repeat past errors, make a violent and cataclysmic confrontation between Urizen and Orc, law and revolution, inevitable. This prophetic confrontation takes place in Night VII.

Night VIIa

The enduring struggle between priestly legalism and prophetic wrath informs the poetic situation of Night VII. Historically, the clash between Urizen's and Orc's forces in the late eighteenth century promises to be the last. Orc's revolt repeats the insurrectionary war in heaven, and all subsequent insurrections, within an eschatological time frame. Both versions of Night VII inaugurate the poem's movement toward apocalypse. But since Night VII consolidates the conflict between law and revolution narrated in the central Nights, and does so by personalizing that conflict in the character of Los, I will focus on Night VIIa. As the events triggered in VIIb find their consummation in the apocalyptic Nights VIII and IX, I discuss the "final" battle of the Urizen-Orc wars in the next chapter.

Drawing on his *Book of Ahania*, Blake narrates in Night VIIa the fate of a complex revolutionary force that entangles itself in the folds of its reactionary opponent, a story of deferred revolution that stretches back to the Old Testament. In the book of Joshua, Moses's failure to liberate Israel is indicated by the nation's fall into Canaanite bondage after Moses dies. Moses the deliverer had become Moses the legalistic priest: Israel is freed from bondage in Egypt only to be re-enslaved in Asia. This process, symbolized at the end of Joshua by renewal of the Mosaic covenant, is embodied in *The Four Zoas*'s symbols of the oak tree and stone, Blake's Stone of Night and Tree of Mystery. Blake dramatizes this failed revolution by chaining Orc to a rock (the rock of Mosaic law) beneath the tree sacred to the Druids (the oak of mystery): "the twin hazards of legalism and nature worship" (Sandler 1972, 7). The repressive "iron" laws of Sinai trigger Orc's wrath even as they negate his power of action. For while Urizen's debasement of Orc arouses his revolutionary ire, Los, parent of prophetic wrath, also is infected by the life-denying moral repression and succumbs to Urizen's power: "Los felt the Envy in his limbs like to a blighted tree." When the Tree shoots up from Orc's rock, it "Branches into the heaven of Los" (77:26; 78:6; 352–53). This event, as it ensnares Los and Orc, replays Los's capitulation to Urizen in Nights IV and V.

The Tree of Mystery—a purposely ambiguous and multivalent symbol—includes within its range of reference the Genesis tree of good and evil, Milton's banyan tree from which Adam and Eve clothe their nakedness, the Druid oak of human sacrifice, and Christ's cross (developed in Night VIII). The core meaning of *mystery* remains central to all four allusions: the sacrifice of human energies to natural morality depends upon the deluded acquiescence of those whose energies are sacrificed. Thus Urizen, attempting to rationalize Orc's sacrificial bondage, dissimulates before the rebel, pretending to pity him and, in Urizen's words, "to reveal myself before thee in a form of wisdom" (78:32; E 354). That form materializes as the Tree of Mystery.

But like his opponents the Deists, Blake exposes the psychosocial basis of Urizen's priestly mystification. He shows that Urizen's cruel daughters "knead the bread of Orc" with iron hands, the hands of Urizen's iron book, which makes the "feeding" of Orc a peculiarly apt metaphor for Urizenic moral law. Urizen "feeds" Orc by depriving him of gratification. Yet deprivation occurs at a social level as well. Urizen commands his daughters to turn their hearts to stone and to "let Moral Duty tune" their tongues as they bring Enitharmon, the "space" of prophetic England, "beneath our wondrous tree." A scathingly ironic speech follows as Urizen addresses his ministers in the Malthusian tone of William Pitt:

Compell the poor to live upon a Crust of bread by soft mild arts
Smile when they frown frown when they smile & when a man looks
  pale
With labour & abstinence say he looks healthy & happy
And when his children sicken let them die there are enough
Born even too many & our Earth will be overrun
Without these arts If you would make the poor live with temper
With pomp give every crust of bread you give with gracious cunning
Magnify small gifts reduce the man to want a gift & then give with
  pomp
Say he smiles if you hear him sigh If pale say he is ruddy
Preach temperance say he is overgorgd & drowns his wit
In strong drink tho you know that bread & water are all
He can afford Flatter his wife pity his children till we can
Reduce all to our will as spaniels are taught with art
                                              (80:9–21; E 355)

In this angry piece of irony Blake mercilessly exposes the working of Urizenic ideology, particularly Urizen's plan to "Reduce all to our will," a plan formulated at Night VI's conclusion when Urizen announced construction of a new world.

Yet repetition is built into history, as Blake understands it. In contemporary terms, Erdman finds evidence of Pitt's "Brown Bread Bill" philosophy in Urizen's speech, which, he argues, is meant to restrain the wrath of London's poor by hoodwinking them into thinking that neither war nor the food market is responsible for the scarcity of bread. In effect, Pitt intimidates or tricks the poor, as Urizen tricks Orc, into accepting the kind of austere domestic policies that deprive them of their livelihood. This strategy destroys Orc's sense of purpose and undercuts the spirit of revolution by "depriving it of its rationale in poverty and social injustice (Wilkie and Johnson 1978, 147). In effect Blake yokes a public or political deception with a private or religious one, attributing to England's leaders (the priest-king alliance of the state church) a pretence to "Moral Duty" as a linchpin to their ideological power.

What happens next in the narrative is crucial for Blake's use of typology and his conception of the Orc Cycle. Orc replies to Urizen's dissimulation with his usual wrath—"Curse thy Cold hypocrisy"—but realizes that he has been deceived and drawn into Urizen's morality, which weakens and divides him, turning him into a scaly serpent hung upon Urizen's Tree of Mystery: "In strong deceit / Thou dost restrain my fury that the worm may fold the Tree" (80:32–33; E 356). Urizen too, however, is trapped within his own net, a point made terrifyingly clear to him when Orc identifies himself as the fallen Luvah. Their dual responsibility for history's nightmarish state is confirmed by the narrator's observation: "Terrified Urizen heard Orc now certain that he was Luvah / And Orc began to Organize a Serpent body" (80:43–44). Urizen will also metamorphosize into this serpent body in Night VIII, sealing his ultimate complicity with Orc in perpetuating the tragic dramas of European history.

Blake's sympathies obviously lie with the oppressed and deceived masses (Orc). But he depicts with bitter accuracy both Orc's capitulation to priestly morality and Urizen's lack of real control over history: "He made Orc / In Serpent form compelld stretch out & up the mysterious tree / Into submission to his will nor knew the dred result" (81:3–6 E 356). By compelling Orc to climb the tree, Urizen unwittingly produces two Luvahs: a wrathful Orc-Luvah whose revolutionary rage he can ultimately control; and a dying god Luvah into whom the Lamb enters to preserve the state of revolutionary passion.[11] In a central scene in Night VIII Urizen confronts this second Luvah but is perplexed by the "figure," for he cannot discern in Orc, in passion or the hungry masses, a type of the crucified redeemer. In effect, Urizen cannot read history typologically.

But neither can Luvah, which is why he does not bring the regenerative solution in *The Four Zoas.* In fact, Luvah as dying god is reified into another idol of sacrifice that exonerates the warrior ethos that desolates Europe with war. At this point in the narrative we reach the nadir of another Urizen-Orc cycle; only this time it promises to be the last cycle, for Los has accumulated the wisdom of experience and begins to read history typologically: he sees in Luvah's robes of blood a vaguely redemptive figure (the Lamb). Los, however, cannot communicate his understanding until his composite character—comprised of Urthona's Spectre and Enitharmon—is reformed.[12]

By playing down the legalistic and sacrificial elements of atonement, Blake emphasizes instead the prophet's fundamental self-examination and the reintegration of his personality. The priestly law of atonement runs counter to the spirit of self-sacrifice that Los exhibits in Night VIIa. In Los's speech on the Lamb, we hear the voice of experience, where Blake's system and his personal insight meet and reinforce each other. As Los sees the Lamb in Luvah's robes of blood, in the body, crucified, he grasps the symbolic nature of Jesus's appearance (as Urizen cannot) both because he has prophetic powers and can read "types," but also because he has undergone crucifixion himself:

Los trembling answerd Now I feel the weight of stern repentance
Tremble not so my Enitharmon at the awful gates
Of the poor broken heart I see thee like a shadow withering
As on the outside of Existence but look! behold! take comfort!
Turn inwardly thine Eyes & there behold the Lamb of God
Clothed in Luvahs robes of blood descending to redeem
O Spectre of Urthona take comfort O Enitharmon
Couldst thou but cease from terror & trembling & affright
When I appear before thee in forgiveness of ancient injuries
Why shouldst thou remember & be afraid. I surely have died in
   pain
Often enough to convince thy jealousy & fear & terror
Come hither be patient let us converse together because
I also tremble at myself & at all my former life

                                                (87:39–51; E 369)

Los understands both the Spectre's need for embodiment and
the hells that Luvah (Orc) has endured and, therefore, is able to
internalize the strife between them. More importantly, this internalization exemplifies the essence of apocalyptic typology as Blake
practices it, the empowering ability to "make it new," to break
from what is dead in the past, a move that Yahweh announces as
his special power in the apocalyptic narratives of the Bible.[13]

Los's reunion with his spectre and emanation dismays many
critics, who argue that Blake either shifts too abruptly from despair to recovery or disrupts too cavalierly the narrative sequence
of the poem. Erdman, perhaps the most noted spokesman for
the latter objection, feels that Los's "personal" integration deflects
attention from the poem's social dynamic, a deflection he explains
in terms of the the Amiens peace accord of 1801 (Erdman 1969,
Part 4). For him, Los's embrace becomes not just a delusion but an
ideological compromise that privileges individual over communal
salvation. But John Middleton Murry, in my opinion, sees more
deeply into Blake's situation when he declares that Blake "faced
the problem which most prophets have avoided—the problem of
life between man and woman" (Murry 1964, 185). That is, the
torments of love and jealousy that afflicted Blake at Felpham,
where he evidently revised the later Nights of the poem, make it
apparent that he could not perform his public duty as a prophet
while in his spectre and shadow's power. The social theme of *The
Four Zoas* temporarily slid out of focus. But Erdman's critique is
well taken: combined with Murry's point, it suggests that in the
textual gaps and stitches of the two Nights VII is precisely where
the material relations of Blake's life push into and out of the
narrative, fracturing its surface and disrupting the poem's coher-

ence. But if the social allegory is blurred here, it returns with powerful force in Night VIII.

Los must teach by example the *kerygmatic* interpretation of history. He must persuade readers to identify their individual and communal pasts, which requires integration of the spectre of individualism, of the selfhood, into a public-minded persona. The prophet induces this effort first by demonstrating his own struggle with selfhood, with spectre and emanation, and second by showing that individual struggle anticipates a larger engagement with history. This strategy must be skillfully handled. The narrative must in some way compel readers to feel that personal and social destiny are intertwined, have reached a critical period, are in need of transformation. Unfortunately, this emphasis on a dual individual-social conversion inevitably entails a temporal lag. "How long?" is a question that not even the most confident prophets can answer. Yet it is a question that will confront us in the next chapter.

I believe that in *The Four Zoas* Blake expects us to regard Los's individual apocalypse in Night VII as a prefiguration or "type" of the wider social apocalypse in Night IX, where the zoas and emanations organize into the giant Albion. The proof is in the act of committed reading that can turn the nightmare of historical repetition into the "new dawn" of eternity, Blake's vision of simultaneity. Access to the "Eternal Now" lies individually in the *intellectus spiritualis* of reading; its social realization depends on the transformative power, the spiritual agency, of collective human imagination.

6

Consolidating Error: History and Apocalypse in Nights VIIb–IX

Since first this Subject for Heroic Song
Pleas'd me long choosing, and beginning late
Not sedulous by Nature to indite
Wars, hitherto the only Argument
Heroic deem'd, chief maistry to dissect
With long and tedious havoc fabl'd Knights
In Battles feign'd; the better fortitude
Of Patience and Heroic Martyrdom
Unsung . . .

—Milton, *Paradise Lost*

To find the western path
Right thro the gates of Wrath
I urge my way
Sweet mercy leads me on
With soft repentent moan
I see the break of day

The war of swords & spears
Melted by dewy tears

—Blake, *Morning*

IN the final nights of *The Four Zoas,* Blake presents his apocalypse, which most Blake scholars describe as a fundamentally internal event. Even Donald Ault, who radically disagrees with the best that has been thought and said about Blake, analyzes the last nights through the subjective lens of his perspective ontology.[1] More comprehensive are Northrop Frye and Joseph Wittreich, who, while they privilege the internalized Romantic apocalypse, remain alert to Blake's prophetic sense of history, which qualifies

130

their individualist assumptions. Also, David Erdman and Jackie DiSalvo more assiduously emphasize Blake's political contexts, but they underplay the crucial *narrative* dimension of the apocalypse (see Erdman 1969 and DiSalvo 1983). These positions, while informative, remain polarized and incomplete.

We must, as ever, deal with a Blake paradox. For he insists on a historical basis to apocalypse, yet, to keep his apocalypse symbolic, he mediates it through the individual. While drawing on archetypal, historical, and poststructural perspectives, I do not claim either to transcend my own interpretive scheme or to expose the "totalizing" gestures of the final Nights. Rather, my argument is that Blake reverses the cyclical violence of history embodied in the mythology of the Orc Cycle: first, by recovering the sociopolitical emphases of Judeo-Christian apocalyptic within his own millenial moment in the 1790s; and second, by imagining the revolutionary future in terms that exemplify the passage from individual to collective transformation.

Blake's insistence on the political dimension of apocalypse follows the long tradition of eschatological thought, which maintains that apocalyptic is "a way of reading contemporary history and taking a stance toward it" (McGinn 1984, 23). While acknowledging its crucial personal dimension, D. S. Russell underscores the historical basis of apocalyptic writing: "It is true," he argues, "that in the apocalyptic literature prominence is given to the destiny of the individual and to personal salvation in the age to come; but the overall perspective is still that of the community." Russell adds that the objective of salvation is the creation of a new society "not just in some far-off time or place, but in the struggles of contemporary life" (Russell 1978, 27). Reclaiming this perspective helps us to modify the internal emphases of Romantic apocalypse and to recover the inherent politics of the genre.

While the apocalyptic as message and movement, as socio-political perspective, originates in the literary form, the form is tied closely to the social history of the Near East in the centuries before Christianity, when Israel came into increasingly antagonistic contact with surrounding nations. On the one hand, this contact revives an ancient Jewish fear of cultural violation; on the other hand, it encourages a syncretism that has positive effects on Jewish literature. Leavened with Persian and Hellenistic influences, Jewish writers develop a worldview that anticipates Yahweh's future intervention in history, one that would bring "historical conditions within which the Jews could live in peace with the nations of the world" (Hayes 1971, 273). The important literary result of this

eschatological hope, the genre of apocalypse, rests on two assumptions—one political and the other transcendental. The political
assumption is that Israel's regional peace depends on removing
the threat of foreign domination; the transcendental assumption,
built on the political one, is that Israel (i.e., humanity) is incapable
of removing the threat and so requires divine intervention.

The Book of Revelation inherits the politics of pre-Christian
apocalyptic, as it too addresses contemporary social struggles. Although opinions differ as to the political content of Revelation,
"no one would want to deny," says Bernard McGinn, "that the
Apocalypse was a call to decision in a time of trial" (McGinn 1984,
23). Adela Yarbro Collins points to the tension between "eschatological expectation and the realities of foreign rule," and argues
that in a time of crisis, the Judeo-Christian community had two
responses: violent or peaceful resistance (Collins 1977, 242). Some
groups, such as the Maccabees or Hasidim Zealots, did resist vio-
lently. Those who did not could either patiently endure persecution, trusting in an imminent arrival of the "End," or refuse to
cooperate, even to death. What Milton calls "heroic martyrdom"
derives from an active, nonviolent resistance to imperial rule (in
John of Patmos's case, against Rome). Collins further contends
that Revelation's first readers would search the book for "a pro-
gram of action" against foreign aggression. The cosmic trial in
Revelation between the symbolic forces of light and darkness thus
is rooted in the history of Christian persecution in Asia Minor
late in the first century A.D.

Blake realizes that, despite centuries of literalist commentary,
Revelation advocates nonviolent resistance: not the passive kind
in which the persecuted play no role, but the active resistance of
heroic struggle that hastens divine intervention. The key event in
this drama is the voluntary self-sacrifice that induces "the Lamb"
to act on behalf of the slain martyrs. "How long, Lord?" is determined in Revelation by a magic numerology of the slain: the Lord
avenges the blood of the innocent only when the fixed number
(144,000) of martyrs is reached. Collins describes this collective
power as "synergism," a concept that approximates the work of
"consolidation" in Blake. This concept, which adds a political
depth to Frye's archetypal "consolidation of error" (Frye 1969,
260), refers to the accumulation of deaths (in *The Four Zoas* of the
spectres) that congeals into the figure of Satan, the narrative form
of war's corporeality—i.e., its "error." Synergism, or positive consolidation, emanates from the posthumous power of the Lamb,

who, as the "first begotten of the dead" (Revelation 1:5), sustains the martyrs' faith in supernatural aid, emboldening them to fight a spiritual war of resistance. Drawing on the evidence of things unseen in Revelation 21, in which the woman clothed with the sun and the child are rescued by miraculous power, Collins asserts that Revelation offers "an explicit rejection of the militant option" (Collins 1977, 247).

As for the transcendental assumption, no apocalyptic writer would deny that "the End" is the far goal of time. But since the course of apocalyptic history implies the literary unity of a "total form," the transcendental dimension is linked inextricably to its narrative presentation. The end point of time can be rendered only in the narrative, a fact that returns apocalyptic to its historical roots in prophecy. We must distinguish between an actual "End" of time and the "end-time" (which could last indefinitely). In other words, because eternity is experienced through the narrative, or *sub specie temporis,* apocalyptic remains prefigurative. The narrative end functions as a prelude, a call, to the communal realization of the "kingdom." While Jesus' proclamation in the Gospel is itself apocalyptic—"The time is fulfilled, and the kingdom of God is at hand" (Mark 1:15)—the incarnation is an initial stage in the end-time.[2] The full, or communal, arrival of the kingdom is projected into the still future Second Coming. Thus, because of the Parousia's deferral, the transcendental perspective of apocalyptic is crossed with an historical one, which keeps anticipatory history, or prophetic typology, central to the genre. "Seal not the sayings of the prophecy of this book," John admonishes (Revelation 22:10). Or, as Paul Korshin puts it, "the types of the Apocalypse can only refer to antitypes in history *since the writing of that book*" (Korshin 1982, 334).

Blake adopts the political perspective of apocalyptic literature (especially of John's Revelation), along with the latter's open-ended chronology and prophetic narrative strategies, especially its code of Christian typology. He uses Revelation typology for the symbolic compression it affords and for its encyclopedic compass, which contains the evolving "consolidations of error" that, for him, signal the most pregnant moments in history. Blake derives from Revelation an organic or "Living form" that encompasses movement in time, a form or shaping principle "characterized first by an 'elegant *Simultaneum*,' then by a pattern of gradually sharpening antitheses" (Wittreich 1979, 44). I interpret these "antitheses" as Blake's consolidations, the contending worldviews whose unresolved tension turns the wheel of history in his poem. Blake does not use Revelation to abolish history in the name of visionary transcendence. Rather, as Wittreich cogently argues:

> A model like the Book of Revelation suggests that form is a means to an end, which may "contradict . . . form and even deny it"; the final objective of form is not, then, to "prevail as . . . 'timeless designs' or eternal paradigms" but to effect liberation. (Wittreich 1979, 44)

Blake retains the liberation ethic of Revelation as he develops its dramatic structure, its series of contending perspectives, that raises corporeal into spiritual war. This series is enacted through the mythological from of the Orc Cycle.[3]

While Frye offers important formal insights into Blake's apocalypse, his structuralism erases the political inscription of the genre. To recover this dimension of meaning, we must return Blake to his own historical moment—the revolutionary crises of late eighteenth-century Europe. Like his millenarian seventeenth-century forerunners, Blake compresses previous historical stages within the "end-time" of his own age, which exceeds the previous one in apocalyptic urgency. The last apocalyptic moment was deferred by what Blake calls "Deism, or Natural Religion." While Blake lumps together these two distinct theologies in his narrative, he makes a crucial point in his typically unanalytical way.[4] He realizes that when the Deists claim that natural law provides a more certain model of religion that revelation (without of course denying revelation), they help the Anglican state church distance scripture from history and so defuse the socially radical message of the Puritan sects. This distancing (this ideology of "nature") is the target of Blake's critique of Deism or natural religion in the final nights of *The Four Zoas*.

But if the ages never actually culminate, or merge into an ideal simultaneity, then how can each cycle be an advance? What power or pattern guarantees that a term is set to history's awful, cyclic bloodshed? Here I must revert to Frye, who in his best moments understands that the conjunction of history and imagination forms the "axis on which all Blake's thought turns" and which distinguishes his work from other "attempts to get along without a redeeming power *in time*" (Frye 1969, 299—italics mine). Blake works his way out of this logical difficulty by recourse to an imaginative strategy:

> Blake . . . postulates a historical process which may be described as the opposite of the Hegelian one. Every advance of truth forces error

to consolidate itself in a more obviously erroneous form, and every advance of freedom has the same effect on tyranny. Thus history exhibits a series of crises in which a sudden flash of imaginative vision (as in the French Revolution) bursts out, is counteracted by a more ruthless defense of the *status quo,* and subsides again. The evolution comes in the fact that the opposition grows sharper each time, and will one day present a clear-cut alternative of eternal life or extermination.

(Frye 1969, 260)

Blake's apocalypse operates by a kind of negative dialectic that cuts across three broad cultural epochs. Blake makes this point by juxtaposing typical events from Old Testament, New Testament, and contemporary British history, condensing them into a figurative moment capable of being transformed by his readers. For Blake, contemporary natural religion repeats the ancient "error" of abstracting moral law from prophetic vision, or of reifying imaginative into institutional forms of worship. In effect, the Hebraic priesthood reduces the visionary scripture of prophecy to a legalistic morality, and this reduction is replicated by the Roman Catholic Church, which transposes the "poetic tales" of Jesus into the formulae of Christian doctrine. Blake thus accosts his readers and beckons them to interpret their age as one of history's consolidating errors. Once they reverse this error, turning abstract moral law back into vision, they free themselves from the compulsive repetitions of the Orc Cycle and help ready their society for apocalyptic reconfiguration.

At least that is the long goal that informs the apocalyptic tradition to which Blake—never blindly—subscribes. Before tracing this historical vision into the grain of Blake's text, we must deal with the thorny textual problems of Nights VIIa and b.

Night VIIb

I base my reading of the two Nights VII on Andrew Lincoln's textual analysis in *Blake: An Illustrated Quarterly* 46 (Summer 1978).[5] While Erdman reverses Lincoln's arrangement, placing VIIb between VIIa, both writers admit that since Blake did not leave editorial instructions for his two Nights VII, editors are free to choose a sequence that works best in the context of the entire poem. Both also agree that neither relegating VIIb to a postscript nor simply placing the two versions in tandem (the Doubleday and Longman choices) is adequate to the common reader's need for "an inclusive yet coherent narrative or thematic sequence or structure" (Erdman 1982, xxvi). I prefer Lincoln's arrangement because it supports my theory of Blake's historical vision.[6] My contention is that Night VII of *The Four Zoas* is incomplete, not just in textual but in narrative-historical terms. For Los-Enitharmon's personal integration in VIIa cannot arrest the larger social and cultural fragmentation that ensues in Night VIII.

But what is the relation between the narrative-historical consolidations of VIIb and Los and Enitharmon's individual integration in VIIa? The "plot" of VIIb takes its cue from its structural position between the Spectre of Urthona's account of the creation-fall and the reunion of the Spectre, Los, and Enitharmon. At the stitch between VIIa and VIIb, Urthona's Spectre gives Vala dominion over Orc, which brings the awful "night of Carnage" in VIIb and VIII that frames VIIa's individual redemption. While Los struggles with the complex image of Orc's crucifixion on the Tree of Mystery in VIIa, he continues to view crucifixion in personal terms, which blocks his insight into the eschatological meaning of this event. Consolidation, therefore, goes on without him. It is sewn into the fabric of the time process, which the prophet must mythologize as the "dragon" form of imperial war to signal the end-time. As Andrew Lincoln aptly puts it, after Los and Enitharmon reconcile, the narrative returns to "the confrontation between Vala and Orc, prepared for in 85:22," and so, thematically and textually, "VIIb pages 91–95 would follow effectively from the end of VIIa2" (Lincoln 1978, 132). For after the "nameless shadow" embraces Orc and spreads through Urizen's web, the Dead ascend upon her clouds and take up the form of Satan, which prepares for the "epiphany" of Satan in Night VIII.

Two key repetitions from earlier Nights occur in VIIb: Urizen's construction of a "Temple" and Tharmas's ensuing wrath and "Flood." VIIb opens with Urizen, sitting beneath the "Roots of Mystery," announcing dramatically: "The time of Prophecy is now revolvd & all / This Universal Ornament is mine & in my hands / The ends of heaven" (95:15–20; E 360). The cycles have turned into the contemporary end-time as Urizen rebuilds his cosmos, the Great Chain of Being, with the "chains" of British industry and empire. Boasting "in power & majesty" of his ability to control the planets, Urizen deems himself a "God and not a Man a Conqueror in triumphant glory," a boast which the narrator follows with this potent description of Urizen's imperialist policy:

First Trades & Commerce ships & armed vessels he builded
 laborious

To swim the deep & on land children are sold to trades
Of dire necessity still laboring day & night till all
Their life extinct they took the spectre form in dark despair
And slaves in myriads in ship loads burden the hoarse sounding
   deep
Rattling with clanking chains the Universal Empire groans

And he commanded his Sons to found a Center in the Deep
And Urizen laid the first Stone & all his myriads
Builded a temple in the image of the human heart
(95:25–33; E 360)

The passage recapitulates the construction of Solomon's temple in Night II; only now the building depicts the complex relations between religion and war in the contemporary industrial context, with its "immense machines" and "hoarse wheels" (96:10, 14; E 361). The recently mechanized (Newtonian) cosmos, Urizen's "intricate wheels . . . Wheel without wheel," undergoes a transformation into England's dark satanic mills. Blake suggests that this policy allows Urizen's "Sons" to press British workers and African slaves into factories and ships built for colonial expansion, and that this policy combines religious and commercial interests in what, to Blake, is a modern replication of ancient Egypt, Babylon, or Rome—what he will identify in Night VIII as "Natural Religion."

As with Urizen's triumph in Night II, Tharmas returns to spread confusion, complicit in Urizen's policy of displacing prophetic anger into corporeal war. Under Tharmas's power, Orc's apocalyptic rage for more than law and order, initially a positive revolt against repression, becomes, literally, a "night of Carnage" (96:24; E 361). This modern deferral, however, links the ancient tribal past to the industrial present, as Tharmas, parent power of Los and Orc, boasts that he will "rend the Nations all asunder" because the people are divided—"vain their combinations." But Los too capitulates to Urizenic policy—"by night or day Los follows war" (97:21; E 362). The organ of prophecy collaborates with repressive religion: as the "Prester Serpent," in the voice of the "Priest of God," authorizes the night of carnage, the war "vibrates" through the cosmic spaces of "Urizen's Web," his tormenting religious ideology.

In Night VII, Orc is sacrified to a new mysterious deity, the God of Newtonianism or "physico-theology." In this mechanistic cosmos, Orc's transformative power is neutralized as the ground of religion shifts from history to nature. From Blake's Romantic visionary perspective, by grounding religion in natural science, rather than in "con-science," the Newtonians forsake the real basis of religion—the imagination—and rely instead on the delusive veil of nature that the Shadow personifies. She emerges as the irrational "mystery" of an unknowable and inhuman God. The irony, as Blake bitterly portrays it in Night VIIb, is that as the Shadow "absorbs" Urizen's "Sciences" by distilling Orc's repressed, and hence destructive, power into her own "indefinite" regions, she destroys the rational capacity in Urizen's system, his web of ideas.

In Blake's historical allegory, such contradiction lies at the heart of the social policy erected in eighteenth-century England. The designers of this policy, Urizen's "Sons," in fear of prophetic vision and revolutionary anger, clutch onto natural law as their fundamental organizing principle. By identifying this merger of law and nature (of Urizen and Rahab) with Judaism, Roman Catholicism, and Anglicanism, Blake assails the law and order morality that benefits the privileged few, those who undercut and malign the transformative power of apocalypse latent in each historical period.

Yet, in my estimation, Blake retains a Jacobin belief that revolutionary rage can be redeemed in a way that reactionary fear cannot: thus the complexity of Orc's crucifixion on Urizen's Tree of Mystery. The mistake, in the context of Blake's prophetic history, is not Orc's violent, and thus collusive, participation in the delusions of natural religion: it is also Los's failure to read in Orc's crucifixion the heroic martyrdom of the Lamb clothed in Luvah's robes of blood. Without regarding the Lamb as the sole, transcendent locus of meaning, I argue that Blake's Lamb is as crucial to his historicized apocalypse as John's Lamb is to Revelation. For both writers, redemption lies *through* the "gates of wrath," not in apolitical escapism. Orc's revolutionary violence is redeemable.

Night VIII

Night VIIb connects directly with Night VIII and shows that, despite Los and Enitharmon's regenerative reunion in VIIa, war continues to drive the proverbial chariot over heaps of the slain. Los's individual regeneration cannot automatically arrest the bloodshed and renovate the world. My sense, however, is that in *The Four Zoas* Blake aligns the internal and historical dimensions of apocalypse by creating a double form of time: the "lyrical moment" of self-awakening and the "epic moment" that announces the communal "Second Coming." Critics deny that *The Four Zoas* achieves this double perspective, but what W. J. T. Mitchell accords to *Milton* applies to the final nights of the *Zoas*. The problem is how to balance Los's discovery of the visionary moment that eludes Satan and his watchfiends with the prophetic task of delineating the larger shape of history. Blake resolves the problem by making Los a direct personification of time:

> The struggle of the artist with time could in this way be recast as a struggle with the self. The drama of the poet's combat with his own doubts and fears becomes a metaphor for the prophet's quarrel with history, and the lyric moment of individual human time can be identified with the epic of collective, historical time. (Mitchell 1978, 169)

I would not oppose "human" to "historical" time in quite the way that Mitchell does. In my view, the metaphor or "type" of the prophet's regeneration, the personal victory over "selfhood," must move through the medium of art into the minds of auditors, who in turn "go and do likewise." The individual apocalypse in fact points to the dual burden of the prophet, who must clarify history for both himself and his readers. This clarification, the consolidation of the psychological, political, and religious contexts of the poem, is the daunting task Blake sets himself in Night VIII.

The major symbol that connects the final Nights of the poem is the Tree of Mystery. This Tree functions as the center of a series of "births" that generate the narrative action of Night VIII. Several characters resurface from earlier Nights and take on meanings obliquely hinted at before. The male characters include Orc's serpent and "eternal" forms as well as the seminal Lamb (depicted as suffering within "Luvah's robes of blood"), the Spectre of Urthona, and Satan, who replaces the Spectre once Los achieves his integration in VIIa. The female characters all derive from Vala, originally the titular spirit of the poem, and include the complex Shadow of Enitharmon, (Enitharmon being Los's female counterpart who, with Los's Spectre, gives birth to the seminal figure of Rahab). Blake identifies Rahab with Revelation's Whore of Babylon, but her narrative function is elusive, related both to Vala and one "Shadowy Female," whose activities in VIIb are incorporated into Rahab's in Night VIII. The Whore of Babylon and Blake's Rahab are the female components of John's "Great Red Dragon," his Antichrist, what Blake calls the "hermaphroditic" union of religion and the state whose eighteenth-century manifestation is "Deism, or Natural Religion."

Night VIII, for all its complexity, sets up Blake's apocalypse through a series of consolidations that condenses the prolific activity of previous Nights. The consolidations identify, on the one hand, Urizen, Orc, and Blake's Satan with Revelation's Great Red Dragon, and, on the other hand, Los, Luvah, and Blake's Jesus with John's symbolic Lamb. As Orc "organizes" his serpent form— allegorically, in Napoleon's wars of conquest—Urizen "in self-deceit his warlike preparations fabricated," "Communing with the Serpent Orc in dark dissimulation / And with the Synagogue of Satan in dark Sanhedrim / To undermine the world of Los & tear bright Enitharmon." Blake incorporates the imperialistic French aggression into the British reaction, exposing each side as an aspect or version of the other. His narrator embodies this exposure in the figure of Satan and shows that the providential logic of consolidation lies beyond any individual zoa's control.

> Terrified & astonished Urizen beheld the battle take a form
> Which he intended not a Shadowy hermaphrodite black & opake
> The Soldiers namd it Satan but he was yet unformd & vast
> Hermaphroditic it at length because hiding the Male
> Within as in a Tabernacle Abominable Deadly

(101:33–37; E 374)

The soldiers' naming the war "Satan" signals a decisive turning point in the narrative: for they are the Spectres of the Dead whose synergism, like that of the slain martyrs in Revelation, the Lamb, Los, and Enitharmon make their primary concern. More particularly, the soldiers indicate their awareness of Urizen and Orc's (England and France's) dual complicity in the war. For while they do not seem to recognize Rahab's role—the hermaphrodite is "yet unformd"—Satan, Blake's Antichrist, is comprised of Rahab and the combined serpent forms of Urizen and Orc.

The term *Antichrist* appears only in the Letters of John, but traditionally it has been attributed to the Beast-Whore symbol in Revelation. II Thessalonians provides an interesting allusion since it presents the exposure of error that precedes the revelation of Jesus as Christ. The Geneva Bible identifies Antichrist with the "son of perdition" of II Thessalonians, a figure who sits in the temple opposing and exalting himself "above all that is called God." Blake transplants this apocalyptic figure into his revolution-reaction allegory of modern Europe:

> The war roard round Jerusalems Gates it took a hideous form
> Seen in the aggregate a Vast Hermaphroditic form

Heavd like and Earthquake labring with convulsive groans
Intolerable at length an awful wonder burst
From the Hermaphroditic bosom Satan he was namd
Son of Perdition terrible his form dishumanized monstrous
A male without a female counterpart a howling fiend
Forlorn of Eden & repugnant to the forms of life
Yet hiding the shadowy female Vala as in an ark & Curtains
Abhorrd accursed ever dying an Eternal death
Being multitudes of tyrant Men in union blasphemous
Against the divine image. Congregated Assemblies of wicked men.
                                        (104:19–30; E 377–78)

The political context emerges more clearly than usual—Erdman,
for example, sees the congregated assemblies as "the armies and
war councils of Britain, France, Prussia, Russia, and Spain in
1804" (Erdman 1969, 401). But in linking the assemblies with the
"ark & Curtains," Blake collapses Old and New Testament allusions to point out the collusion of Church and State, religion and
politics, in repressing vision. As his Revelation source makes clear,
when prophetic vision is institutionalized into a state church, religion turns into another morality that excuses tyranny and imperial conquest. The language of sexual repugnance enforces this
insight, suggesting the closest possible association of psychological
and political tyranny in all versions of natural religion.
   "Deism, or Natural Religion" repeats the contradiction that
Revelation exposes and denounces in the Beast-Whore symbol—
the pernicious imposture of state religion masquerading as "Law."
Interweaving his language closely with his Revelation source,
Blake situates Rahab within the assemblies—"The Synagogue cre-
ated her from Fruit of Urizen's Tree"—where she functions as
the motive for war, ancient and modern, but now "vegetated," like
Orc, into her most delusive manifestation: "The Synagogue of
Satan Clothd her with Scarlet robes & gems / And on her fore-
head was her name written in blood Mystery" (105:14–15; E 378).
Blake takes us both backward, to Old Testament legalism (Rahab
descends from Urizen's Tree), and forward to his own age, using
Revelation as a clarifying point of departure. The Anglican-Whig
state, incorporating and yet containing the millenial thrust of
radical Protestantism, spills blood in the name of natural religion.
In Blake's view, Anglican natural religion combines a "druidic"
worship of natural law with an expansionist economic and social
policy, a conjunction of religious and civil power that not only
legislates the construction and defense of the British empire, but
conceals the ritual of death that attends it. Blake thus appro-

priates and updates the political perspective of Revelation, drawing particularly on those chapters (17 and 18) focused centrally on the "Mystery" of Roman imperialism, on the Whore of Babylon, which helps him to integrate the various contexts of the poem into a "Living Form."

Blake expands his Revelation typologies both backward and forward in the section on the Lamb's crucifixion, which is the ultimate scene of consolidation. In Blake's antinomian view, natural religion underwrites the state church's power because its obsession with moral law blocks the realization of apocalyptic desire. The contradictory nature of this law is exposed when Los sees the Lamb descend to judgment "thro Jerusalem's gates. . . . to put off Mystery time after time" (104:32–3). Perhaps *because* "all his words were peace," the Lamb is condemned to death "as a murderer & robber," as a threat to law and order. Yet when the Lamb suffers crucifixion in "Luvah's robes of blood," the desire for apocalypse is raised to a symbolic level: Luvah-Orc's serpent form is "cut off" and the Lamb rends the veil or net of morality, revealing the impotence of natural law in the process. The apocalyptic moment has arrived that not only exposes the Beast (or monarchical tyranny) and the Whore (of natural religion), but transmutes Luvah-Orc into the Lamb of peace:

> But when Rahab had cut off the Mantle of Luvah from
> The Lamb of God it rolld apart, revealing to all in heaven
> And all on Earth the Temple & Synagogue of Satan & Mystery
> Even Rahab in all her turpitude
>
> (113:38–41; E 379–80)

The Lamb's "posthumous presence," as Mark Bracher terms it, contravenes the mortal law of nature and sets up the potential for annulling moral law as well. For belief in the posthumous presence can affect individuals in society, "freeing them from the fear of death and even encouraging self-sacrifice." And once self-sacrifice spreads from the text to the body politic, then compassion and forgiveness can render the morality of natural religion obsolete. But individuals must adopt the principle of self-sacrifice over sacrifice of others, for if they realize that "such perishing is ultimately a creative transformation of their own being and that of other individuals which they influence, the very being of the Shadowy Female [Rahab] will vanish" (Bracher 1985, 93).

Blake's hope is that, once his audience (re)learns to read history figuratively, the power of Rahab, or the whole system of natural religion, will self-destruct. Blake features this self-destruction at the conclusion of Night VIII. When Rahab is exposed "in all her turpitude," Urizen undergoes his ultimate transformation into the biblical Leviathan, equated in Revelation with "the dragon, that old serpent . . . and Satan"—i.e., with Antichrist. Rahab goes to Urizen and the "Prince of Light beheld / Reveald before the face of heaven his secret holiness"; he feels her "stupor" while "sitting in his web of deceitful Religion" and "[f]orgetful of his own Laws pitying he began to embrace / The Shadowy Female" (116:5, 18–24; E 381). This embrace symbolically enacts the contemporary consolidation of error into "Deism, or Natural Religion," a crowning moment in eighteenth-century English literature.

On the level of historical allegory, the Anglican state church, complicit with liberal and revolutionary forces, promulgates a religion of nature that degenerates into a lawless parody of Christian community. This is an inevitable result of its literalist worldview. Orc has already transposed himself into this "satanic" state by declaring revolutionary war in the name of the Supreme Republic and "*Vertu.*" Blake consolidates this error by showing how Urizen, as rational monarchical state, and Orc, his irrational revolutionary counterpart, become one "state" through Rahab, the "harlot" of nature who draws them both into corporeal war.

> Satan divided against Satan resolvd in open Sanhedrim
> To burn Mystery with fire & form another from her ashes. . . .
> The Ashes of Mystery began to animate they calld it Deism
> And Natural Religion as of old so now anew began
> Babylon again in Infancy Calld Natural Religion.
> (111:19–24; E 386)

Based on a self-righteous sacrifice of others—whether in the name of English or French "virtue"—the architects of natural religion carry on a campaign against revelation as religious mystery while, as Blake shows, instituting yet another form of mystery in its place. This exposure and critique in Night VIII prepares for the apocalyptic reversals of Night IX.

Night IX

After consolidation: transformation. The spiritual agent of this transformation is the Lamb in Luvah's robes of blood, a being that can direct and thus redeem the revolutionary violence of Orc. The mediating charge of this redirecting, however, falls to Blake's "eternal prophet," Los. As Wittreich puts it, Los must respond to history like the two witnesses of Revelation, who "testify to the spirit of prophecy and . . . embody it; they witness to the truth of a new birth . . . and thus precipitate a revolution that reforms the world" (Wittreich 1975, 227–28). Reformation, unfortunately, is not equivalent to individual conversion. The artist-prophet must spread the Lamb's "posthumous presence" or "spiritual agency" through the community for the *kerygma* to be realized. Thus, to activate a desire to reverse the "fallen" system of Rahab's natural religion, Blake depicts in Night IX the very process he would inculcate: the integration of the individual into the collective form he calls "Universal Humanity."

The Lamb bears crucially on the transvaluation of war and division that constitutes the main narrative of *The Four Zoas*. Of particular importance is, again, the Lamb's victory over natural law, the visionary force that nullifies death and the power of the literal sword. Night IX exhibits the fundamental prophetic principle that the higher heroism lies in intellectual war, in the struggle to reshape the figures of cultural and individual identity. In the opening lines of Night IX, the Lamb teaches Los and Enitharmon to separate the body (ideology) of nature from that of vision, coaxing them off the battlefield into the prophetic workshop. In effect, they enter narrative space and take control of the action, tearing down the poetic world constructed in the first eight Nights. Perspectives rather than human beings do battle: Los "burns" mystery and "cracks" Urizen's cosmology (his Mundane Shell) by the hammer of his imaginative faith. He aims to free Orc from Urizen's branches, which also entangle Los, by first freeing himself. He must clarify the historical problematic in individual terms, showing that Orc's hatred of tyranny and injustice, while based in honest indignation, is crossed by a debilitating emotional fury. But we should not forget that Los's regenerative embrace of Urthona's Spectre in Night VIIa was meant not only to cleanse Los's vision, but "to comfort Orc in his dire sufferings" (90:13; E 370). Los preserves and raises Orc's revolutionary wrath by self-sacrificing the Spectre, the Urizen within himself. In effect, Los's task is to transfigure wrath, Luvah's robes of blood, into a symbolic form of warfare: "and the remnant were slain with the sword of him that sat upon the horse, which sword proceeded out of his mouth" (Revelation 19:21).

Blake attempts to draw readers into the field of his symbolic war by "rouzing" their faculties, testing their responses to his apocalyptic imagery. Signs of violence are everywhere. Yet Blake provides ample clues for understanding the signs *as* signs: he underscores the *written* nature of Urizen's Newtonian cosmos and its reversal in Night IX's conflagration:

Then fell the fires of Eternity with loud & shrill
Sound of Loud Trumpet thundering along from heaven to heaven
A mighty sound articulate Awake ye dead & come
To Judgment from the four winds Awake & Come away
Folding like scrolls of the Enormous volume of Heaven & Earth
(117:10–14)

Rahab and Tirzah wail aloud in the wild flames they give up
  themselves to Consummation
The books of Urizen unroll with dreadful noise the folding Serpent
Of Orc began to Consume in fierce raving fire his fierce flames
Issud on all sides gathring strength in animating volumes
(118:7–10)

Blake can give Orc full vent of his rage within the imaginative space of Los's narrative, for his symbolism belies a literal interpretation. One could argue that Blake's apocalypse is wish fulfillment of a particularly gruesome kind; indeed, Blake could see a terrible beauty in the violent terror of the French Revolution. But he continually emphasizes the symbolic nature of his warfare, as when the linchpin of the Anglican state church, the accusatory morality embodied in the Tree of Mystery, is burned by "living flames winged with intellect," and which "march in order flame by flame" until all priests and kings, all "Mysterys tyrants are cut off & not one left on Earth" (119:12–13). Obviously, the final overthrow of these tyrants has occurred within the mind of our eternal prophet. Los's activity, however, while paradigmatic of individual regeneration, must affect the other zoas and emanations in order to bring a communal liberation. Blake thus finally awakens the "hero" of his poem, Albion (England), the composite being of Los, Urizen, Orc, and all the rest, whose speech to Urizen constitutes one of the most crucial exchanges in the poem.

Albion's first speech since Night II focuses on the war theme. Hearing Mystery howl in the flames, he demands to know "Whence is this sound of rage of Men drinking each others blood" and, suspecting Urizen, commands: "Shake off thy cold repose . . . great opposer of change" (120:20). Two more commands follow, indicating Albion's (England's) repossession of his powers. Enlightened by Los's activity within him, Albion separates Urizen from the unreasonable satanic state he has generated in history.

"Lie down before my feet O Dragon let Urizen arise," Albion says, and he then gives the solution to the nightmare of the Orc Cycle: "Let Luvah rage in the dark deep even to Consummation / For if thou feedest not his rage it will subside in peace" (120:29–33).

Albion here penetrates to the psycho-social roots of Urizen's preoccupation with war. Blake's particular target is the internal repression by moral law whose objective correlative, the exploitation of nature's energies, is sanctioned by the theology of natural religion, which, for Blake, has engineered the social upheavals of the late eighteenth century. Vowing unending war on Urizen if he refuses to unite with Orc, Albion threatens him with his own "self-destroying beast formd Science," the scientific religion of Newtonianism that defers and distances the promise of apocalypse from its personal and historical realization.

> My anger against thee is greater than against this Luvah
> For war is energy Enslavd but thy religion
> The first author of this war & the distracting of honest minds
> Into confused perturbation & strife & honor & pride
> Is a deceit so detestable that I will cast thee out
> If thou repentest not & leave thee as a rotten branch to be burned
> With Mystery the Harlot & with Satan for Ever & Ever
>
> (120:41–7)

The whole Newtonian cosmos must be dismantled, both within the individual and, subsequently, in the society: not because Newtonian physics is wrong per se, but because the Newtonian "synthesis" legitimates imperial war and domestic oppression.[7]

Los's activity in Night IX reverses the cosmic construction of Night II. It depicts a process of narrative decomposition and reconstruction, translating the literal war of nations into a war of contending perspectives. But Los's reconstruction is not enough: Urizen's ruined world cannot be remade until the other zoas and emanations organize into a collective body. That is why Albion cannot "Enter the Consummation" with Urizen: communal work must still be done to bring in the apocalyptic harvest.

Thus Albion's first policy decision is to replace the war production that has plagued the nine Nights of fallen history. "The noise of rural work" resounds as Albion's children alter their former activity: "They sing they seize the instruments of harmony they throw away / The spear the bow the gun the mortar they level the fortifications / They beat the engines of destruction into wedges," which Urthona's sons use to forge rollers that "break the clods to pass over the nations" (124:17–22). History has ripened for the harvest—"The field is the world . . . the harvest is the end of the world" (Mark 13:38)—which signals apocalypse. Yet, as ever, Blake sustains the symbolic nature of his narrative action; "Then follows the golden harrow in the midst of mental fires," and Urizen announces dramatically: "Times are Ended" (131:31).

On the brink of apocalypse, Blake inserts a feast between harvest and vintage that repeats essential motifs from his entire narrative history. Only in this eschatological context, the alternatives between literal and symbolic war, between extermination and eternal life, are finally clear cut.

The "Feast of the Eternals" separates harvest and vintage, the treading of the winepress of wrath that "consumes" six thousand years of toil.[8] It also sets up the zoas' reunion with their emanations, manifesting the synergism and collective unity toward which the poem aspires. The coherence of Blake's structural design is indicated also by the feast. On the one hand, it offsets the violent feast of Los and Enitharmon in Night I, which celebrated Orc's struggle with Urizen. The "nervous wine" of the first feast is replaced by the "wine of eternity" of the second, and the "Bloody sky" is replaced by Luvah's "flames" as the source of activity. "Clearly," James Evans writes, "the feast in Night I is a feast honoring a false semblence of victory in corporeal battle; the feast in Night IX is a feast of the victory of mental harmony" (Evans 1972, 320). On the other hand, the feast in Night IX provides a setting for one of the "Eternals" to proclaim the principles of solidarity. This proclamation enables not just the zoas and emanations to integrate in the risen Albion, but for Albion himself to reunite with *his* family, the Eternals.

In what, for my purposes, is the definitive speech in the poem, an Eternal rises and recasts the story of the first nine nights in the apocalyptic context of Night IX ("Being the Last Judgment"). The situation calls for a reversal of the narrative history put in motion by two seminal zoic figures, Tharmas and Enion, the "parental powers" of humanity who create the Circle of Destiny, the tormenting warp and woof of time that generates the Orc Cycle. The Eternal consolidates and then unpacks the "error" of earthly life, syncretizing the psychological, social, and cosmological dimensions of Blake's narrative.

> Man is a Worm wearied with joy he seeks the caves of sleep
> Among the Flowers of Beulah in his Selfish cold repose
> Forsaking Brotherhood & Universal love in selfish clay
> Folding the pure wings of his mind seeking the places dark

Abstracted from the roots of Science then inclosd around
In walls of Gold we cast him like a Seed into the Earth
Till times & spaces have passd over him duly every morn
We visit him covering with a Veil the immortal seed
With windows . . . we cover him & with walls
And hearths protect the Selfish terror till divided all
In families we see our shadows born. & thence we know
That Man subsists by Brotherhood & Universal Love
We fall on one anothers necks more closely we embrace
Not for ourselves but for the Eternal family we live
Man liveth not by Self alone but in his brothers face

(133:11–25)

The solution of empathic brotherhood, which Los witnesses in the Lamb donning Luvah's robes of blood, is buttressed in this passage by a marginal allusion to Ephesians 3:10. The only other glosses in the poem appear on the title page, and one in particular (it introduces the poem) forms a counterpart to the Ephesians gloss. Blake in fact ties them closely together: the title page epigraph about spiritual wickedness in high places is reversed by the passage on page 133 of Blake's text. In Ephesians 3:10 Paul tells his audience that he has been blessed with grace to preach "fellowship," but with the radical "intent that now unto the principalities and powers in heavenly places might be known by the church the manifold wisdom of God." The primitive Christian church is the spiritual agency of this direct challenge to the authorities. Its anger, however, has coupled with the visionary courage inspired by the Lamb, so that a new gospel emerges: the Eternal then embraces Albion "the New born Man" as part of the "Eternal family," an embrace that completes the individual integration of Los with his Spectre in Night VIIa.

The Eternal's speech shows Blake's firm grasp of the function of prophetic narrative. In Blake's conception of prophecy, as in the "fourfold" hermeneutic scheme of the medieval church, the figural movement from prophetic types to antitypes occurs but is not completely contained within the polysemantic space of the narrative. A *kerygmatic* dimension to prophecy challenges its audience to take direct action on a text, to make a dialectical turn from text to history, which Albion does when he embraces the Eternal following the proclamation of brotherhood. This turn begins in individual readers, but it also opens the internalized apocalypse to the larger community. As in the medieval scheme of four levels, Blake's narrative shifts gears from the literal to the typological through the "tropological" (moral) levels of meaning, so that the destiny of the people (Israel) is rewritten in terms of individual biography (Christ). But, with Fredric Jameson, I believe that the "tropological" level of individual moral biography "is clearly insufficient by itself, and at once generates the fourth or anagogic sense, in which the text undergoes its ultimate rewriting in terms of the destiny of the human race as a whole" (Jameson 1981, 30–31). Although Blake's narrative does not need the medieval scheme to make sense, his multivalent text does move from the individual trajectory of Los to the collective destiny of Albion.

Once Albion embraces the Eternal, the narrative is poised for apocalyptic consummation, which Blake dramatizes as the vintage that ferments the grapes of wrath into the wine of spiritual communion. Luvah's robes of blood, the garments of war, undergo a figurative transformation into the Lamb's "vesture dipped in blood," a garment John of Patmos identifies with the "Word of God" (Revelation 19:13). Blake presents the vintage as an inherently social event, a fulfillment of the Second Coming anticipated in Christ's first incarnation in the individual. Adapting a passage from *America a Prophecy,* Blake places it into the more fully realized context of Night IX to highlight the political perspective of his apocalypse. The passage begins "Let the slave grinding at the mill run out into the field" and concludes: "Are these the Slaves that groand along the streets of Mystery / Where are your bonds & task masters are these the prisoners / Where are your chains. . . . The good of all the Land is before you for Mystery is no more" (124:18–29).

The reference to the conclusion of *Paradise Lost* is apt, particularly in the collective context under discussion. For Adam and Eve's departure from Eden points to the extratextual dimension of Milton's poem, or to the fact that Milton's protagonists do not fulfill Michael's prophecy in the narrative space of the epic. And if, as Milton scholars argue, Adam and Eve somehow represent Milton's readers, then one could argue that these readers do not fulfill prophecy in the region of the narrative either. Individual readers enact the *kerygmatic* demand of prophecy when they become part of the community trying to work out the metanarrative of liberation. Once this collective goal is grasped, the (self) divisions of war can vanish, and Blake's prophet of rage (Luvah-Orc) can be released from the burden of sacrificial atonement for others.

Luvah's liberation is precisely what is accomplished in Night IX of *The Four Zoas.* As he drinks the "wine of ages" and sings a new song, a song of Los, "his crown of thorns fell from his head"

(135:23). Luvah has ceased to define himself in opposition to Urizen: he realizes that Urizen is a "Man" and not a "God," for the
mysterious, abstract deity of natural religion embodies a fundamental error: "Attempting to be more than Man We become less
said Luvah." With Luvah and Urizen now in harness, Tharmas
and Urthona (the regenerated Los) resume their ancient partner-
ship at the controls of history. They take over harvest and vintage,
creating bread and wine from Urizen's thresher and Luvah's
wine presses.

The communal transformations of Night IX correct the errors
instigated by the Urizen-Luvah conspiracy, the Orc Cycle, and the
subsequent attempts at domination by each of the zoas. As the
most creative zoa, Urthona becomes the key figure: indeed, it is
his "fall into Division & his Resurrection to Unity" that Blake
announces as his epic theme in the opening pages. As Urthona
(re)emerges as the prodigal hero of the final pages, the narrator
describes his activity as confronting the insidious social effects of
the Urizenic philosophy, as "Men are bound" to sullen contempla-
tions, feeling the "crushing Wheels" of life and death contend
"in their inmost brain" (138:11–14). In a difficult but suggestive
passage, the narrator says "Urthona made the Bread of Ages. . . .
then took his repose . . . in the night of Time." Harold Bloom
sees an apocalyptic reversal taking place between lines 19 and 20
of manuscript page 138, between Urthona's "night of Time" and
the "Morning" of Albion's resurrection into unity (Erdman 1982,
967). Whether or not Bloom is right, the significant gap between
night and morning effectively hands the poem over to its readers.
Urthona does not reverse the world *for* Blake's audience; he attempts to enact symbolically a mode of perception that, if adopted,
can effect a change of perspective that leads to "vision." Readers
then become responsible for realizing vision in act, for becoming
witnesses to imaginative truths that can transform a war-torn
world into a community. When Urthona reposes, our work begins.

We thus return to the problem of an individual and social
apocalypse and the concomitant issue of literalism. The Romantic
poets, unlike their pre-Enlightenment forerunners of the seventeenth century, tend to stress the symbolic nature of apocalypse
to avoid the literal closure of history. But they do so in the subjective terms that Frye and M. H. Abrams have reiterated (see Abrams 1963, 53). Wittreich, building on Frye and Abrams, anchors
the Romantic apocalypse more securely in this world, and he
makes the notable observation that "Blake is the only Romantic
poet to present a united vision of apocalypse in the mind and in

history" (Wittreich 1987, 59). But when we move from archetypal to "actual" history in *The Four Zoas,* from the seven-phase eschatological frame to within the frame where the wars are being fought, we see that history eludes Los the prophet's individual control. Los relies on the Lamb's provident power, on the "Universal hand", when he despairs of arresting the cycles of bloodshed. No need to deny the essential role of individual conversion, the paradigmatic experience of self-examination that the prophet undergoes. For the solution to the "error" of literal apocalyptic lies in the *kerygmatic* conception of apocalypse that requires a move from individual to collective conversion.

If conversion is traditionally a matter of vision or perception, related to how we see, we should also realize that perception itself is determined by the ideological constraints blocking vision. In *The Four Zoas* Blake does not portray an apocalyptic annihilation of the external world; he suggests that the world, in addition to its materiality, is a construct of human experience. I believe that Blake does want to induce, or at least encourage, his readers to alter their ingrained perceptions of reality. That is why we get the same objects, the Urizenic cosmos, in Night IX as in earlier nights, only from an entirely different epistemological perspective (Evans 1972, 329). Again, those who stress the individual apocalypse make a crucial but, I believe, partial contribution to understanding Blake's version of apocalypse, particularly (and perhaps primarily) in *The Four Zoas,* where Blake tries to carry history with him into the Last Judgment. War will continue to mar history unless both the mental constructs *and* their social correlatives are challenged and broken. While the individual is responsible for breaking his or her own mind-forged manacles, defeating spiritual wickedness in high places requires the collective opposition of "Brotherhood & Universal Love."

Blake, then, compels us to come to terms with the forceful illogic of his position, the paradox of summing up history in an eschatological narrative while keeping the future open for collective conversion. The point lies in the fundamental and enabling gap between fiction and the world, between narrative and its audience, a gap that enables readers to embrace apocalypse without literally seeking to annihilate history. Hence the importance of poetry as a mediation between history and "the End." Blake's apocalypse operates in the gap between fiction and the world and opens into history by virtue of its transactive focus. His radically open-ended narrative thus reveals a truth about all narrative: that it is constituted by the interaction of an internal form and a *kerygmatic* force. If *The Four Zoas* is not a perfect poem, it remains a powerful one: it is the prophetic workshop where Blake matures his epic vision, where he forges his "spiritual agents" to challenge and admonish readers to carry that vision into their communities.

Plates

Οτι ουκ εστιν ημιν η παλη προς αιμα και σαρκα, αλλα προς τας αρχας, προς τας εξουσιας, προς τας κοσμοκρατορας τυ σκοτυς τυ αιωνος τυτυ, προς τα πνευματικα της πονηριας εν τοις επουρανιοις.

Εφεσ. VI κεφ 12

VALA

Night the First

1 The Song of the Aged Mother which shook the heavens with wrath
2 Hearing the march of long resounding strong heroic Verse
3 Marshalld in order for the day of Intellectual Battle
6 The heavens quake: the earth moved & shudderd & the mountains
7 With all their woods, the streams & valleys: waild in dismal fear

4 Four Mighty Ones are in every Man: a Perfect Unity
Cannot Exist. but from the Universal Brotherhood of Eden
The Universal Man. To Whom be Glory Evermore Amen

Los was the fourth immortal starry one. & in the Earth
Of a bright Universe. Empery attended day & night
Days & nights of revolving joy, Urthona was his name

John XVII c. 21 22. 23

John 10. 14 v
και εγνωσθεν
εν ημιν

In

Page 3. Night I. Pencil and ink drawing with brown, blue, gray, and black watercolor washes.

Page 25. Night II. Chalk drawing.

Page 40. Night III. Pencil drawing.

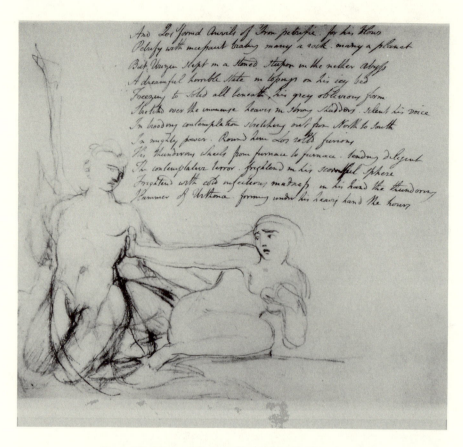

Page 52. Night IV. Pencil and chalk drawing.

Once how I walked from my palace in gardens of delight
The sons of wisdom stood around the harpers followd with harps
Nine virgins clothd in light compos'd the song to their immortal voices
And at my banquets of new wine my head was crownd with joy   200

Then in my ivory pavilions I slumberd on the noon
And walked in the silent night among sweet smelling flowers
Till on my silver bed I slept & sweet dreams round me hoverd
But now my land is darkend & my wise men are departed

My songs are turnd into cries of Lamentation
Heard on my Mountains & deep sighs under my palace roofs
Because the Steeds of Urizen once swifter than the light
Were kept back from my Lord & from his chariot of mercies

O did I keep the horses of the day in silver pastures
O I refusd the lord of day the horses of his prince
O did I close my treasuries with roofs of solid stone
And darken all my Palace walls with envyings & hate

O Fool to think that I could hide from his all piercing eyes
The gold & silver & costly stones his holy workmanship
O Fool could I forget the will that filld my bright spheres
Was a reflection of his face who calls me from the deep
I well remember for I heard the mild & holy voice
Saying O light spring up & shine & I sprang up from the deep
He gave to me a silver sceptre & crownd me with a golden crown
& said Saying Go forth & guide my Son who wanders on the ocean

I went not forth I hid myself in black clouds of my wrath
I calld the stars around my feet in the night of councils dark
The stars threw down their spears & fled away naked
We fell. I siezd thee dark Urthona In my left hand falling
I siezd thee beauteous Luvah thou art faded like a flower
And like a lily is thy wife Vala witherd by winds
When thou didst bear the golden cup at the immortal tables
Thy children smote their fiery wings crownd with the gold of heaven

Page 64. Night V. Pencil and chalk drawing.

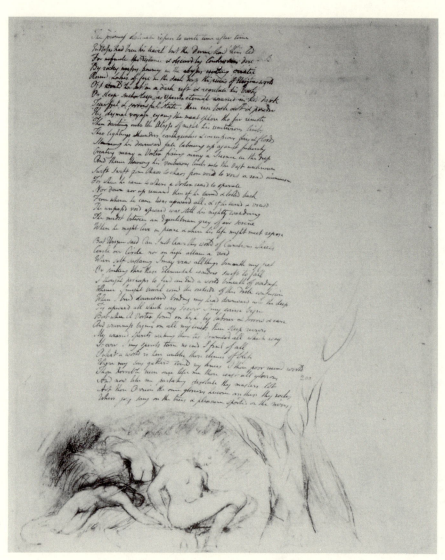

Page 72. Night VI. Pencil and chalk drawing.

Page 84. Night VII. Pencil drawing.

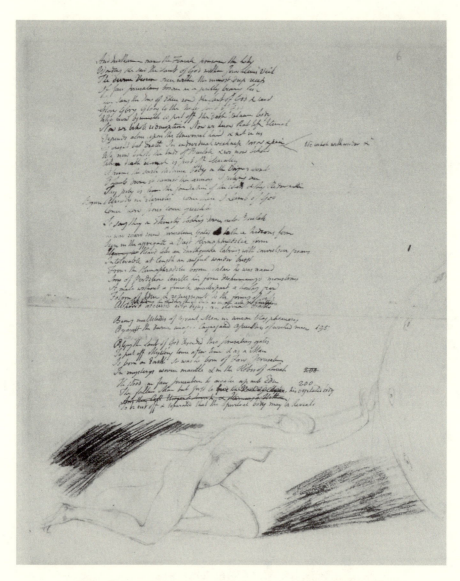

Page 104. Night VIII. Pencil drawing with chalk shading.

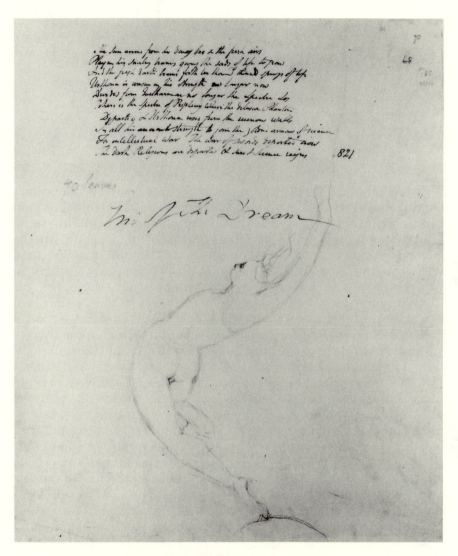

Page 139. Night IX. Pencil drawing.

Appendix:
A Commentary on the Drawings

I<small>N</small> what follows I consider some correlations between the poem's narrative and visual components. While no definitive statement can be made about this unruly, incomplete manuscript, my sense is that the sketches and drawings in *The Four Zoas* and in the *Night Thoughts* proofs work roughly by a twofold strategy: first, analogous to his narrative method, Blake *repeats* key images in various frames to signal changing context or development; second, he exposes visually what his narrative represses, often (but not always) in graphic sexual detail. To facilitate this discussion, I focus on the creation-fall narratives examined in chapter three.

While I am indebted to the Erdman and Magno facsimile edition, which consistently pairs text and design, I draw particularly on two studies (by John Beer and John Grant) for my twofold thesis.[1] Although Grant dismisses Beer's brief commentary on the drawings as "worthless," Beer does link the drawings closely to the text: the designs "make clear that the phallic significance which one senses from time to time is really a part of the poem" (Beer 1969, 344). And though Grant is interested mainly in visual language, he does formulate a broad enough principle about the drawings to apply to the text-design connection: "What one finds in Blake's iconography . . . is a series of metamorphic variations on a large repertoire of key images" (Grant 1973, 148). Aligning Grant's "variation" principle with Beer's insight into the "phallic" aspect of the narrative, I argue that pictorial contexts broaden the creation-fall accounts in the *Four Zoas* manuscript, helping to create a distinctly Blakean plurality of sexual, social, and cosmological meanings.

Night I

The first three pages of the manuscript supply important generic and thematic signals for understanding the creation-fall narratives. The first page retains two titles, suggesting two versions of Albion's fall: the strife among the four zoas and the generation of a separate female will (Stevenson 1972, 123). These versions, in turn, summon two ancient myths that permeate Blake's thinking about cultural origins, as implied on the opening page of text (manuscript page 3): "The Song of the Aged Mother which shook the heavens with wrath / Hearing the march of long resounding strong heroic Verse" (3:1–2). Blake invokes the Great Mother and War in Heaven myths, which according to Jackie DiSalvo record the breakup of a "tribal Eden" or egalitarian clan—Blake's "Universal / Brotherhood of Eden" (3:5).[2] Blake places this brotherhood in contentious relation to both the matrilineal ("pagan") and the patriarchal (Jewish) traditions behind the Genesis cosmogony.

In typically iconoclastic style Blake inserts two marginal glosses from the Gospel of John (to support the theme of Edenic brotherhood) that are challenged by the female figure drawn below. She appears in brown and blue wash, her body in a V (for Vala) shape, her pose provocatively sexual. Her right arm extends behind her head, in marked contrast to the male "resting" on page 2.[3] Blake sets this paganized figure against Judeo-Christian brotherhood, for Vala's left leg (sketched in) extends up the right margin, nearly kicking the Gospel glosses off the page.

Blake prepares for the first account of the creation-fall, the Song of Vala by Enitharmon, with a series of sketches (pages 3–7) that anticipate Los and Enitharmon's birth from Enion on page 8. Tharmas plunges *in medias res* into his lament on page 4, which displays an intensely focused Cupid, crouching on a large phallic serpent, aiming bow and arrow from the snaky cloud he rides. Even though Tharmas sits on a cloud bemoaning the absence of his emanation, the drawing implicates him in this loss. For as Tharmas speaks of love and liberty, the Cupid figure (portrayed in various contexts throughout the poem—pages 4–5, 19, 25, 40, 108, 134, and 136) uncovers the erotic nature of his fall.

The Cupid-Tharmas identity is illustrated on page 5, the page on which Tharmas turns the "circle of Destiny." Tharmas-Cupid buries his head in his hands and weeps as his Spectre and Enion (textually) generate the "woven shadow" of creation (5:27). Page 6 shows a still-winged Tharmas sleeping while Enion, in the text, draws out his zoic potential on her loom of vegetation. The text states that both Tharmas and Enion are ensnared in fallen creation—"mingling their bodies"—which the horror-struck figure on page 7 confirms. This "Half Woman & half Spectre," trailing a serpent tail, embodies the male-female split that marks each account of the Fall. Generation from mothers and fathers is a step down from Edenic brotherhood.[4]

While the pages on which the first creation-fall narrative appears (10 and 11) are faint and disappointing, they are flanked by illustrations of Los and Enitharmon's fallen existence. Page 9, which follows a picture of Enion nursing Los and Enitharmon, shows the children's sadistic glee in watching the aged mother stumble after them. Page 12 manifests the basis of their actions: Los and Enitharmon, engaged in a vicious duel, compulsively repeat their parent's tormented love and jealousy, which at least establishes a pattern or kind of experience that possibly may be understood, worked through, and transformed.

Two minor details, one visual and one textual, point to this redemptive possibility. One is the small drawing at the top of page 9, depicting Jesus in a globe, his arms outstretched in a gesture that "corrects the jealous tilt of Los's arms (below)" (Erdman and Magno 1987, 30). (This open-armed gesture reappears throughout the manuscript, and Blake's work in general, and is unfailingly positive.) Two, directly above the dueling couple on page 12, Blake inserts these lines: "Los saw the wound of his blow he saw he pitied he wept / Los now repented that he had smitten Enitharmon he felt love" (12: 40–41). In context, these lines and the englobed Jesus remain dialectic *potentialities,* but they do intersect and broaden the meaning of the first creation-fall account.

The other creation-fall narrative of Night I, by the Messengers of Beulah, also appears on pages with faint and insignificant sketches. It ends, however, with Cupid pursuing his sexually devious antics on manuscript page 21[19]. The Messengers' account clarifies the political context and details Urthona's division into emanation and spectre. They explain that when Enitharmon appears, Tharmas takes her in and Enion embalms her; Urthona's Spectre then flees to Enion and Tharmas watches him fall as "a raging serpent." The textual image is correlated with a depiction of Cupid in the act of firing his arrow into a female's crotch. This Cupid can be identified as an aspect of Luvah (he has been Tharmas *and* Urthona's Spectre), responding to Urizen's plot; Luvah has been tricked (as Urizen absconds to the North) and left to "smite" Albion alone.

The politics of the Urizen-Luvah plot, unmasked in graphic sexual detail, are also cosmological. In fact, the cosmic-sexual politics of this war in heaven so horrify the "Divine Family" that they draw up the "Universal tent" *above* Snowdon and cast the Messengers in a cloud "Till the time of the End" (21[19]:90). This withdrawal of responsibility—repeated by Albion at the opening of Night II—is mitigated by their election of seven prophetic "Eyes" to watch over "the Man" as he "wanders" through the rest of the poem. The dialectic of fallen and redeemable creation works by such contradiction: as the Lamb of God "followd the Man," a female figure is shown laying on her back, slain by Cupid's arrow-penis stuck in her vagina. However, while the fallen Venus-Vala is (visually) penetrated, Enitharmon's "Gates" remain closed (textually), not to be opened until a new creation emerges in Night VII to replace the fallen creations of Nights I and II.

Night II

In this Night, the ancient religion of the Great Mother is absorbed into Urizen's patriarchal cosmology. As the opening of Nights I and II are linked through Enion's lamenting "voice" (which induces Albion's abdication), Urizen's Mundane Shell becomes a variant of Enion's "filmy woof" or "created Phantasm." The drawing on page 23 suggests as much. A spectral figure, immersed in a chalky veil, illustrates either Albion or Urizen-in-Albion rising on his "couch of Death" while just above the figure's eyes, we read: "pale he beheld the Abyss / Where Enion . . . wept in direful hunger craving" (23: 15–16). This Night and Night III exhibit, par excellence, the strategy of exposing narrative repression—in cosmological and sexual terms—while they also constitute Blake's grim satire on Genesis.

Blake alternates the sexual and cosmological terms between pages 24 and 29. On 24 a faint sketch of a naked female (perhaps Enion) falls in the margin (of "Non Entity") as a phallus extends up the left margin, its head drawn across from the lines: "Build we the Mundane Shell" (24:8). On page 25, the narrator describes Urizen's sealing of Luvah-Vala in the "furnaces of affliction" (25:40) while the drawing visualizes its cosmological import. A male figure (Urizen) wields three sets of "poles" in his hands, two of them drawn over the stanza about the sealing. For Grant, the figure "is conceptually related" to the Cupid on page 19, perhaps because of the phallic poles. Two poles circle parts of the words "affliction" and "necessity," while the third extends from Urizen's left hand below the text through the final "r" of the phrase "iron power." Blake's deft irony is revealed by these touches, and by drawing Urizen's head directly below the final line on the page: "in woe & fear he saw" (25:44).

Page 26—the most discussed in the manuscript—illustrates Luvah's tale of Vala's "evolution." I do not have much to add, except to suggest that it uncovers what Urizen fears to see on page 25: the polymorphous perversity of the mystery religions he absorbs into his cosmos. More crucially, Urizen is, like Luvah, deeply dependent on both the pagan goddess and her minions, his source of slave labor. Page 27, which depicts a skeletal Urizen veiled inside a net with Vala, indicates his actual subjugation to her sexuality, as do the highly-charged erotic illustrations on pages 28 and 32. On page 28, the Sons of Urizen "divide the deep" with compasses and strong scales as the word "erect" is written above a lewd drawing of a naked youth and half-naked woman next to him, her left arms wound behind her head (reversing Vala's gesture on page 3). "There is," Butlin writes, "an erasure between them, suggesting an erotic scene" (Butlin 1981, 278–79). These pages unveil, so to speak, the sexually repressive nature of Urizen's "sublime" creation.

Where page 32 visually exposes the monstrous fertility rites involved in Urizen's creation, page 33 textually links it to the cosmic politics of Night I. We learn that Urizen is doing the work of the Divine Family, walling the universal tent from mortality below. This attempt to evade a temporal realm is doomed on two counts: the "Divine Lamb" permits Urizen to create a golden chain to "bind him to heaven" and keep him "from falling into the Abyss"; and Urizen cannot silence Enion's cry of discontent. The drawing on page 36 shows that Ahania, his female consort, also suffers from his blindness. As Enion delivers her moving lament—"I am made to sow"—Ahania is drawn literally into the margin with her, where she delivers her "Vision."

Night III

As Ahania narrates her account of the creation-fall, the drawings in Night III expose in graphic detail the perversions that support Urizen's deified power. Blake choses the two *Night Thoughts* proofs for this Night with care. The first (page 43) follows Ahania's narrative and the most erotic series of manuscript drawings, and in context reveals the hypocrisy of Urizen's tablet of law. The second (page 45), one of many parallel sets of drawings, illustrates the Lazarus story: with Lazarus countering Urizen's

gesture on page 44, these designs counterpoint Blake's antinomian and institutional versions of Christianity.

Ahania's eloquent account of the "Fall" begins on the last line
of the sexually graphic page 38: "O Prince the Eternal One hath
set thee leader of his hosts" (38:15). Erdman and Magno describe
the visual context thus: "In the left margin our friend Cupid . . .
appears to be mounted (as in page 21) on a vague phallic erasure
. . . thrust upward from the cluster of naked copulating bodies at
the bottom of the page" (Erdman and Magno 1987, 44). Not an
auspicious beginning, although Urizen and Ahania suppress this
information. When Ahania shifts into the "Fall" narrative proper,
she hints that Urizen's delusion about his own purity actually generates Albion's "holy" Shadow, which in turn induces Albion's guilt
for some unspecified sin—revealed in both the (erased, censored)
drawing on page 39 and the text of page 40.

With pointed irony, Blake shows that the sin occurs when Albion
turns his back on Vala, on his own desire (41:4), a repression that
spills out of the text and into the margins of the manuscript.
That this repression is engineered by Urizen, Ahania can only
insinuate. But when she closes Albion's insert at the bottom of
page 40—"the shadowy voice was silent; but the cloud hoverd
over their heads"—Blake places her "Vision" in a graphically dis-
turbing context. As in the opening pages of the poem, the cloud
is mounted by Cupid: only this time he is wearing spurs "with
sharply spiked rowel," pulling reins attached to Vala's arms, which
are bent back over her head. He is "astride not the female but
the male, the Luvah figure who in turn is astride Vala, in the
posture of coitus from the rear" (Erdman and Magno 1987, 46).
Although Ahania cannot verbalize it, the maintenance of Urizen's
system requires such degradations of human desire. Its cost, the
"torments of love and jealousy," is revealed on page 41, one of
the most interesting parlays of text and design in the manuscript.
It shows that in Urizen's cosmic system, "Love" (Luvah) is forced
to seek dominion on its own (exploited) terms.

The gnarled syntax that connects pages 40 and 41—"but the
cloud hoverd over their heads / In golden wreaths, the sorrow
of Man & the balmy drops fell down"—performs a number of
functions. The "balmy drops" that (textually) come from the cloud
are drawn as drops of semen falling onto the face of a female
figure in the margin below. In the text, as Luvah-Love descends
from the cloud and Albion turns his back on Vala, Ahania reports
that Urizen "rolls" *his* cloud in "sickning mists" (41:5). In the

drawing, this sequence of actions is illustrated as Vala ejaculating the erect penis of a half-drawn headless torso. The irony is crude but lends urgency to Ahania's claim that she cannot contain the "dismal vision," that "Prophetic dreads" compel her to speak.

This visionary urgency is underscored by a phrase that Blake inserts at the center of the page, which—with the twisted syntax of line 1—supplies a sense of prophetic relief. Ahania claims simply: "Rent from Eternal Brotherhood we die & are no more" (41:9). If the key figure in this Brotherhood of Eden is that Man of Sorrow, Jesus or the "Lamb in Luvahs robes," then Blake connects line 1 of page 41 to the "cloud" of page 40 in a redemptive if highly unorthodox manner: syntactically he links the "sorrow of Man" to the "balmy drops" of Luvah descending from the cloud. The Man of Sorrow (drawn on page 45) offers a more human "balm," if you will, than what falls from the male organ.

Pages 43 and 45, the two *Night Thoughts* proofs, continue these lessons in the art of visual contrast. Following the uninhibited eroticism of pages 38 to 42, the design of Urizen's scroll of law on page 43 makes a stunning point: law equals repression. This insight from the "Everlasting Gospel" is confirmed textually on pages 43 and 44 and visually on 44 and 45. Textually, the corrupt system is exposed by Ahania's vision and demolished by Tharmas's flood. Visually, pages 44 and 45 depict male figures gesturing upward (Urizen on page 44 with his left arm, Lazarus on page 45 with his right). On page 44, Butlin sees a man with body torn open and woman wearing a spiked crown with "a sort of Gothic tabernacle at her loins" (Butlin 1981, 281): that the female *does not* offer to help the male, although it has psychological and political logic, contrasts with Jesus touching the heart of Lazarus on page 45. His gesture is redemptive, even if Urizen's contradicts it at this narrative-historical juncture. Blake's brilliant evocation seals the union between Vala's natural and Urizen's patriarchal religions.

Night IV

This is the Night of Tharmas's flood, his transfer of power to Los, and Los's re-creation (binding) of Urizen. Where Night I explores the ancient context behind Genesis, and Nights II and III explore the Elohist cosmogony, Night IV draws on the Jahwist strand, which includes the story of Adam and Eve. The two drawings and the proof on pages 48, 49, and 52 visualize Eve's birth; pages 49 and 50 present the Tharmas–Spectre of Urthona creation account. As these pages illustrate the narrative rather than expose its suppressed content, they remind us that in this experimental manuscript Blake did not always execute his visual strategies with consistency.

The Night begins with Tharmas lamenting for Enion, which recalls not only the epic opening but the ends of Nights II and III. Blake signals the later narrative context by bringing Los-Enitharmon back in "strength" and "scorn" after successfully planting division in Ahania-Urizen's soul. Cursing Urizen and Luvah, Tharmas commands Los—"Son" and "comforter"—to rebuild the universe and reform "endless corruption." But Los too is corrupt and rashly opposes Tharmas, claiming in confusion that Urizen is his God, that he is God, and that his own zoic power, Urthona, is merely his shadow. "Doubting," Tharmas looks on half enraged, half pitying, until Enitharmon calls him an "abhorred Demon" for overthrowing Urizen's creation.

Tharmas's response—"What Sovereign Architect . . . dare my will controll" (49:1)—is to rip Enitharmon from Los's side in a bleak parody of Eve's birth from Adam's rib. As Los howls in torment and his right arm stanches the blood (page 48), a "Dark Spectre" appears in the text. In Blake's brilliant textual-visual correlation, the Spectre of Urthona falls upon the shore (where Los lies in pain) and delivers his creation-fall account directly above the illustration (page 49), which shows a serpent poised to strike a male connected by his left side to the lower spine and buttocks of a woman. This hermaphroditic creation is also depicted on page 52: Los with female genitals giving birth to Eve-Enitharmon.

Genesis imagery augments the Spectre's account, in which he reenacts Urthona's division from Enitharmon, who emerges (in text and drawing) as a separate female on page 50. She is supported by the waves (of Tharmas) from which Los rebuilds the universe: Tharmas groans upon the tide "till underneath the feet of Los a World / Dark dreadful rose" (51:8–9). On this same page, Tharmas hands power over to Los in terms that look toward the prophetic humanism of the epic's final lines: "Is this to be a God rather would I be a Man / To know sweet science & to do with simple companions. . . . / Take thou the hammer of Urthona and rebuild these furnaces" (51:29–33). This transfer is accompanied by another redemptive sign. On the last page (56), as a limit is put to "Eternal Death," an old man is raised by a young figure that Erdman and Magno identify as Orc, whose birth is narrated in Night V.

Night V

In this Night of Orc's birth—"the night of prophecy" Urizen deems it—the drawings again expose sexually repressed content, namely the incestual family dynamics between Los, Orc, and Enitharmon on pages 60, 62, and 64. The drawing on page 64, which features Urizen's confessional account of the Fall, shows a dual cosmo-sexual configuration matched in complexity only by page 27 of Night II. Significantly, Urizen utters his confession only after Orc's "birth" opens the furnaces in which Luvah and Vala were sealed in Nights I and II. And since Los has bound him in a body, Urizen must confront the temporal form of his adversary Luvah in Orc. That the confrontation is providential is corroborated by a clearly redemptive signal: Orc's birth (page 58) is followed by the first (of five in all) full-page drawing of Jesus.

Ironic counterpointing comes thick and heavy on pages 60, 62, and 63, preparing the way for Urizen's confession. On page 60, as Los binds Orc with the cosmo-sexual "chain of Jealousy," the drawing portrays *Los* chain-bound, looking jealously on as Orc and Enitharmon fondle each other. Los throws a tantrum on page 62, which illustrates Orc's chaining to the rock: as he is crowned naked, Los is implicated with Urizen as he too fears an alliance between the aged mother and the wrathful son of prophecy. The *Night Thoughts* proof on page 63 deepens these ironies: it depicts a happy holy family, with smiling child and joyous mother, the proud father's hand spanning the length of the child's body in a gesture of loving confinement. Despite Los's repentance for chaining Orc and professing love for him (page 62), the relation between text and design (page 63) suggests that Los becomes what he beholds—an oppressive father.

On the sexually graphic page 64, Blake piles on layers of meaning, although irony intersects both the text and drawing. It dramatizes an Oedipal scene: Enitharmon sits on the ground, her head bent back to kiss Orc above her, Los straddling her leg. As Los gazes intently into the cosmic net he holds, Orc cups Enitharmon's breasts as she reaches back with her left hand, seizing his "tumid organ." The scene moves literally into the text, next to Urizen's line: "We fell. I seized thee dark Urthona In my left hand falling"

(64:28). The textual-visual pun yokes the sexual and cosmological levels of meaning in a graphically striking way.

The social level, while less visible, can be found with attention to minute detail. Below Enitharmon's vagina crawls a tiny crab, which on closer inspection turns into a "grinning jester Cupid," as Erdman and Magno put it, sporting cap and bells. Grant regards the scene as a version of the "cuckholding of Hephaestus by Aphrodite and Ares": "According to Homer," he writes, "the illicit lovers were netted by Los's prototype, but here Blake's blacksmith-to-be seems snared in his own (Urizenic) gins" (Grant 1973, 171). This interesting classical allusion is apt but needs to be situated in another, less urbane, context: that of the radical pornographers of Blake's day, the lower-class artisans and disaffected intelligentsia that Iain McCalman discusses in his *Radical Underworld.* Their bawdy iconography echoes in the drawings of *The Four Zoas,* even if Blake's sketches shame anything in print. He shows, perhaps, more affinity with the Marquis de Sade, although Blake's ironic self-awareness and human empathy keep him from validating sadomasochism.[5]

Night VI

Night VI witnesses Urizen's return to narrative and visual prominence as he "explores his dens" and reasserts theocratic control after the Flood.[6] Through repetition of key images, the Night also enacts a major symbolic metamorphosis: the chain and net imagery of Night V merges with the serpents and phalluses of previous nights, turning Urizen's "cumbrous wheels" into menacing dragons. The most complex example of this merging occurs on pages 72 and 73, which present Urizen's second creation account and introduce (visually) one of the crucial typological symbols in the poem—Urizen's Tree of Mystery. These narrative and visual developments expand into Nights VII, VIII, and IX.

Pages 72 and 73 resume Blake's strategy of exposing the narrative's repressed sexual content: except that by repeating images in this context, he points to a strangely compulsive development. While Urizen echoes his confessional version at the end of Night V, the scene below his lament—"Can I not leave this world of Cumbrous wheels / Circle oer Circle" (72:22)—draws out the sexual implications, providing a tragic contrast to his text. Where Urizen reminisces of "those climes of Bliss" when "joy sang in the trees," Blake draws a tree that enfolds the corner of the text and overarches three naked women who "languish in various postures of despair" (Grant 1973, 177). This "Oak" of mystery bears a large "vaginal" slit that clutches a fallen figure by the waist, his left elbow touching the ground and his lower half bound to the right of the "vaginal" line. To consider, with Grant, that the "serpentine tree . . . is Urizen himself" makes the exposure all the more revealing (Grant 1973, 177).

As we turn to page 73, Blake unveils further textual-visual contrasts that move us toward the apocalyptic consolidations of the final Nights. Urizen prefaces his creation by acknowledging that he is compelled to "eternally" lose his powers, regenerate, and wander in perpetual discontent. At the same time he declares: "Here will I fix my foot & here rebuild." As if this irony were not enough, he binds "all futurity" in his vast chain and "fixes his sciences" to terrify "every human soul" with his "turning wheels." These textual ironies are woven into the web image that the narrator introduces to describe Urizen's "New Dominion," his new cosmology. Further, the web is drawn out of Urizen's soul and vibrates, as in Night II, with the torment of his victims. The instability of his creation, however, while it produces real pain, is offset by the providential signs that circumscribe it.

The design (a proof from *Night Thoughts*) depicts a large serpentine dragon, an *ouroboros,* that surrounds the textual frame. The design includes a starry-haired woman whose open-armed gesture counteracts both the dragon and the oppressed women on page 72. Redemptive signs also appear textually—Urizen is conducted toward Urthona's world by "Providence divine" (74:31)—and visually, in the male-female figure on page 76, which separates Nights VI and VII. Erdman and Magno name the figure "War as hermaphroditic Satan," the Beast-Whore symbol that Blake adapts from Revelation. This figure not only embodies the sexual politics of Urizen's chain-web of religion, but condenses the serpentine tree and dragon into one apocalyptic form.

Night VII

As the iconographic problems are compounded by the textual ones, I will not venture into a discussion of the two Nights VII. Instead I will focus on the final creation-fall account in the manuscript, presented on pages 83 and 84 of Night VIIa, although pages 81 and 82 provide an arresting visual introduction.

The introduction to Enitharmon's account on page 82 repeats

a key image that, in the new context, indicates how far we have come. The naked female figure is not exposing sexually repressed content. This condition is made possible by the previous design, the first state of a *Night Thoughts* proof that Blake redeploys on page 133 in Night IX. Although the Night VII narrative context belies finality, page 81 reveals an apocalyptic image: Death, dart in hand, is pulling down the sun and trampling on dead kings, ready "to tread out empire" as Erdman and Magno put it (Erdman and Magno 1987, 70). As Urizen realizes, the "time of Prophecy has now revolvd" (95:4; E 360), which means that the Circle of Destiny is about to turn. But who is in control? Page 83 unveils the answer: the reader-viewer. The spry female figure holding the eight-starred circle open toward page 83 shows that destiny is finally in *human* hands. And as Erdman and Magno further suggest, the eight stars are the "Eyes of God," of which "the seventh will be Jesus, the eighth the present reader" (Erdman and Magno 1987, 71). Blake's *kerygmatic* narrative strategy includes a visual correlative.

Apocalyptic imagery is carried forward in the proof from *Night Thoughts,* on page 83, which frames the creation-fall account by Urthona's Spectre and Enitharmon's Shadow. Blake's use of the design at this moment in Night VII adds allusive depth to the narrative. It depicts a huge winged creature—the "Darkness" of Young's poem—with face buried behind the text and arms cradling the text's frame. In the bottom right margin, a female figure in white looks through the frame into a flowing stream of human forms. While the design illustrates the "Vale of Death" that Enitharmon places Vala in, Young's text provides the proper gloss: "darknesse, brooding o'er Unfinisht fates, / With Raven wing . . . waits the Day / (Dread Day!) that interdicts all future change" (Young 1970, 43–44). Blake's minor alteration of the design accents the point: in the river, in front of everyone, a tiny Urizen, replete with beard and fearful look, cowers in the circle of his head as he is driven forward by the current of destiny.

As Urizen is borne along, the Spectre of Urthona delivers his response to Enitharmon on the next page, directly above his own illustration. Claiming to "view futurity" in the Shadow, the Spectre declares that he will bring Vala and Orc together beneath the Tree to destroy "that Creation I created" (84:31; E 359). Blake's bizarre sketch captures the Spectre's 'deformity', as his face—"something in the special effects department" (Erdman and Magno 1987, 72)—is a vortex of swirling lines. Crouching on his right leg and left hand, the Spectre extends his right arm upward past his face, gesturing toward a line drawn from an asterisk to a stanza added in the top right corner of the page. The gesture is peculiarly positive: in both narrative and visual terms, the Spectre exposes *himself:* "Thou knowest that the Spectre is in Every Man insane brutish / Deformed that I am" (84:36–7; E 360). With the pathos of Frankenstein's creature, the Spectre gives voice to a timely utterance that produces two major changes: he inspires Los's "brotherly" integration with himself and Enitharmon; and he copulates with Enitharmon's Shadow below the Tree of Mystery, generating Rahab, that aspect of Vala that *contains* the psychosocial (t)errors of Urizen's creation in Night VIII.

Night VIII

While no creation account appears in Night VIII, pages 104 and 105[113] correlate text and drawing in a fascinating and characteristic way. Repetition of a major visual symbol (the circle) and a full page narrative insertion recapitulate the zoic contention in the poem. The return of the circle image in this new context clears the way for the Lamb-Jesus entrance, both in text and design. As the Sons of Eden and Los-Enitharmon realize, however, this symbolic clearing comes only with the kind of intense struggle represented by the heroic female, knees to the ground, pushing the wheel off of page 104.

The Sons of Eden give a symbolic summary of the epic action on page 104. They point to the urgency of the present context by uttering the word "now" five times in five lines, accenting the female figure's struggle with the stellar circle. Indeed, as the female visually labors with the wheel, Los and Enitharmon work against the "perverse" wheels of Satan and Rahab in the text. And when the Sons proclaim insight into the providential process—"Now we know that life Eternal / depends alone upon the Universal hand & not in us / Is aught but death In individual weakness"—they 'behold' Los and Enitharmon at the cosmic loom and forge.[7]

The Sons discover that the Lamb—"Universal Humanity"—can put on the clothing of Vala-Rahab, of mortality, without losing identity in individual weakness. Los and Enitharmon see this also and, while engaged in battle, watch the Lamb descend from Eden to "Give" his mortal body in order "that the Spiritual body may be Reveald." Blake writes the word "Reveald" immediately above the laboring female in the drawing: it seems to inspire her gesture and open the circle's eyes. By repeating the circle image in this context, Blake not only signals development but affirms his *kerygmatic* strategy: as Erdman and Magno put it, "she cannot see the eyes—but we can" (Erdman and Magno 1987, 81).

Page 104 (with text page 113) crowns Blake's critique of natural religion and patriarchal cosmology and ushers in a series of finely executed full-page drawings of Jesus. This heavy artillery is backed by a *Night Thoughts* proof that recasts an important image from the title page: the trumpeter blowing a wake-up call to a half-rising spectre. This page enacts a subtle irony: the trumpeter appears on a page that narrates the (false) judgment of Jesus the Lamb as a criminal (murderer and robber). The irony extends into the drawings that follow (pages 110–115), which alternate signs of redemption with scenes of exploitation and war. Just when the horror seems to abate, Blake reminds us that the dialectic never rests.

Night IX

Several key repetitions appear in Night IX that deserve comment. They occur on page 133 (which contains a key speech in the poem), its verso page 134, and the final page of the manuscript. These repetitions are attended by narrative and visual reversals, as appropriate in the Night of apocalypse.

The first is a *Night Thoughts* proof used on page 81, which takes on deeper meaning in this later narrative context. *Both* text and drawing on page 133 render apocalypse: the "atmosphere of eschatology thickens from here to the end" (Grant 1973, 196). Urizen announces "Times are Ended" on page 131 and Tharmas— "Sounding his trumpet to awake the dead"—embraces Enion on page 132, which evokes the poem's opening. Indeed, on page 133 Albion "The Eternal Man" welcomes the zoas and emanations to his feast while the Eternals relive (from a distance) the creation-fall, shuddering at the "female form now separate" (133:6).

In the narrative, an Eternal associates the fall with a basic selfishness endemic to family life and proclaims that the solution is to replace motherhood and fatherhood with brotherhood. While the Eternal Man articulates the philosophy that fuels the poem's drive toward unity—"Man subsists by Brotherhood & Universal Love"—the design features a king-stomping Los who is pulling down the sun of the old world in an unequivocally re-

demptive context. This claim is substantiated by the text: upon
finishing his speech, the Eternal is hailed as "the New born Man."

Personal and cultural transformation are affirmed visually and
textually on the next page (134). As Mystery—the Beast-Whore
of state religion, "religion hid in war"—is demolished, Blake inverts its visual image. He transforms the hermaphroditic dragon
into a human-headed beast with a bird's body and serpent's tail,
ridden by a Cupid sans wings, bow, or arrow. Indeed, the sexually
deviant Cupid undergoes metamorphosis into a *human* child, one
who is also divine, as he repeats the redemptive open-armed gesture of Blake's Jesuses. This visual change is attended by another
apocalyptic reversal. As Mystery goes down in flames, the slaves
from all over Urizen's "Universal Empire" are set free, and one
of them comes forward to sing "a New Song" that is composed,
significantly, by "an African Black" (134:34). Truly a cultural
coup, this Song.

One final figure awaits liberation: the Emanation—lost from
the narrative's opening line. On the final two pages of text, after
depiction of the struggling males on page 137, Blake closes *The
Four Zoas* with a study of contrasting females. While he does not
offer a feminist perspective on the woman question, Blake does
give the Emanation the last gesture.

On the penultimate page (138), as Urthona's lions converse with
Albion, a female figure (probably Vala) looks a bit sadly and skep-
tically at their apocalyptic conclusion: "How is it that we have
walkd thro fire & yet are not consumd / How is it that all things
are changed even as in ancient times" (138:39–40). She reclines
on her right side, bound to the margin on which she lies. On page
139, in contrast, the female (perhaps Enitharmon or the generic
Emanation) seems able to spring joyously over the "End of the
Dream" scribbled above her. While both figures are in touch with
the worlds below them, the latter rises and gestures past the "sweet
Science" of the text and beyond: indeed, a line from her hand
scurries upward and off the page, reversing her earlier marginali-
zation. This figure also inverts the posture of the male figure on
page 2 of the manuscript, the worker-prophet, whose "rest before
labour" motto is complemented by the female's postpartum vi-
brancy.

More importantly, the figure on page 139 remains a *human*
character, one whose gender ultimately is indeterminate. Its sexual nature has baffled critics—some identify a female and others
a male. Erdman and Magno argue correctly, I believe, that the
figure need not be recognized as gendered, but perhaps "as the

unity of Enitharmon and Urthona, purged of the hermaphroditic Spectre and of the "Female Will"" (Erdman and Magno 1987, 101). This cultural androgyny, I would suggest, is what Blake means by "Brotherhood." He doesn't say "Sisterhood," and one could take issue with him, but the evidence of the *Four Zoas* manuscript indicates that Blake struggled mightily to come to terms with the relation of the sexes in his prophetic history of the human race.

I would submit, however, that Blake retains a plebeian sense of humor to the end. Conspicuously marking the figure on page 139, aligned with the "End," is "a very carefully drawn anus" (Erdman and Magno 1987, 101). It should indicate something about Blakean *kerygma:* that he would not send us forward into the world, armed with prophetic hope in history's future, without a spirited sense of irony about apocalyptic ends.

Notes

Preface

1. I emphasize "actual" to distinguish my approach from that of Donald Ault, whose most recent work, *Narrative Unbound*, magnifies Newton into a trope for *all* traditional, linear narratives. In Ault's view, the "Newtonian" is equivalent to metaphysical reductionism.

2. See Whitehead 1976, 193–200; and DiSalvo 1983.

3. Blake did stretch for the long view of history, moving from protozoa origins to a post-zoa future. And we should be aware that early in his artistic life Blake immersed himself in antiquarian traditions that bear only indirectly on modern notions of history. However, as Stuart Piggott points out in a highly relevant and informative study, antiquarians of Blake's day sought to construct an "absolute chronology" from the ancient to the modern world, one capable of universal application. He counted seventy-five "systems of the world" current in 1757, the year of Blake's birth (Piggott 1989, 38).

4. See the exchange between Paul Mann and Peter Otto in *Blake/An Illustrated Quarterly* 22 (Spring 1989). The Mann-Otto debate has roots in an earlier exchange, dating from articles in *Blake/An Illustrated Quarterly*, Spring 1985 and Spring 1987.

5. See the essay by the Santa Cruz Blake Study Group (1986), p. 324.

Chapter 1. A Reception History of *The Four Zoas*

1. On Blake's relation to the artisans, see E. P. Thompson's classic account in *The Making of the English Working Class* (New York: Vintage Books, 1966), especially part 1; Marilyn Butler says that in the early 1790s Blake wrote in collective solidarity with radical London artisans: "Their [his prophecies'] corporate author is the urban sub-class which emerged through its opposition to Britain's national policy," in *Romantics, Rebels, and Reactionaries* (Oxford: Oxford University Press, 1982), 43.

2. See F. B. Curtis, "Blake and the Booksellers" in *Blake Studies* 6 (1975): 167–78; and Erdman 1969, 153–58.

3. See also R. K. Webb, *The British Working Class Reader, 1790–1848* (London: George Allen & Unwin, 1955), chap. 2.

4. Blake's contemporary engraver, John Landseer, did acknowledge this di-

chotomy: he blames the "dictation of ignorant capitalists, co-operating with those parts of the academical code which respect the profession of engraving" for separating "the mechanical from the mental part of the art." Quoted in John Pye, *Patronage of British Art* (1845; Rpt. London: Cornmarket Press, 1970), 255.

5. Jack Lindsay argues that censorship and the reactionary turn in the mid-1790s contributed to Blake's obscurity and isolation, especially in relation to his artisan public: see *William Blake: His Life and Work* (London: Constable, 1978), 120–21.

6. A reconstruction of Blake's audience would need to consider reading publics of other writers popular in the 1790s: radical preachers like James Bicheno and Elhanan Winchester, fringe millenarians such as Richard Brothers, speculative mythologists like Jacob Bryant, mystic followers of Emanuel Swedenborg and William Law, and literary artists, especially Miltonic epic poets like Robert Southey and Walter Savage Landor. What would constitute "the obscure" to such a diverse audience? Consider the bizarre and heterogenous group of speculative mythologists studied by Edward Hungerford, who argues that from the "eccentric systems" of the mythologists "it was but a step to Blake" and that if Blake deployed "equally nebulous figures" as they, "the contemporary reader would at least have recognized the misty region in which he trod," in *Shores of Darkness* (New York: Columbia University Press, 1941), 12. Hungerford contends that Blake's Los and Urizen "were no more implausible" than Bryant's Noah or J. S. Bailly's Atlas.

7. Gilchrist's first effort in biography, *The Life of William Etty* (1854), was modeled after Carlyle's *Life of John Sterling* (1851). After Carlyle praised his work in a letter, Gilchrist moved next door to his hero in London, helped see the sage's *Works* through the press, and researched Carlyle's biography of Frederick the Great.

8. Samuel Palmer, one of Blake's "Ancient" disciples and a key source for Gilchrist's *Life*, writes: "I never saw a more perfect embodiment of Mr. C's [Carlyel's] *ideal* of a *man in earnest*, but in the person of Mr. Blake" (Dorfman 1969, 65).

9. For Ruskin's influence on the Pre-Raphaelites, see Lionel Stevenson, *The Pre-Raphaelite Poets* (New York: Norton, 1972), 4–5. After reading Gilchrist's *Life*, Ruskin commented: "There is a deep morality in his horror—as in Dante's"; and when Ruskin felt depressed with the burden of Carlyle's death, he found a kindred frustrated prophet in Blake, whose mind, he said, was "disturbed, but not deceived" (quoted in Dorfman 1969, 39).

10. Rossetti's introductory note to *Songs of Innocence and Experience* identifies Blake's social concerns as the source of his obscurity: he argues that the distance between the sets of songs "proved sufficient for obscurity and the darker mental phases of Blake's writings to set in and greatly mar its poetic value"; Rossetti favors "The Chimney Sweeper" or *Innocence* because it is not "tinged," as is the later version, with "the commonplaces, if also with the truths, of social discontent" (in Gilchrist 1969, 2:27).

11. In 1866 Swinburne turned from erotic love songs to verse celebrating the Italian Risorgimento and was introduced, kneeling, to Mazzini in 1867. But he denies in a note to the *Essay* that such political poets as Dante or Shelley "did ever tend to alter the material face of things; though they may have desired that it should, and though their unwritten work may have done so. . . . that is beside the point" (Swinburne 1970, 93).

12. In a later chapter, Benjamin writes: "The non-conformists rebel against

the surrender of art to the market. They rally round the banner of *l'art pour l'art*. From this slogan there springs the conception of the total work of art, which attempts to isolate art against the development of technology. . . . Both abstract from the social being of man. Baudelaire succumbs to Wagner" (Benjamin 1976, 172). Benjamin's bitter conclusion must be seen in context: Germany between the wars, when Romantic ideas had drifted toward fascism.

13. The section that contains the essay on Blake is titled after Rossetti's "Ideas of Good and Evil," a section from the Aldine edition (1874) of Blake's works edited by the Rossetti brothers.

14. In his *Autobiography*, Yeats claims that a "young workman" in William Morris's Marxist study group drove him from socialism to Irish myth: see Yeats 1965, 99–100.

15. The work of D. J. Sloss and J. P. R. Wallis, S. Foster Damon, and subsequent *Four Zoas* critics comes out of an institutional setting foreign to nineteenth-century bohemians and aesthetes. For the historical background, see Rene Wellek, *Concepts of Criticism* ed. Stephen G. Nichols, Jr. (New Haven: Yale University Press, 1963), 256–58; and Gerald Graff, *Literature Against Itself: Literary Ideas in Modern Society* (Chicago: University of Chicago Press, 1979), 49–52, and *Professing Literature: An Institutional History* (Chicago: University of Chicago Press, 1987), chapter 4.

16. Even with Murry's, and Max Plowman's, emphasis on a "this-worldly" Blake, it is not until the 1940s that a "social" Blake emerges in Bronowski's *A Man Without a Mask* (1944) reprinted as *William Blake and the Age of Revolution* (New York: Harper, 1965). Between Murry and Bronowski arrives one of the most significant books on Blake from the perennial philosophy school, Milton Percival's *William Blake's Circle of Destiny* (1938), which suggests the overlapping, contradictory, always fertile contexts summoned by Blake's work. I exclude Bronowski from the main narrative of the chapter because he did not write about *The Four Zoas.*

17. For an advanced discussion of this vexing issue, see Michael Löwy and Robert Sayre, "Figures of Romantic Anticapitalism" in *Spirits of Fire: English Romantic Writers and Contemporary Historical Methods* ed. G. A. Rosso and Daniel Watkins (Rutherford, NJ: Fairleigh Dickinson University Press, 1990), 23–65.

18. Margoliouth is more interested in textual than in interpretive issues: see Margoliouth 1956.

19. The term comes from W. J. T. Mitchell's article by that title in *Studies in Romanticism* 21 (Fall 1982).

20. Modern theology recognizes two senses of the term *kerygma:* the content of the Gospel message and the act of preaching. The theologian Rudolph Bultmann writes: "the communicating of the past does not have the meaning of a historical report, but rather is a call, in which the past is contemporized" (quoted in Robinson 1968, 42). I draw on *Kerygma and Myth: A Theological Debate,* a collection of essays by Bultmann and five critics, edited by H. W. Bartsch (New York: Harper & Row, 1961).

Chapter 2. The Uses of Obscurity: *The Four Zoas* in Eighteenth-Century Literary History

1. Donald Ault has recently suggested that because *The Four Zoas* subverts traditional (what he calls "Newtonian") narrative, it evades generic classification.

The statement, however, remains either too general or incomplete: Which particular Newtonian narratives does *The Four Zoas* subvert? This chapter offers an answer. See Ault 1987, 3–4.

2. Quoted in Paul D. Sheats, ed., *The Poetical Works of Wordsworth* (Boston: Houghton Mifflin, 1982), 801–2. See also Curran 1986, 180–203.

3. Many generic or descriptive terms could serve: Josephine Miles examines Blake's work in relation to the "sublime poem" in her *Eras and Modes in English Literature* (1964). Like Joseph Wittreich, she places Blake in a "bardic line" that descends from Spenser and Milton, but she adds the eighteenth-century context of Thomson, Gray, Collins, and the Wartons, who form "a line of scenic and spiritual concern" that supplies the material and forms the community of Blake's art (78, 82). Miles locates in *The Seasons* "a compendium of the language of eighteenth-century Whiggish verse which would reach its height of power in Blake" (62). While Miles restores an important tradition, she underplays Blake's critique of his "sources."

4. In his *Lectures on the Sacred Poetry of the Hebrews,* Lowth comments on the condensed energy of the parabolic or sententious style used by the biblical prophets: "a degree of obscurity was not infrequently attendent upon this studied brevity" (Lowth 1829, 42–3).

5. David Morris argues that the dramatic focus of Young's *Night Thoughts* "allies it with various Restoration and eighteenth-century works of Christian apologetics," although he realizes that the poem lacks traditional "coherence": "[P]robably he intended a certain formless spontaneity in his presentation to suggest a mind coping with passion too real for method. A logical structure is surely not what Coleridge, or earlier readers [Blake?], sought in the *Night-Thoughts*" (Morris 1972, 146).

6. The poems I discuss in the chapter can also been viewed as responses to *Paradise Lost* in the age of Newton, which makes Fredric Jameson's observation relevant to the tradition being sketched: "The failure of a particular generic structure, such as epic, to reproduce itself not only encourages a search for those substitute textual formations that appear in its wake, but more particularly alerts us to the historical ground, now no longer existent, in which the original structure was meaningful" (Jameson 1981, 146).

7. In this section I draw on the work of Arthur Lovejoy (1965), Robert Hurlbutt (1965) and Richard Westfall (1973), who discusses Newton's work in relation to the virtuosi. See also Rosso 1994.

8. All subsequent citations from *The Seasons* are to Thomson 1981; references are to the Season and line numbers.

9. See Maynard Mack's introduction to the Twickenham edition of *An Essay on Man,* where he lists the numerous translations of Pope's widely-read work (Mack 1951, xii, note 1). All citations to *An Essay on Man* are from Mack's edition and are cited by Book and line number.

10. These remarks, interestingly enough, are echoed by Blake scholar G. E. Bentley, whose editing strictures remind us of Lowth's complaint that the prophetic events "are often improperly connected, without any marks of discrimination," and that their "injudicious arrangement" creates "insuperable difficulties" for textual and thematic analysis (Lowth 1829, 176–77). See also my discussion of Bentley in chap. 1.

11. Earl Wasserman has given a succinct formulation of the problem in *The Subtler Language:* he explains that the Medieval-Renaissance "system of correspondences" became detached "from any worldview" and left the "cosmological

groundwork," what he calls the language of *concordia discors*, in shambles. See the chapter entitled "Metaphors for Poetry" (Wasserman 1968, 169–88). See also M. H. Abrams, *The Mirror and the Lamp: Romantic Theory and the Critical Tradition* (New York: Norton, 1958), 272–85.

12. Leslie Tannenbaum has examined the Genesis tradition in relation to Blake's *Book of Urizen*, concentrating on the various narrative and theological strands of the argument.

13. Tilottama Rajan explores the connections between the higher critical hermeneutic, Romanticism, and deconstruction in *The Supplement of Reading*. See Rajan 1990, part 1, and Ault 1987.

Chapter 3. Plotting the Fall: Creation Narratives in *The Four Zoas*

1. I am building on Leslie Tannenbaum's analysis in "Blake's Art of Crypsis: *The Book of Urizen* and Genesis," in *Blake Studies* 5 (Fall, 1972), 141–64. Tannenbaum argues that *Urizen*, Blake's first articulation of a "cosmogonic myth," parodies Genesis by its "dual creation account." I argue that, as with *Urizen*, *The Four Zoas* "transposes, condenses, and often inverts the material in [its] source" (p. 143): the J (Jahwist) and E (Elohist) narrative strands.

2. Since the voices of the narrator and characters often coincide, both within the dialogues and between narration and dialogue, readers need to look for formulas that point to the beginnings and endings of narrative units. The narrator often tilts what characters say or summarizes their dialogue without clarifying complex, even contradictory, passages, Or he may repeat dialogue verbatim, either to direct attention back to an exchange or to highlight the way a character's perspective diverges from the narrator's supposedly authoritative report. In effect, Blake compromises the narrator's third-person position, in part to bridge larger units of direct speech, but also to dramatize conflicts in the varied points of view. See Ault 1987, chapter one. My view differs from Ault's "perspective ontology" in that I would separate readers from the narrative rather than conflate them as one "being."

3. All quotations of Blake's works are from *The Complete Poetry and Prose of William Blake*, edited by David V. Erdman (Berkeley: University of California Press, 1982). Because of complexities in citing the *Four Zoas* manuscript in Nights VIIa, VIIb, and VIII, I include the page and line number in these Nights: thus (95:1 E 360) means page 95, line 1 of the *Four Zoas* manuscript found on page 360 of the Erdman text.

4. I am indebted to Milton Percival's discussion of this episode: "The spiritual body, like the natural body, labors to throw off infection and in the end succeeds. The path of experience is therefore circular. . . . This cycle, which descends from Beulah into Ulro and ascends from Ulro by way of Generation, where it joins the supernal cycle, is the Circle of Destiny" (Percival 1938, 12).

5. For example, Blake inserts a thematic stanza that suggests creation is both fallen and fortunate. Enion weaves for "nine days . . . & nine dark sleepless nights," the symbolic length of the poem; yet the narrator informs us that in "Eden Females sleep the winter in soft silken veils / Woven by their own hands to hide them in the darksome grave" (5:1–2). This imagery recalls Young's *Night Thoughts*, which also interprets the grave in typological terms, as prefiguring immortality, not eternal death.

6. For Blake's gnostic tendencies, see Stuart Curran's urbane treatment in "Blake and the Gnostic Hyle: A Double Negative," in *Blake Studies* 4 (1972), 117–33 and Damrosch 1980, 255–80.

7. On page 47, the opening page of Night IV, Tharmas reenacts Los and Enitharmon's birth from Tharmas's Spectre and Enion's Shadow. The drawing from *Night Thoughts* shows Young's narrator holding a dead Narcissa and looking up at the Sun-Chariot, despairing of immortality (as Tharmas despairs of Enion).

8. The Spectre's remembrance of "the Day" harkens back to the incomplete version by the Messengers of Beulah in Night I and anticipates his later version in Night VII, which branches in two directions: on the one hand, to the birth of Rahab and, on the other, to Los's embrace. That is, the narrative moves toward historical consolidation and individual regeneration.

9. All citations to *Paradise Lost* are from Milton 1957; subsequent references are to Book and line numbers.

10. This typology of Nimrod-Satan suggests that Blake's creation-fall also draws on Milton's portrayal of the biblical Creation as a by-product of Satan's war in heaven. In Book VII of *Paradise Lost,* God assures the Son concerning Satan's rebellion: "I can repair / That detriment . . . and in a moment will create / Another World" (7:152–54).

11. Analyses of Night VII have become a critical genre. For an overview of the Night VII problem, see my Note on the Manuscript. For interpretive stances, consult Sloss and Wallis 1926, 137–39; Bentley 1963, part 3; Wagenknecht 1973, 298–302; Wilkie and Johnson 1978, 239–54; and Ault 1987, 475–79.

12. In *The Art of Logic* Milton defines "crypsis" as a method of concealment in which something implied is left unsaid. Michael Fixler writes that while "crypsis is, strictly speaking, a technical principle, it . . . has affinities with the traditional attitude toward scriptural obscurity." See "The Apocalypse in *Paradise Lost,*" in *New Essays on Paradise Lost,* ed. Thomas Kranidas (Berkeley: University of California Press, 1971), 147–48. Milton's practice bears importantly on Blakean cosmology and typology.

Chapter 4. Blake's Typology in Historical Context

1. I draw mainly on Sartre 1988, 48–70, and Charity 1966, chap. 2, for my notion of affective aesthetics. For a related account of Blake's theory of art, see Eaves 1982, part 4; and for a critique, see Mann 1985, 4–6.

2. The most informed contextual studies of Blakean typology remain Frye 1969, chap. 5, and Tannenbaum 1982, chap. 4.

3. My understanding of the historical and especially the *kerygmatic* nature of biblical typology is indebted to Charity's erudite and impassioned study.

4. Erich Auerbach's is still the classic discussion of biblical typology and this chapter draws heavily on his view—see Works Cited. For a critique of Auerbachian typology, see Timothy Bahti, "Vico, Auerbach, and Literary History," *Philological Quarterly* LX (1981), 239–55, and William Walker 1989.

5. As Tannenbaum elaborates: "Through its typological structure, the text is always pointing to and impinging upon realities beyond the text, realities which in turn modify it" (Tannenbaum 1982, 105).

6. For this sense of radical engagement with history, see James M. Robinson's cogent discussion of *kerygma* in *A New Quest of the Historical Jesus* (London: SCM Press, 1968), especially 38–58.

7. See Victor Harris, "Allegory to Analogy in the Interpretation of Scripture," in *Philological Quarterly*, 45 (January, 1966), 1–23; W. Neil 1963, 238–39; and Drury 1989, 1–20.

8. Frei 1974, 75. On Locke's theory of language, see Hans Aarsleff, *The Study of Language in England, 1780–1860* (Minneapolis, MN: University of Minnesota Press, 1983), 21–35.

9. Gay equates Christian rationalism with "the treason of the clerks" because it aids and abets the Enlightenment attack on revealed religion: "Deeply as the issue of religion divided philosophes from their Christian culture, they could count on allies even there. But most of the alliances were unwitting" (Gay 1973, 199).

10. Coleridge quoted in Shaffer 1975, 53–54; see Stephen 1962, 1:65, Frei 1974, 74, and Neil 1963, 243.

11. Gay writes insightfully: "It was not Bayle or Erasmus singly or both together but Bayle and Erasmus allied with Newton and Locke that created the atmosphere hospitable" to Enlightnment; "The treason of the clerks did the rest" (Gay 1966, 374).

12. For a deconstructionist account of the concept of *understanding* in relation to the higher critical project, see Rajan 1990, 15–36.

13. See also Isaiah Berlin, "Herder and the Enlightenment," in *Aspects of the Eighteenth Century*, ed. Earl Wasserman (Baltimore: Johns Hopkins University Press, 1965), 69.

14. On this Blakean position, see also Herder 1969, p. 181 and Herder's *Outline of a Philosophy of the History of Man*, trans. T. Churchill (New York: Begman, nd), 163.

15. Marjorie Reeves explains: "Just as, in the understanding of the individual mind, from meditation on the letter of the Old and New Testaments there proceeded one Spiritual Intelligence, which gathered all truth into one comprehension, so in the history of mankind, from the work of God the Father and God the Son, there must proceed the work of the Holy Spirit.... [A]lthough Joachim certainly believed in the equality of the three Persons, he did see the work of the Third Person as the culmination of history in the third *status*, just as in the life of the individual the Spiritual Intelligence *[intellectus spiritualis]* was the crowning illumination." Quoted in *Joachim of Fiore and the Prophetic Future* (New York: Harper & Row, 1977), 5–6.

16. I allude to such writers as Joseph Priestley, *The Present State of Europe Compared with Antient Prophecies* (London: J. Johnson, 1794) and James Bicheno, *The Signes of the Times* (London: J. Johnson, 1794), who saw the political violence of the French Revolution as confirmation of biblical prophecy. Blake took a more subtle view, as Raymond Williams aptly perceives: "his intensity of desire is as much a response, a deciding response, to the human crisis of that time as the more obviously recognizable political radicalism. Indeed, to give that kind of value to human longing and need, that absolute emphasis on commitment to another, the absolute love of the being of another, is to clash as sharply with the emerging system ... as in any assault on material poverty." See his *The English Novel: From Dickens to Hardy* (London: Chatto & Windus, 1970), 60–61.

17. Priestley, quoted in Garrett 1975, 143.

Chapter 5. Repetition and Simultaneity: Typological History in *The Four Zoas* Nights I–VIIa

1. For a critique of my (Auerbachian) view of typology, see William Walker 1989 and Robert Gleckner, *Blake and Spenser* (Baltimore: Johns Hopkins Univer-

sity Press, 1985), 308–10. Walker's critique of typology targets Erich Auerbach's concept of "figura," which he finds problematic because it posits both the historical type and transcendent antitype as different "quantities and degrees of the same thing"; Walker invokes the term's binary structure (type/antitype, shadow/ substance) to deconstruct or unravel its putative intellectual coherence (Walker 1989, 254–55). In my view, Walker's approach erases extrinsic reference altogether and swallows up history, subsuming it within the empire of textuality.

2. See Erdman 1969, 298–312; Frye, 1969, chap. 9; and DiSalvo 1983, chap. 7.

3. See the entry "William Stuckeley" in *The Rise of Modern Mythology, 1680–1860,* ed. Burton Feldman and Robert Richardson (Bloomington: Indiana University Press, 1972), and Edward B. Hungerford, *Shores of Darkness* (New York: Columbia University Press, 1941), 67ff.

4. On Wilford, see Damon, 1979 under "Druids"; Hans Aarsleff, *The Study of Language in England 1780–1860* (Minneapolis: University of Minnesota Press, 1983), chap. 4; and Hungerford, cited above, 30.

5. This situating the type is what A. C. Charity means when he argues that the Old Testament prophets subject myth to "the controlling categories of history" (Charity 1966, 53) and what Florence Sandler has in mind when she speaks of the Hebrew "habit of historicizing the mythological" (Sandler 1972, 37).

6. Albright illuminates the Los-Enitharmon argument: "At this dangerous moment in the history of Yahwism," when threatened by the "Canaanizing encroachments of the temple-cult," "came the prophetic movement like a refreshing west wind" (Albright 1957, 301). While he welcomes the prophetic west wind, Blake is not so sanguine about the Old Testament: he sees in Jehovah's vow of vengeance the diabolic underside of his pathos for justice.

7. I do not proffer this view of Blakean eschatology without awareness of serious objections by other scholars. Donald Ault's views have been examined in chap. 1. Tilottama Rajan uses Blake's early prophecies to counter the "totalizing impulses" of the longer works, whose "imaginative imperialism" goes against the grain of post-structural "intertextuality."

8. For distinctions between Blake and Vico, see Lowith's discussion of Vico's rationalism (Lowith 1949, 134). For a view critical of the idealist version of Vico, see Timothy Bahti 1981, "Vico, Auerbach, and Literary History," *Philological Quarterly* 60: 239–55.

9. As John Middleton Murry put it; "The Law achieves its typical and perfect form in the mechanical motions of the starry heavens" (Murry 1964, 56). This view is supported by Newton's obsession with Solomon's temple: see Feldman and Richardson 1972, 125, cited in note 3.

10. David Punter interprets Blake as a Hegelian and argues that in *The Four Zoas* all the individual zoas lack "agency," and that "an everpresent historical process," "a continual dialectic of division and regeneration," is the "true agent of the poem" (Punter, 1982, 174. In "Further Reading.")

11. Blake's *Lamb* typology derives from the Gospel of John, which interprets Moses's act of raising the brazen serpent on a pole as a type of Christ's crucifixion. But Blake's powerfully condensed symbol of Orc wrapped around Urizen's tree embodies a number of referents: not only to Christ's crucifixion but also to God's sacrifice of his Son in *Paradise Lost,* to Abraham's "druidic" sacrifice of Isaac, and to the "crucifixion" of modern revolution (Orc) by reactionary forces in England and France. Significantly, all these sacrifices are examples of what Blake sees as "false atonement." See Sandler 1972 and Tannenbaum 1982.

12. The relations between these character are extremely complex and the

Spectre of Urthona poses a special challenge. D. J. Sloss and J. P. R. Wallis state
that the "relation of Los and the Spectre of Urthona in Night VII is without
parallel elsewhere, and constitutes a peculiar difficulty" (Sloss and Wallis 1969
2:194); Northrop Fyre more radically argues that the Spectre of Urthona "occa-
sioned the rewriting of Night VII" and that it ultimately "burst the whole Zoa
scheme altogether," forcing Blake to abandon the poem (Frye 1969, 298); Paul
Youngquist, while ultimately in agreement with this view, offers a sympathetic
analysis of the Spectre. See Youngquist 1989, 128–31.

13. This theme runs throughout the book of Isaiah and Revelation; see J.
F. C. Harrison's Introduction to his *The Second Coming: Popular Millenarianism
1780–1850* (London: Routledge and Kegan Paul, 1979).

Chapter 6. Consolidating Error: History and Apocalypse in Nights VIIb–IX

1. Many of Northrop Frye's works touch on the internalized apocalypse. See
Frye 1969, and "The Keys to the Gates" in *The Stubborn Structure: Essays on
Criticism and Society* (Ithaca: Cornell Univ. Press, 1970). See also Abrams 1963;
Bloom 1970; Wilkie and Johnson 1978; Ault 1987.

2. I draw on the theologian Wolfhart Pannenberg: "What it means that in
the person of Jesus the end of history is already anticipated can itself be understood only within the apocalyptic concept of history. Thus the historical framework remains intact. History is by no means abolished." From "Redemptive
Event and History," in *Essays on Old Testament Hermeneutics*, ed. Claus Westermann
and trans. James Luther Mays (Atlanta: John Knox Press, 1979), 333–34.

3. I agree with Frye that the Orc Cycle mythologizes the movement of history
within an even larger cosmological scheme that Blake names the "Circle of Destiny," and that this larger cycle is guided by a "providential" vision sealed in
Blake's "Seven Eyes of God" construct. But Blake associates the "Eyes," the seven
ages of history, with the Urizen-Orc struggle that never reaches culmination,
despite the potential finality of each period. Frye erroneously concludes that
Blake's historical cycles thus are not sequential, but rather a "seven-time-recur-
ring phenomenon" that contains the three stage Orc-Urizen struggle (Frye, 211).
Blake certainly disrupts linear narrative patterns and strives for simultaneity.
But his nine Nights cover three distinctly *historical* stages, while Frye's stages are
structural and occur within each of the seven frames.

4. For a concise, informed discussion of the distinction between Deism and
natural religion, see Force 1990, 43–73.

5. Erdman's new edition of *The Complete Poetry and Prose of William Blake*
(Berkeley: University of California Press, 1982), follows the sequence proposed
by Mark Lefebvre in *Blake: An Illustrated Quarterly* 46 (Fall 1978), 134.

6. This inbuilt interpretive dimension of the text leads deconstructionist
critics, in opposition to "logocentric" assumptions of unity and coherence, to
tease out the *aporias* or warring contraries that "subvert" the narrative's own
logic. But, with Erdman, I do not believe that Blake left his versions unfinished
because he "got a twentieth-century charge out of narrative discontinuities." See
also Erdman's comments on Ault and Mitchell (Erdman 1978, 137) and Lincoln
(133). Certainly the "unfinished" nature of the manuscript, as well as Blake's
narrative strategies, contributes to the text's centrifugal rhetorical structure. Yet
I do not equate its unfinshed state with Blake's intention.

7. I am not arguing that Blake blames Newtonianism for British imperialism or the French Revolution: only that it is a key social and cultural factor in these developments. For another view, see Stuart Peterfreund, "Blake and Newton: Argument as Art, Argument as Science" in *Studies in 18th-Century Culture* 10 (1981), 205–26. Peterfreund claims that (for Blake) implementing Newtonian physics into social policy meant that "there was something wrong with the physics itself" (207). True, in a humanistic sense, but I doubt that Blake read Newton's *Principia* on its own terms or that he anticipated relativity physics.

8. I draw on E. J. Rose, "'Forms Eternal Exist Forever': The Covenant of the Harvest in Blake's Prophetic Poems," in *Blake's Visionary Forms Dramatic*, edited by David V. Erdman and John E. Grant (Princeton: Princeton University Press, 1970), 452. Rose, as his title indicates, bases his reading of *The Four Zoas's* internal apocalypse on Blake's late commentary *A Vision of the Last Judgment* and *Jerusalem*. While his work is instructive, I resist the tendency to resolve the historical anxiety in *The Four Zoas* by reference to Blake's later, more neatly structured apocalypses.

Appendix

1. For citation in the appendix, I follow the page numbering of Erdman and Magno's 1987 facsimile edition instead of Erdman's 1982 text.

2. DiSalvo traces the war in heaven to Canaanite, Greek, and Hebrew myth. She believes, however, that Blake's view of the goddess is distorted by biblical sources (DiSalvo 1983, 178–90).

3. Page 2 ushers us into Blake's workshop. It is a full page drawing of a male figure with cloven foot and left leg ready to spring into action, with the phrase "Rest before Labour" written below. Erdman and Magno contrast the figure with the titlepage trumpeter and name him the "poet as workman" who must "respond with labour that will create the poem" (Erdman and Magna 1987; 26). I would link them as a composite worker-prophet.

4. DiSalvo writes: "The poet has to project from history an alternative to its two dominant ideologies, worship of the Mother Goddess and of the Father God, both of which obscured the path through which history, Generation, might open again to heaven" (DiSalvo 1983, 183).

5. *See* Iain McCalman, *Radical Underworld: Prophets, Revolutionaries and Pornographers in London, 1790–1840* (Cambridge: Cambridge University Press, 1988). McCalman draws relevant parallels for Blakeans between Jacobin revolutionaries and lower-class religious enthusiasts. McCalman also notes that as the demand for pornography increased in the Victorian era (a Blakean logic there), so did the drive to eradicate it, which may account for the Linnell erasures (see page 215).

6. Urizen's return to dominion is rendered palpable on the pages of Night VI. He appears *in effect* on pages 68–69: a trunkless female figure buries her head in the margin and a fully-drawn queen holds the scales of justice. He appears in symbolic form as the gaping-mouthed alligator dragon on page 70. And he shows up in person on the closely paralleled pages 74–75, lugging a globe in his right hand, moving with implacable and pitiless gaze toward the terrified figure on 75. On pages that Urizen regains narrative control, Blake supplies counterpoint visual effects.

7. Los and Enitharmon wage intellectual battle with the forces of Urizen

and Vala (now become Satan and Rahab) over the "spectres of the dead." Los and Enitharmon forge and weave "gems & gold of Eden" for the spectres while Satan and Rahab, in a reactionary strategy, build mills of "resistless wheels to unwind the soft threads," clothing the spectres in "webs of torture," despair, and ignorance. But precisely because Los and Enitharmon engage in struggle, the Sons of Eden are able to see that Satan's mills derive from Urizen's Tree of Mystery—an apocalyptic realization.

Works Cited

Abrams, M. H. 1963. "English Romanticism: The Spirit of the Age." In *Romanticism Reconsidered,* edited by Northrop Frye. New York: Columbia University Press.

Albright, W. J. 1957. *From the Stone Age to Christianity.* New York: Doubleday.

Albright, W. J. 1963 [1949]. *The Biblical Period from Abraham to Ezra.* New York: Harper and Row.

Allen, D. C. 1963 [1947]. *The Legend of Noah: Renaissance Rationalism in Art, Science, and Letters.* Urbana: University of Illinois Press.

Auerbach, Erich. 1984 [1944]. "Figura." In *Scenes from the Drama of European Literature.* Minneapolis: University of Minnesota Press.

Ault, Donald. 1987. *Narrative Unbound: Revisioning Williams Blake's "The Four Zoas".* Barrytown, NY: Station Hill Press.

Bate, Walter Jackson. 1970. *The Burden of the Past and the English Poet.* New York: Norton.

Battestin, Martin C. 1974. *The Providence of Wit: Aspects of Augustan Literature and the Arts.* Oxford: Clarendon Press.

Beales, Derek. 1969. *From Castlereagh to Gladstone, 1815–1885.* New York: Norton.

Beer, John. 1969. *Blake's Visionary Universe.* New York: Barnes & Noble.

Benjamin, Walter. 1976. *Baudelaire: A Lyric Poet in the Era of High Capitalism,* Translated by Harry Zohn. London: New Left Books.

Bentley, G. E. 1963. *William Blake: Vala or The Four Zoas.* Oxford: Clarendon Press.

Bentley, G. E. 1975. Ed. *William Blake: The Critical Heritage.* London: Routledge & Kegan Paul.

Bloom, Harold. 1970 [1963]. *Blake's Apocalypse: A Study in Poetic Argument.* Ithaca: Cornell University Press.

Bloom, Harold. 1971. *The Ringers in the Tower: Studies in Romantic Tradition.* Chicago: University of Chicago Press.

Bracher, Mark. 1985. *Being Form'd: Thinking Through Blake's "Milton".* Barrytown, NY: Station Hill Press.

Brisman, Leslie. 1978. *Romantic Origins.* Ithaca: Cornell University Press.

Butlin, Martin. 1981. *The Paintings and Drawings of William Blake. Text & Plates.* 2 vols. New Haven: Yale University Press.

Butt, John. 1979. *The Mid-Eighteenth Century.* Edited and Completed by Geoffrey Carnall. Oxford: Clarendon Press.

Cassirer, Ernst. 1955 [1951]. *The Philosophy of the Enlightenment.* Boston: Beacon Press.

Charity, A. C. 1966. *Events and Their Afterlife: The Dialectics of Christian Typology in the Bible and Dante.* Cambridge: Cambridge University Press.

Collins, Adela Yarbro. 1977. "The Political Perspective of the Revelation to John." In *Journal of Biblical Literature* 96.

Collins, Anthony. 1976 [1724] *A Discourse on the Grounds and Reasons of the Christian Religion.* New York: Garland.

Crehan, Stewart. 1984. *Blake in Context.* Atlantic Highlands, NJ: Humanities Press.

Curran, Stuart. 1986. *Poetic Form and British Romanticism.* New York: Oxford University Press.

Damon, S. Foster. 1958 [1924]. *William Blake: His Philosophy and Symbols.* Gloucester, MA: Peter Smith.

Damon, S. Foster. 1979 [1965]. *A Blake Dictionary: The Ideas and Symbols of William Blake.* Boulder, CO: Shambhala.

Damrosch, Leopold, Jr. 1980. *Symbol and Truth in Blake's Myth.* Princeton: Princeton University Press.

DiSalvo, Jackie. 1983. *War of Titans: Blake's Critique of Milton and the Politics of Religion.* Pittsburgh: Pittsburgh University Press.

Dorfman, Deborah. 1969. *Blake in the Nineteenth Century: His Reputation from Gilchrist to Yeats.* New Haven: Yale University Press.

Drury, John. 1989. *Critics of the Bible, 1724–1873.* Cambridge: Cambridge University Press.

Eaves, Morris. 1982. *William Blake's Theory of Art.* Princeton: Princeton University Press.

Eliot, T. S. 1972 [1920]. "Blake." In *The Sacred Wood: Essays on Poetry and Criticism.* London: Methuen.

Ellis, E. J., and W. B. Yeats. 1893. *The Works of William Blake.* 3 vols. London: Bernard Quaritch.

Erdman, David V. 1969 [1954]. *Blake: Prophet Against Empire: A Poet's Interpretation of the History of His Own Times.* Princeton: Princeton University Press.

Erdman, David V. 1978. "Night the Seventh: The Editorial Problem." In *Blake: An Illustrated Quarterly* 46 (Fall).

Erdman, David V., and Cettina Tramontano Magno. 1987. *The Four Zoas by William Blake.* Lewisburg: Bucknell University Press.

Erdman, David V. 1982. Ed. *The Complete Poetry and Prose of William Blake.* Berkeley: University of California Press.

Ernesti, Johann A. 1827. *Elements of Interpretation.* Translated by Moses Stuart. London: Marc Newman.

Essick, Robert, and Jenijoy LaBelle. 1975. Ed. *Night Thoughts or, The Complaint and The Consolation.* New York: Dover.

Evans, James. 1972. "The Apocalypse as Contrary Vision: Prolegomena to an

Analogical Reading of *The Four Zoas.*" In *Texas Studies in Language and Literature* XIV 2 (Summer).

Ferber, Michael. 1985. *The Social Vision of William Blake.* Princeton: Princeton University Press.

Fisher, Peter. 1961. *The Valley of Vision: Blake as a Prophet and Revolutionary.* Toronto: University of Toronto Press.

Foucault, Michel. 1973 [1970]. *The Order of Things: An Archaeology of the Human Sciences.* New York: Vintage.

Force, James E. 1990. "Newtonianism and Deism." In *Essays on the Context, Nature, and Influence of Sir Isaac Newton's Theology,* edited by James E. Force and Richard H. Popkin. London: Klumer Academic Publishers.

Frei, Hans. 1974. *The Eclipse of Biblical Narrative: A Study in Eighteenth and Nineteenth Century Hermeneutics.* New Haven: Yale University Press.

Frye, Northrop. 1976. "The Responsibilities of the Critic." In *Modern Language Notes* 91.

Frye, Northrop. 1964. *The Educated Imagination.* Bloomington: Indiana University Press.

Frye, Northrop. 1963. "Toward Defining an Age of Sensibility." In *Fables of Identity: Studies in Poetic Mythology.* New York: Harcourt, Brace, and World.

Frye, Northrop. 1969 [1947]. *Fearful Symmetry: A Study of William Blake.* Princeton: Princeton University Press.

Garrett, Clark. 1975. *Respectable Folly: Millenarians and the French Revolution in France and England.* Baltimore: Johns Hopkins University Press.

Gay, Peter. 1966. *The Enlightenment: An Interpretation. Vol I. The Rise of Modern Paganism.* New York: Alfred A. Knopf.

Gay, Peter. 1973. Ed. *The Enlightenment: A Comprehensive Anthology.* New York: Simon and Schuster.

Gilchrist, Alexander. 1969 [1880]. *Life of William Blake.* 2 vols. New York: Phaeton.

Grant, Douglas. 1951. *James Thomson: Poet of the Seasons.* London: Cresset Press.

Grant, John E. 1973. "Visions in *Vala:* A Consideration of Some Pictures in the Manuscript." In *Blake's Sublime Allegory: Essays on The Four Zoas, Milton, Jerusalem,* edited by Stuart Curran and Joseph Anthony Wittreich, Jr. Madison: University of Wisconsin Press.

Harrison, J. F. C. 1979. *The Second Coming: Popular Millenarianism 1780–1850.* London: Routledge and Kegan Paul.

Hayes, John. 1971. *An Introduction to the Bible.* Philadelphia: Westminster Press.

Herder, Johann G. 1969. "Yet Another Philosophy of History." In *Herder on Social and Political Culture,* translated and edited by F. M. Bernard. Cambridge: Cambridge University Press.

Hough, Graham. 1961 [1947]. *The Last Romantics.* London: Methuen.

Hurlbutt, Robert H. 1965. *Hume, Newton, and the Design Argument.* Lincoln: University of Nebraska Press.

Jacob, Margaret C. 1976. *The Newtonians and the English Revolution, 1689–1720.* Ithaca: Cornell University Press.

Jameson, Fredric. 1982. "Imaginary and Symbolic in Lacan: Marxism, Psycho-analytic Criticism, and the Problem of the Subject." In *Literature and Psycho-analysis: The Question of Reading: Otherwise.* Baltimore: Johns Hopkins University Press.

Jameson, Fredric. 1981. *The Political Unconscious: Narrative as a Socially Symbolic Act.* Ithaca: Cornell University Press.

Jones, William Powell. 1968. *The Rhetoric of Science: A Study of Scientific Ideas and Imagery in Eighteenth-Century English Poetry.* Berkeley: University of California Press.

Korshin, Paul. 1982. *Typologies in England, 1650–1820.* Princeton: Princeton University Press.

Lincoln, Andrew. 1978. "The Revision of the Seventh and Eighth Nights in *The Four Zoas.*" In *Blake: An Illustrated Quarterly* 46 (Fall).

Lindsay, Jack. 1978. *William Blake: His Life and Work.* London: Constable.

Lovejoy, Arthur O. 1965 [1936]. *The Great Chain of Being: A Study in the History of an Idea.* New York: Harper and Row.

Lowith, Karl. 1949. *Meaning in History.* Chicago: Chicago University Press.

Lowth, Robert. 1829 [1787]. *Lectures on the Sacred Poetry of the Hebrews.* Translated by Richard Gregory. London: Codman.

Mack, Maynard. 1951. Ed. *An Essay on Man.* New Haven: Yale University Press.

Mann, Paul. 1985. "Apocalypse and Recuperation: Blake and the Maw of Commerce." In *English Literary History* 52 (Spring).

Manuel, Frank. 1974. *The Religion of Isaac Newton.* Oxford: Clarendon Press.

Margoliouth, H. M. 1956. *"Vala": Blake's Numbered Text.* Oxford: Clarendon Press.

Marshall, Donald. 1982. "Plot as Trap, Plot as Mediation." In *Horizons of Literature,* edited by Paul Hernadi. Lincoln: University of Nebraska Press.

McCalman, Iain. 1988. *Radical Underworld: Prophets, Revolutionaries and Pornographers in London, 1795–1840.* Cambridge: Cambridge University Press.

McGann, Jerome. 1986. "The Idea of an Indeterminate Text: Blake's Bible of Hell and Dr. Alexander Geddes." In *Studies in Romanticism* 25 (Fall).

McGinn, Bernard. 1984. "Early Apocalypticism: The Ongoing Debate." In *The Apocalypse in English Renaissance Thought and Literature,* edited by C. A. Patrides and J. A. Wittreich. Ithaca: Cornell University Press.

McNeil, Helen. 1970. "The Formal Art of *The Four Zoas.*" In *Blake's Visionary Forms Dramatic,* edited by David V. Erdman and John E. Grant. Princeton: Princeton University Press.

Mellor, Anne Kostelanetz. 1974. *Blake's Human Form Divine.* Berkeley: University of California Press.

Miles, Josephine. 1964 [1957]. *Eras and Modes in English Poetry.* Berkeley: University of California Press.

Milton, John. 1957. *Complete Poems and Major Prose.* Edited by Merritt Y. Hughes. New York: Odyssey.

Mitchell, W. J. T. 1978. *Blake's Composite Art: A Study of the Illuminated Poetry.* Princeton: Princeton University Press.

Morris, David B. 1972. *The Religious Sublime: Christian Poetry and the Critical Tradition in 18th-Century England.* Lexington: University of Kentucky Press.

Murry, John Middleton. 1964 [1933]. *William Blake.* New York: McGraw-Hill.

Neil, W. 1963. "The Criticism and Theological Use of the Bible, 1700–1950." In *The Cambridge History of the Bible,* vol. 3, *The West from the Reformation to the Present Day,* edited by S. L. Greenslade. Cambridge: Cambridge University Press.

Newton, Isaac. 1966 [1729]. *Sir Isaac Newton's "Mathematical Principles of Natural Philosophy".* 2 vols, translated by Andrew Motte, revised by Florian Cajori. Berkeley: University of California Press.

Paine, Thomas n.d. [1794]. *The Age of Reason.* New York: Thomas Paine Foundation.

Paley, Morton D. 1970. *Energy and the Imagination: A Study of the Development of Blake's Thought.* Oxford: Clarendon Press.

Paley, Morton D. 1983. *The Continuing City: William Blake's "Jerusalem".* Oxford: Clarendon Press.

Parr, P. J. 1975. "History of Syria and Palestine." In *Encyclopaedia Britannica,* vol 17.

Percival, Milton O. 1938. *William Blake's Circle of Destiny.* New York: Columbia University Press.

Piggott, Stuart. 1989. *Ancient Britons and the Antiquarian Imagination: Ideas from the Renaissance to the Regency.* New York: Thames and Hudson.

Rajan, Balachandra. 1985. *The Form of the Unfinished: English Poetics from Spenser to Pound.* Princeton: Princeton University Press.

Rajan, Tilottama. 1990. *The Supplement of Reading: Figures of Understanding in Romantic Theory and Practice.* Ithaca: Cornell University Press.

Rosso, George Anthony. 1994. "Newton's Pantocrator & Blake's Recovery of Miltonic Prophecy." In *Milton, the Metaphysicals, and Romanticism,* edited by Anthony Harding and Lisa Low. Cambridge: Cambridge University Press.

Russell, D. S. 1978. *Apocalyptic: Ancient and Modern.* Philadelphia: Fortress Press.

Sandler, Florence. 1972. "The Iconoclastic Enterprise: Blake's Critique of 'Milton's Religion'." In *Blake Studies 5.*

Santa Cruz Blake Study Group, 1986. "What Type of Blake?" In *Unnam'd Forms: Blake and Textuality,* edited by Nelson Hilton and Thomas A. Vogler. Berkeley: University of California Press.

Sartre, Jean-Paul. 1988 [1949]. *'What is Literature?' and Other Essays.* Cambridge, MA: Harvard University Press.

Schorer, Mark. 1959 [1946]. *William Blake: The Politics of Vision.* New York: Vintage.

Scrivener, Michael. 1990. "The Rhetoric and Context of John Thelwall's 'Memoir'." In *Spirits of Fire: English Romantic Writers and Contemporary Historical Methods,* edited by Daniel P. Watkins and G. A. Rosso. Rutherford, NJ: Fairleigh Dickinson University Press.

Shaffer, Elinor S. 1975. *'Kubla Khan' and the Fall of Jerusalem: The Mythological School in Biblical Criticism and Secular Literature, 1770–1880.* Cambridge: Cambridge University Press.

Sloss, D. J., and J. P. R. Wallis. 1926. *The Prophetic Writings of William Blake.* 2 vols. Oxford: Clarendon Press.

Stephen, Leslie. 1955 [1904]. *English Literature and Society in the Eighteenth Century.* New York: Barnes and Noble.

Stephen, Leslie. 1962. [1876]. *A History of English Thought in the Eighteenth Century,* 2 vols. New York: Harcourt.

Stevenson, Warren. 1972. *Divine Analogy: A Study of the Creation Motif in Blake and Coleridge.* Salzburg: University of Salzburg Press.

Swinburne, Algernon Charles. 1970 [1867]. *William Blake: A Critical Essay.* Lincoln: University of Nebraska Press.

Tannenbaum, Leslie. 1982. *Biblical Tradition in Blake's Early Prophecies: The Great Code of Art.* Princeton: Princeton University Press.

Thayer, H. S. 1974 [1953]. *Newton's Philosophy of Nature: Selections from his Writings.* New York: Haffner Press.

Thomson, James. 1981. *The Seasons,* edited by James Sambrook. Oxford: Clarendon Press.

Wagenknecht, David. 1973. *Blake's Night: William Blake and the Idea of Pastoral.* Cambridge: Harvard University Press.

Walker, William. 1989. "Typology and *Paradise Lost,* Books XI and XII." In *Milton Studies* 25.

Wasserman, Earl R. 1968 [1959]. *The Subtler Language: Critical Readings in Neoclassic and Romantic Poems.* Baltimore: Johns Hopkins University Press.

Webster, Brenda. 1983. *Blake's Prophetic Psychology.* Atlanta: University of Georgia Press.

Westfall, Richard S. 1973 [1959]. *Science and Society in Seventeenth-Century England.* Ann Arbor: University of Michigan Press.

Whitehead, Fred. 1976. "William Blake and Radical Tradition." In *Weapons of Criticism: Marxism in America and the Literary Tradition,* edited by Norman Rudich. Palo Alto, CA: Ramparts Press.

Whitehead, Fred. 1982. "Visions of the Archaic World." In *Sparks of Fire: Blake in a New Age,* edited by James Bogan and Fred Goss. Richmond, CA: North Atlantic Press.

Wilkie, Brian, and Mary Lynn Johnson. 1978. *Blake's "Four Zoas": The Design of a Dream.* Cambridge: Harvard University Press.

Wittreich, Joseph Anthony Jr. 1975. *Angel of Apocalypse: Blake's Idea of Milton.* Madison: University of Wisconsin Press.

Wittreich, Joseph Anthony Jr. 1979. *Visionary Poetics: Milton's Tradition and His Legacy.* San Marino CA: Huntington Library.

Wittreich, Joseph Anthony Jr. 1987. "The Work of Man's Redemption: Prophecy and Apocalypse in Romantic Poetry." In *William Wordsworth and the Age of Romanticism,* edited by Kenneth Johnston and Gene Ruoff. New Brunswick, NJ: Rutgers University Press.

Yeats, W. B. 1961. *W. B. Yeats: Essays and Introductions.* New York: Collier Books.

Yeats, William Butler. 1965 [1924]. *The Autobiography of William Butler Yeats.* New York: Collier Books.

Young, Edward. 1970. *The Poetical Works of Edward Young,* vol 1. Westport, CT: Greenwood Press.

Youngquist, Paul. 1989. *Madness and Blake's Myth.* University Park and London: Pennsylvania State University Press.

Further Reading

These items update and supplement the bibliography supplied by Erdman and Magno's *The Four Zoas by William Blake*.

Chapters in Books

Adams, Hazard. 1968 [1955]. "The Growing Image." In *Blake and Yeats: The Contrary Vision*. Rpt. New York: Russell and Russell.

Bidney, Martin. 1990. "Fourfold Visions: Mind-Mapping and the 'Pulse of Life'." In *Blake and Goethe: Psychology, Ontology, Imagination*. Columbia: University of Missouri Press.

Brisman, Leslie. 1978. "Re: Generation in Blake." In *Romantic Origins*. Ithaca and London: Cornell University Press.

Cantor, Paul A. 1984. "The Myth Unbound." In *Creature and Creator: Myth-Making and English Romanticism*. Cambridge: Cambridge University Press.

Damrosch, Leopold Jr. 1980. "The Zoas and the Self." In *Symbol and Truth in Blake's Myth*. Princeton: Princeton University Press.

Deen, Leonard. 1983. "Priest and Poet, Serpent and Human Form, in *The Four Zoas.*" In *Conversing in Paradise: Poetic Genius and Identity-as-Community in Blake's Los*. Columbia: University of Missouri Press.

Fisher, Peter. 1961. "Human Existence: The Epic Theme." In *The Valley of Vision: Blake as Prophet and Revolutionary*, edited by Northop Frye. Toronto: University of Toronto Press.

Frosh, Thomas R. 1974. "The Fallen World." In *The Awakening of Albion: The Renovation of the Body in the Poetry of William Blake*. Ithaca: Cornell University Press.

Fuller, David. 1988. "Creation and Redemption and Judgement: *The Four Zoas.* In *Blake's Heroic Argument*. London: Croom Helm.

Gallant, Christine. 1978. "The Balance of Archetypes in *The Four Zoas.* In *Blake and the Assimilation of Chaos*. Princeton: Princeton University Press.

Hall, Mary S. 1988. "*The Four Zoas.*" In *Materialism and the Myths of Blake*. New York: Garland Press.

Hirsch, E. D. 1975 [1964]. "Return to Innocence." In *Innocence and Experience: An Introduction to Blake*. Chicago: University of Chicago Press.

King, James. 1991. "The Female Will 1798–1800." In *William Blake: His Life*. New York: St. Martin's Press.

Punter, David. 1982. *"The Four Zoas."* In *Blake, Hegel, and Dialectic.* Amsterdam: Rodopi.

Weiskel, Thomas. 1976. "Darkning Man: Blake's Critique of Transcendence." In *The Romantic Sublime: Studies in the Structure and Psychology of Transcendence.* Baltimore: Johns Hopkins University Press.

Articles

Ackland, Michael. 1983. "Blake's Critique of Reason in *The Four Zoas.*" *Colby Library Quarterly* 19:173–89.

Aers, David. 1987. "Representations of Revolution: From *The French Revolution* to *The Four Zoas.*" In *Critical Paths: Blake and the Argument of Method,* edited by Dan Miller, Mark Bracher, and Donald Ault. Durham, NC: Duke University Press.

Ault, Donald. 1986. "Re-Visioning *The Four Zoas.*" In *Unnam'd Forms: Blake and Textuality,* edited by Nelson Hilton and Thomas A. Vogler. Berkeley: University of California Press.

Bidney, Martin. 1990. "Urizen and Orc, Cortés and Guatimozin: Mexican History and *The Four Zoas* VII." *Blake/An Illustrated Quarterly* 23:195–98.

Dawson, P. M. S. 1987. "Blake and Providence: The Theodicy of *The Four Zoas.*" *Blake/An Illustrated Quarterly* 20:134–43.

Essick, Robert. 1985. *"The Four Zoas*: Intention and Production." *Blake/An Illustrated Quarterly* 18:216–20.

Fisher, Peter F. 1959. "Blake and the Druids." *The Journal of English and Germanic Philology* LVIII: 589–612.

Fox, Susan. 1977. "The Female as Metaphor in William Blake's Poetry." *Critical Inquiry* 3:507–19.

George, Diana Hume. 1979. "Is She Also the Divine Image? Feminine Form in the Art of William Blake." *The Centennial Review* 23:129–40.

Glausser, Wayne. 1985. "The Gates of Memory in Night VIIa of *The Four Zoas.*" *Blake/An Illustrated Quarterly* 18:196–203.

Haigney, Catherine. 1987. "Vala's Garden in Night the Ninth: Paradise Regained or Woman Bound?" *Blake/An Illustrated Quarterly* 20:116–24.

Ide, Nancy M. 1987. "Image Patterns and the Structure of William Blake's *The Four Zoas.*" *Blake/An Illustrated Quarterly* 20:125–33.

Kilgore, John. 1984. "On Reading *The Four Zoas*: Some Basic Principles." *Journal of English Language and Literature* 30:687–99.

Mann, Paul. 1988–89. "Finishing Blake." *Blake/An Illustrated Quarterly* 22:139–42.

Otto, Peter. 1987. "Final States, Finished Forms, and *The Four Zoas.*" *Blake/An Illustrated Quarterly* 20:144–46.

Otto, Peter. 1987. "The Spectrous Embrace, the Moment of Regeneration, and Those Two Seventh Nights." *Colby Library Quarterly* 23:135–43.

Pierce, John B. 1988–89. "The Shifting Characterization of Tharmas and Enion in Pages 3–7 of Blake's *Vala or The Four Zoas*." *Blake/An Illustrated Quarterly* 22:93–102.

Pierce, John B. 1989. "The Changing Mythic Structure of Blake's *Vala* or *The Four Zoas*: A Study of Manuscript Pages 43–84." In *Philological Quarterly* 8:485–508.

Signet, Charles J. 1976. "The Role of Christ in Blake's *The Four Zoas*." *Essays in Literature* 3:167–80.

Storch, Margaret. 1981. "Blake and Women: 'Nature's Cruel Holiness'." *American Imago* 38:221–46.

Ward, Aileen. 1972. "The Forging of Orc: Blake and the Idea of Revolution." In *Literature in Revolution*, edited by George Abbot White and Charles Newman. New York: Holt, Rinehart, and Winston.

Index

Abraham, 80–81, 185n.11

Abrams, M. H., 150, 183–84n.11

Adam: and Eve, 78; in FZ, 79, 85, 170–71; and Jesus, 33; in *Paradise Lost*, 123, 125, 149

Ahania: account of creation-fall, 73–76, 169–70; division from Urizen, 72; exchange with Enion, 92–93; exposes Urizen's defective creation, 118; hurled into abyss, 73, 77, 82, 118. *See also* Urizen; Enion

Akenside, William, 56

Albion: abdication of, 65, 112; autism of, 44; as composite figure, 30, 65, 107, 145; as England, 41; fall of, 69–72, 74–76, 78, 86–87, 165; at Feast of Eternals, 177; integration with Eternals, 147, 149; as the people, 35; resurrection of, 145, 146, 150; smitten by Luvah, 166; commands Urizen, 146

Allen, D. C., 96

Antichrist, 139–40. *See also* Satan

Apocalypse: biblical, 36, 108; Blake's individual vs. collective, 10, 131, 133, 146, 151; "end-time" in, 136; genre of, 132–33; history and, 37, 133, 138; political perspective of, 132, 149; revolution and, 40–41, 124, 134, 138; and "New Song" by African, 178; symbolic nature of, 35, 144–45; visual depiction in FZ MS, 174–75, 177–78

Apologetics (Anglican): and cosmology, 79; and Blake's FZ, 63; influence on eighteenth-century long poem, 49, 53, 56, 60

Artisans: and Blake's aesthetic, 31, 40–41, 94; and Blake's social class, 11, 24, 63, 180–81n.4

Auerbach, Erich, 96

Ault, Donald, 9, 13, 86, 184n.2; and

Blake's apocalypse, 130; and Blake's post-structural reception, 10, 40–43, 44; on Blake and Newton, 180n.1, 182–83n.1

Babylon: as symbol of oppression, 113–14. *See also* Revelation

Battestin, Martin, 55

Baudelaire, Charles, 27, 28

Bayle, Pierre: *Critical and Historical Dictionary*, 98–99, 101

Beer, John, 164

Benjamin, Walter, 28, 181–82n.12

Bentley, G. E., 26, 38, 40; and facsimile edition of FZ, 15–16; and FZ reception, 39–40; on FZ as failure, 13, 42; on workshop metaphor, 11

Bentley, Richard, 51

Beulah. *See* Daughters of Beulah; Messengers of Beulah

Bible: Frye's myth criticism and, 36; Geneva, 140; Jahwist (J) and Elohist (E) creation stories in, 62, 64, 71, 170, 184n.1; Lowth on, 59; Old Testament history in, 110–20, 122–25, 165, 170; universal history in, 95. *See also* titles of individual books; Typology; Enlightenment

Blackmore, Richard: *Creation*, 53

Blackwell, Thomas, 55

Blake, William: *America a Prophecy*, 120, 149; *The Ancient Britons*, 100, 102; "Annotations to Watson's *Apology*," 104; *The Book of Ahania*, 124–25; *The Book of Los*, 80; *The Book of Urizen*, 25, 80, 184n.1; "Edward & Eleanor," 15; *Europe a Prophecy*, 116; *The French Revolution*, 35; *Jerusalem*, 25, 26, 28, 39, 90; Letter to Butts, 60; Letter to Trusler, 60; *Milton*, 26, 37, 39, 60, 90, 139; *Night Thoughts*, Blake's illustrations to, 49; *Songs of*